Interpreting Politics

READINGS IN SOCIAL AND POLITICAL THEORY

Edited by William Connolly and Steven Lukes

Language and Politics *edited by Michael J. Shapiro*
Legitimacy and the State *edited by William Connolly*
Liberalism and Its Critics *edited by Michael J. Sandel*
Power *edited by Steven Lukes*
Rational Choice *edited by Jon Elster*
Feminism and Equality *edited by Anne Phillips*
Interpreting Politics *edited by Michael T. Gibbons*

Interpreting Politics

Edited by MICHAEL T. GIBBONS

New York University Press
Washington Square, New York

First published in the USA in 1987 by
NEW YORK UNIVERSITY PRESS
Washington Square, New York, N.Y. 10003

Library of Congress Cataloging-in-Publication Data

Interpreting politics/edited by Michael T. Gibbons.
p. cm. – (Readings in social and political theory)
Bibliography: p.
Includes index.
ISBN 0–8147–3018–3 ISBN 0–8147–3019–1 (pbk.)
1. Political science. I. Gibbons, Michael T., 1939–
II. Series.
JA66.I563 1987
320 – dc19 87–16472
CIP

Typeset in Sabon 10 on 11 pt
by Joshua Associates Limited, Oxford
Printed in Great Britain by
Billing & Sons Ltd, Worcester

Contents

Introduction: the Politics of Interpretation

MICHAEL T. GIBBONS

INTERPRETATION AND POLITICAL SCIENCE

Interpretive theory, or hermeneutics,[1] emerged in political inquiry as an alternative to positivist political science. The latter had adopted a position of methodological monism. That is, it argued that the method appropriate to the study of social and political life was, in principle, the same method used in the study of the natural world. In the practice of political inquiry this translated into empirical political science. The ideal goal of empirical political science is the objective explanation of political and social life through statistical correlations and causal laws that are empirically discovered. The assumption on the part of this mode of inquiry is that there are units of data (e.g. overt political behavior such as voting and subjective attitudes regarding issues) that are identifiable and that exist independently of the method used to reveal them.

Accompanying the empiricist philosophy of political inquiry is the view that the language of everyday political life, because it is vague, ambiguous, and value-laden, must be replaced by a more precise, scientific language. Consequently, the vocabulary of political explanation must be operationalized. Concepts must be redefined in order to eliminate the evaluative dimension and to ensure uniformity of measurement among researchers. In effect, the vocabulary of political inquiry must be made as transparent as possible in order to ensure that scientific explanation only re-presents the political world. From this perspective, the reconstruction of political concepts would purge language not only of its evaluative dimension; it would purge it of ambiguity and imprecision as well.

There are several problems with this mode of inquiry, argue interpretive theorists. First, the empiricist approach assumes a disjuncture between political life and the language of that political life. More specifically, it assumes that there is a political reality that exists and that in principle can be discovered that is independent of the language of that polity. This view downplays the internal connection between social and political life on the one hand and the language that is embedded in it on the other. Our political practices are expressed and constituted by the language that is lodged in them, and the language that is lodged in them gets its sense from the form of political practice within which it grows. Our political practices, in Charles Taylor's words,

> cannot be identified in abstraction from the language we use to describe them, or invoke them, or carry them out. . . . The situation we have here is one in which the vocabulary of a given social dimension is grounded in the shape of social practice in this dimension; that is, the vocabulary wouldn't make sense, couldn't be applied seriously, where the range of practices didn't prevail. And yet this range of practices couldn't exist without the prevalence of this or some related vocabulary. . . . The language is constitutive of the reality, is essential to its being the kind of reality it is.[2]

One of the most important consequences of this internal connection between language and action is that the explanation of political life must go beyond the registration of theories substantiated by appeal to subjective attitudes and empirically identifiable behavior. It must delve deeper in an attempt to uncover those meanings and practices of language and political life that form the social matrix against which subjective intentions are formed. These more basic intersubjective and common meanings and practices require a depth hermeneutics that goes beyond the evidence (data) required of empirical inquiry. Because they are practices and meanings that are informed by language, they often are inchoate, tacit and imperfectly articulated. Because they are inchoate, tacit and imperfectly articulated, they require interpretation to make them manifest. And because they are made manifest by interpretation, any particular interpretation is contestable.

From this perspective, the explanation of political life available to empirical social science is insufficient for explaining the most fundamental aspects of political and social life. Explanation in terms of subjective attitudes and empirical indicators of behavior is too thin to identify and account for the more profound meaning and sense of political life. Finally, because from this interpretive view man is a self-interpreting agent, political inquiry cannot be value-free. To make manifest and give expression to that which is inchoate, tacitly understood or imperfectly articulated opens up the possibility of self-reflection and political change. Moreover, to support any particular interpretation is to endorse one set of political alternatives while undermining others. Consequently, interpretive theory is not value-neutral.

BETWEEN RECOVERY AND SUSPICION

Unfortunately several misunderstandings and misconstruals, on the part of critics and defenders alike, accompanied the emergence of interpretive theory. One misconstrual of the interpretive project attributes to it a dichotomy between explanation and understanding. According to this reading, interpretive theory aims at understanding while the methods of the natural sciences aim at explanation.[3] In fact most interpretive theorists reject this dichotomy. The attempt to understand the intersubjective meanings embedded in social life is at the same time an attempt to explain why people act the way they do. And explanation in terms of intersubjective meanings leads to greater understanding.

A second misinterpretation of interpretive theory suggested that the latter claimed all social inquiry was reducible to linguistic analysis of one type or another at the expense of social action.[4] But this reading of interpretive theory ignores two points. First, it overlooks the claim that language cannot be understood outside of the practices and institutions within which it grows. Second, it ignores the fact that the interpretation of intersubjective and common meanings is an interpretation of practices, institutions, and political life as a whole. It is not an analytic approach to language divorced from the practices within which that language exists.

But a more long-standing problem in the discussion of interpretive theory lies in a third misunderstanding.

Until recently the terms of discourse concerning the application and possibilities of interpretive theory for the study of political life were constrained by two models. On the one hand the hermeneutics of recovery insists that the goal of interpretation is the recovery of the original meaning of a political or social practice. Historically, it is rooted in the theological hermeneutics of the nineteenth century which was concerned with the Word of a divine subject. In contemporary thought the object of interpretation shifted to the ideas, beliefs and intentions of authors and actors.

From this conception of the aims of interpretation, several implications follow. First, since the ideas, beliefs and intentions of actors and authors constitute the meaning of social actions and texts, explanations of political life in large part must be in terms of the self-understanding of participants in a way of life. Secondly, and flowing from the first point, one aim of interpretive theory is to uncover the internal coherence amongst ideas, beliefs, intentions, actions and practices, to show how the understanding of participants makes sense in terms of the institutions and relationships within which they are located. Thirdly, this conception of the aim of interpretation means that hermeneutics would be seen primarily as a set of methodological techniques required for this type of textual understanding. Finally, from this vantage point language plays a constitutive role with respect to the world. That is, language is seen as constituting the world and specifically the social and political relationships it establishes. In its more extreme versions this conception effectually claims a relationship of identity between language intentions, passions, and the relations embedded in language, and the meaning of political and social life.

In contrast to the hermeneutics of recovery, a second version, the hermeneutics of suspicion, insists that the self-understanding available to political and social actors is fundamentally flawed. Rather than being constitutive of social reality, such an understanding actually masks the underlying reality. In other words, the self-understanding of participants in a way of life hides a more fundamental meaning to texts or practices. Consequently, a hermeneutics concerned primarily with the explication of that self-understanding will only be able to develop a limited critical perspective on the social life it attempts to explain, and in fact will fail to explain the most significant aspects of that polity. The appropriate goal for hermeneutic social science is to penetrate the self-understanding of everyday life and uncover the real or true meaning of social and political practice. The works of Freud, Nietzsche, and Marx are often offered as examples of this second version of interpretation.[5]

Unfortunately, neither model of hermeneutics seemed able to deliver on the promise that it could provide a convincing interpretive theory of politics. The hermeneutics of recovery, with its emphasis on the constitutive role that ideas, beliefs and intentions play in social action, seemed unable to address one of the most important and interesting aspects of political life, that is, those situations in which the actual development or functioning of a way of life is at odds with the participants' understanding of it.

A more ironic difficulty faced the hermeneutics of suspicion. Marx, Freud, and Nietzsche occupy at best an ambiguous position with respect to interpretation. Specifically, the critical dimension in each respective thinker's work, that is, the economic laws of development, the structural theory of the mind and the genealogy of modernity, does not fit neatly into the category of interpretation. And other theorists often classified under the rubric of the hermeneutics of suspicion, notably Habermas, deny that interpretive theory can provide sufficient foundation for political and social theory. Consequently, to place such thinkers within the confines of interpretive theory would require that one recast the boundaries of interpretation.

Perhaps, then, the limits of interpretive theory are significantly greater than proponents believe. Or perhaps the value of interpretation lies primarily in its critique of positivist conceptions of political inquiry and social science, rather than its own ability to explain social life. Perhaps the critical possibilities of interpretive theory are muted by its emphasis on internal standards of rationality and constitutive meaning. And perhaps the claims made for interpretive theory are inflated.

Or, is it possible that the terms of discourse available to social and political inquiry were at first incapable of capturing completely the meaning of interpretation? Perhaps the discourse of political science and social theory tended to distort the arguments and claims of some interpretive theorists. In fact, the vocabulary available to political and social theorists, the vocabulary of suspicion and recovery, incompletely expresses the nature of interpretive theory as well as the possibilities and implications for politics and political inquiry.

Peter Winch's article 'Understanding a Primitive Society' is often read as a classic statement of the hermeneutics of recovery. Building on his earlier work in *The Idea of a Social Science*, Winch argues that Western social scientists make two fundamental, related mistakes in their attempts to explain the practices of primitive societies. First, Winch argues, they often presuppose that Western accounts of reality, and specifically Western scientific accounts of reality, are privileged in their accuracy and their representation of the real. Consequently, primitive beliefs in phenomena such as witchcraft and magic must be described as mistaken. The assumption here is that there is a pre-existent reality against which competing discourses can be judged for accuracy (and truth) and for which science is the most reliable guide.

Winch agrees that to abandon the possibility of checking our thought by reference to the independent, real world is to 'plunge straight into an extreme Protagorean relativism with all the paradoxes it involves'. But this conception of the issue is deceptively simple, he argues. We need to take care in understanding the place that the 'independently real' has in a particular mode of thought or way of life. In effect, we need to examine the relationship that 'independent reality' has to the practices within a way of life. As Winch puts it

> Reality is not what gives language sense. What is real and what is unreal shows itself *in* the sense that language has. Further, both the distinction between the real and the unreal and the concept of agreement with reality themselves belong to our language. . . . we could not in fact distinguish the real from the unreal without understanding the way the distinction operates in the language. If

then we wish to understand the significance of these concepts, we must examine the use they actually do have – *in* the language.

Winch makes a similar point with respect to the issues of rationality. We cannot judge the practices of other cultures as irrational simply by reference to some objectivist standard,[6] e.g. that of science. Rather, Winch insists that standards of rationality are in large part internal to a way of life: 'Something can appear rational to someone only in terms of *his* understanding of what is and is not rational. If our concept of rationality is a different one from his, then it makes no sense to say that anything either does or does not appear rational to *him* in *our* sense.'

This language of 'our concept of rationality' versus others' raises important concerns. It suggests (1) that standards of rationality are completely, internally generated; (2) that internal standards of rationality are sufficient for evaluating practices; and (3) that different standards of rationality are completely exclusive. Moreover, Winch doesn't address the issue of how we explain violations of even internal standards of rationality when we encounter them. Indeed, the tenor of his argument, perhaps, suggests he assumes complete coherence on the part of the way of life or practices under examination. Consequently, one might infer that Winch is arguing that apparent violations of internal standards of rationality are actually misunderstandings of social practices on the part of the investigator.

Steven Lukes's article, 'On the Social Determination of Truth', addresses these concerns. It is representative of the rationalist response to Winch's argument (and others similar to it) that standards of rationality and reality are largely internal to a way of life. This, argues Lukes, amounts to the claim that truth is socially determined and that our perceptions of reality are completely theory-dependent. But from here theorists who argue for the context-dependency of reality and rationality engage a non-sequitur, he claims: 'The influence, however deep, of theories upon men's perception and understanding is one thing; the claim that there are no theory-independent objects of perception is another.' Similarly, Lukes argues that neither the influence of theories on criteria of consistency and validity, nor the diversity of theories, nor the fact that beliefs are causally constrained (as in the case of the effect of ideology or culture), or finally that people may have what appear to them as good reasons for their beliefs is sufficient for concluding that those theories or beliefs are true or valid.

Moreover, there are good reasons for assuming that there are criteria of rationality and truth that are not context-dependent, that are fundamental and universal. If we are to understand another culture, and if that culture 'has a language in which it expresses its beliefs, it must minimally possess criteria of truth (as correspondence to a common and independent reality) and logic – which are not context dependent.' Without these criteria, a correspondence theory of truth and formal logic, we would be unable to communicate with that culture.

Several implications for the study of social and political life follow from this assumption of universal and fundamental criteria of truth and logic, argues Lukes. Specifically, it allows us to analyse the structure of belief systems, to identify mistaken beliefs and explain why they are believed, to explain the role of ideology and finally to distinguish between traditional, pre-scientific and modern scientific modes of thought.

The ability to identify and explain the effect of ideology is particularly important for Lukes and is a concern he shares with Brian Fay and Jürgen Habermas. Lukes fears that the claim that all standards of rationality and reality are internally generated confines social theorists and actors to conventional standards of critical evaluation. Conventional standards of critical evaluation often mask the effect of ideology or other constraints on self-understanding. It would make it difficult to distinguish the real interests of political actors from those (subjective) interests they identify with as an effect of ideology. Consequently, it would limit the ability of political theorists and actors to identify both the more subtle effects of power (such as ideological constraints on political agendas) and the existence of latent conflict. Without a strong notion of real interests, interests that are not completely determined by conventional standards of criticism and existing political arrangements, the explanatory and critical edge of political theory is limited.[7]

The insistence on universal and fundamental criteria of truth and logic does not preclude us, insists Lukes, from guarding against the type of ethnocentrism Winch is concerned about and that leads us to presuppose a moral or ethical superiority of the Western world. Nor should it lead us to take for granted the content of Western beliefs, which may be mistaken and should always be open to revision.

Brian Fay's criticism of interpretive social theory locates the problem of interpretive theory in its connection to political practice. In the excerpt from his book *Social Theory and Political Practice* reproduced here, Fay begins with a sympathetic account of interpretive theory's potential for understanding social life. Interpretive theory, he quite rightly insists, is concerned with showing how ideas, beliefs and intentions of social actors help constitute their social actions. This is not simply a form of psychologism. It involves reference to the social rules that help make particular practices possible and these in turn are dependent upon deeper constitutive meanings that themselves underlie social relations.

Now this approach to explaining political life has its virtues, according to Fay. Specifically, it reveals the underlying connections amongst different parts of social life, thereby making that life more transparent and available for critical reflection. In doing so, interpretive theory makes possible a dialogue amongst those within a society or between forms of life.

But the critical voice of interpretive theory is muted by its inadequacies. It is flawed in its account of social theory in so far as it ignores, according to Fay, (1) various causal factors (e.g. technological developments) that contribute to the rise of certain meanings; (2) the unintentional consequences of actions; (3) the structural conflicts between different aspects of social life, particularly where actors' accounts are inconsistent with their actual practices; and (4) the explanation of social change, i.e., how constitutive meanings change over time.

These limitations result in more important shortcomings from Fay's perspective. First, they mean that interpretive theory is unable to account for the resistance of social actors to explanations that are at odds with their self-understanding. Secondly, interpretive theory's relation to political practice is unjustifiably conservative. For Fay this latter failure is its most serious, and is a consequence of two inherent features of interpretive theory: its search for internal standards of rationality and its insistence that all social tensions are rooted in communicative misunderstandings rather than in social practices and institutions themselves:

> The upshot of all this is profoundly conservative, because *it leads to reconciling people to their social order*, and it does this by demonstrating to them that . . . actual social practice is inherently rational.

It seems, from Fay's perspective, that the very strengths of interpretive theory, i.e. its emphasis on constitutive meanings, are the source of its limitations.

Given Lukes's and Fay's respective readings of the possibilities of interpretive theory, it is not surprising that each draws the conclusions he does. But by focusing on internal standards of rationality and constitutive meanings, by focusing on those aspects of the interpretive argument most characteristic of the hermeneutics of recovery, both may misread the claims and possibilities of interpretation.

Lukes's argument downplays the central theme of Winch's article, i.e. how understanding primitive societies is possible when those practices at first seem unintelligible. This, Winch argues, does not involve simply coming to see things from the perspective of those under examination, which, as he points out, it is unlikely we could do in any event. Rather, it involves an effort to extend our own way of looking at things through engagement with alien and unfamiliar categories and ways of life. Such a move goes beyond either assuming the point of view of other cultures or relying on our own, unrevised categories. It makes possible a new perspective previously unavailable to either our own way of life or that of the culture we are trying to understand and explain.

This conception of the problem of understanding other cultures does not imply complete relativism. Far from insisting upon a total separation of standards of reality and rationality, Winch insists that some similar standards of reality and rationality must be assumed by both cultures:

> Rationality is not *just* a concept *in* a language like any other. . . . It is a concept necessary to the existence of any language; to say of a society that it has a language is also to say that it has a concept of rationality. There need not perhaps be any *word* functioning in its language as 'rational' does in ours, but at least there must be features of its own members' use of language analogous to those features of our use of the word rational. Where there is a language it must make a difference what is said and this is only possible where the saying of one thing rules out, on pain of failure to communicate, the saying of something else.

This does not require that we reject standards of logic. What it does mean is that formal rules of logic are themselves insufficient for determining the rationality of political and social practices.

For example, the First Amendment to the Constitution of the United States of America states that 'The Congress shall make no laws . . . prohibiting freedom of speech . . .'. The interpretation of this prohibition against restrictions on the right to speak one's mind has only in this century been extended to laws passed by state and local governments. Despite the unqualified language of the amendment (it does not say, for instance, that Congress shall make no unreasonable laws, or no laws prohibiting freedom of political speech) a number of limitations are considered completely consistent with this protection of freedom of speech. Students are not allowed to disrupt classes claiming First Amendment protections, citizens are not allowed to libel one another, to publish obscene photos, nor to shout 'Fire!' in a crowded theatre. Indeed, as is commonly known, the Supreme Court has spent considerable effort trying to specify valid limitations to the unqualified language of this ultimate law of the land.

Relying strictly on a narrow conception of the law of contradiction, social scientists from other cultures would be led to conclude that the American political system, at least concerning its claim to protect freedom of speech, is irrational or unintelligible. One would have to go beyond strict laws of identity and contradiction to understand the point behind allowing exceptions to the absolutist language of the First Amendment, to explain what counts as consistency with that law and what does not, and hence to show how those limitations are intelligible. All this merely demonstrates the point that Winch makes concerning logic, that it requires consistency but does not tell us what is to count as consistency or a violation of consistency. Only traditions of and the point behind a way of life can do that, and they are not expressed in the formal rules of logic.

Winch makes a similar point with respect to the reality of Azande witchcraft and their use of it in explaining such things as the failure of their crops. Before passing judgement on the validity of reality of the Azande practice of witchcraft, we need to situate that institution within that way of life:

> A Zande's crops are not just potential objects of consumption: the life he lives, his relations with his fellows, his chances for acting decently or doing evil, may all spring from his relation to his crops. Magical rites constitute a form of expression in which these possibilities and dangers may be contemplated and reflected upon – and perhaps also thereby transformed and deepened.

Having done that, we can perhaps then conclude that the Azande practice is superstition and irrational, and as importantly, we are in a better position to explain why, if inconsistencies exist, they are not detected by the Azande themselves.

Fay's claim that the interpretive concern with constitutive meaning and internal standards of rationality ultimately encourages political complacency on the part of political actors can only be sustained if we presume, as he does, that demonstrating the inherent rationality of a way of life is the overriding goal and ultimate outcome of interpretive explanation. However, it is one thing to claim that the rationality of practices must be judged in terms of their connection to other practices and the way that they help a political culture make sense of the world and quite another to insist that coherence and rationality is to be insisted upon at all costs.

An interpretive account of a polity may in fact bring out the irrationalities and emphasize the tensions within the political life being explained. For example, Charles Taylor's account of a potential legitimation crisis in American political life is cast in terms of what Taylor interprets as the weakening hold that the intersubjective meanings that help constitute the American political economy have on the American worker. The civilization of work that Taylor argues has bound those in our democratic society together and given meaning to those who labour can no longer be sustained, he argues.[8] If Taylor's account of the legitimacy of the American political economy is correct, one could not endorse current priorities in the American economy nor recent proposals for various forms of economic renewal. In short, one could not accept the accommodation to existing political arrangements.

There is none the less a point behind Lukes's and Fay's criticisms of interpretive theory's ability to deal with discrepancies between appearance and reality. Winch fails to address the question of how we go about explaining inconsistencies and discrepancies between actors' self-understanding and their actual behaviour once we have taken the steps towards understanding that he suggests.

At the same time there is an additional theme in Winch's essay, and an integral part of the interpretive project, that Lukes does not squarely address, that Fay undervalues and that went almost completely ignored by other critics of Winch and interpretive theory. The point behind understanding other cultures and modes of thought is not simply technological, as Winch points out: 'More importantly we may learn different possibilities of making sense of human life, different ideas about the possible importance that the carrying out of certain activities may take on for a man, trying to contemplate the sense of his life as a whole.' In the study of other modes of thought, other ways of life and perhaps of our own past, our own conceptions and presuppositions about the possibilities for human life, good and evil, the self and other, are thrown into relief; the openness to others, including their views of rationality and reality, is at the same time a questioning of, a dialogue with ourselves. Interpretation then is not simply a method; it offers not just different possibilities of technological control, but different possibilities of practical wisdom, according to Winch.

BEYOND SUSPICION AND RECOVERY

Oddly enough, one of the most important dimensions to interpretive theory was obscured by the vocabulary of recovery and suspicion. Language, according to expressivist interpretation, is central to understanding human social life. It is only through language that we are able to experience the world in ways that are distinctively human. As Hans-Georg Gadamer puts it, 'Language is the fundamental mode of operation of our being-in-the-world and the all embracing form of the constitution of the world'.[9]

Like the hermeneutics of recovery, this expressivist interpretation recognizes a constitutive dimension to the relationship between language and action, between thought and action. But beyond this constitutive moment lies a much more fundamental dimension to language. It is here that Charles Taylor's essay plays a pivotal role in the articulation of interpretive political theory. Taylor grounds interpretive political theory in an expressivist theory of language. His essay constrasts this view of language with the designative view that has dominated Western scientific thought since the Enlightenment. But it is also at odds with the constitutive theory of language that informs the hermeneutics of recovery. Designative theories of language see it as an instrument, an inventory of signs, which can be used to label and re-present the world objectively. If language functions merely to re-present the world, it follows that the primary task of philosophy is to make language as transparent and manipulative as possible. It is this conception of language which informs the empiricist requirement of an operationalized language within social science.

In contrast to this designative theory, the expressivist theory of language that Taylor endorses sees language as more than an instrument with which to describe the world. For him it is 'a pattern of activity, by which we express/realize a way of being in the world, that of reflective awareness . . .'. At the same time, it is not something that is completely at our disposal. Because it precedes us, because it is always more than any particular use of language can encompass, 'it is a pattern which can only be deployed against a background which we can never fully dominate; and yet a background that we are never fully dominated by because we are constantly reshaping it'. Moreover, because language is not merely the tool of any individual, but the language first of a community of language users, it enables us to express not just subjective preferences, but the possibilities of the self, the relationship between the self and society, and the possibilities for political life in general.

The expressivist articulation of interpretive theory involves several unique implications for the study of political life. Here I will focus on two sets of issues: the relationship between the appearance and reality and the connections amongst the self, politics and the other.

The expressivist interpretation of politics recasts the relationship between appearance and reality along lines significantly different from theories of recovery and suspicion. In contrast to the hermeneutics of recovery, expressivism emphasizes the extent to which the self-understanding of participants, because it does not exhaust that social life, is always potentially incomplete or flawed and therefore always subject to re-examination and revision. In contrast to the hermeneutics of suspicion, expressivism recognizes the reality of appearances. That is, it explains not only how intersubjective meanings help constitute the inchoate pre-understanding against which conscious self-understanding is formed, but also how this underlying reality of social and political life takes the shape it does because of the self-understanding that operates at the level of appearances. It relaxes suspicion, refusing to insist that the underlying reality is either that which in some strong sense determines the apparent world, or to which understanding at the level of appearances by itself has little or no access, little or no affect.

Neither do expressivist theories of social and political life deny the importance of an account of the structural constraints in political explanation. Indeed, they often require it. But at the same time expressivist theories make clear the extent to which the shape that structuralist explanations take depends in some significant part on the intersubjective understandings available to participants in a social or political life. For example, if one accepts the claim made by some interpretive theorists that the underlying motivation for compliance with the felt constraints on the part of blue-collar workers in the American political economy is the quest for dignity rather than the unbridled desire for more material goods, one is unlikely to interpret the structural challenge to the American political economy as one requiring only increased economic growth. If these interpretive theorists are correct in their interpretation of the dilemmas, constraints and problems faced by blue-collar workers in the United States, the problem is much more complex than is commonly perceived within mainstream American political discourse. Indeed, imperatives for economic growth and productivity that currently dominate American political discourse are likely to put additional pressures on those aspects of contemporary social life (e.g. the family) that economic growth is supposed to support.

Similarly, some theorists have argued that advanced liberal capitalism contains the potential for crises of legitimacy despite the fact that citizens of those societies do not perceive the problems in that fashion. Yet the phenomena that theorists of legitimation crisis allude to can only be characterized as potential legitimation crises in light of the intersubjective understandings embedded in American political relationships, practices and institutions. In short, the explanation of structural constraints that one accepts will in large part be determined by the understanding and explanation of meaning that one endorses.

This expressivist dimension to language also has important implications for understanding the self and self-reflection. From this perspective, critical self-reflection is not the description of pre-existent, independent passions, needs, wants and interests that need only be discovered or for which we need only adopt the correct vocabulary to re-present them. Rather, passions, needs, wants and interests are given shape and form by the very process of articulating them; it is a process by which we give our inchoate desires, vaguely articulated hopes, incompletely articulated needs new force. It is the process of bringing that which was undifferentiated and unclear into language, giving it specificity and bringing to bear public standards of criticism and rationality. Deep reflection consists of critical articulation rather than simply the description of sensation.[10] In short, because language is an expression of a way of being in the world it is also that by which we realize the potential for reflective awareness. Because it is an articulation of possibilities, the reflective awareness available to us will encourage the realization of some possibilities of the self and political life and conceal others. And as our language changes, new articulations and understanding of the self and of society will become possible.

Consequently, our understanding of ourselves will always be subject to revision and re-evaluation. Moreover, the language we find ourselves immersed in will shape the possibilities for our conception of the self, its relationship to others and to society as a whole. Consequently, one of the primary tasks of interpretive theory will be the interpretation of the possibilities of the self and its connection to society that are embodied in intersubjective meanings and practices.

Clifford Geertz's article demonstrates this theme of interpretive theory while at the same time addressing the question posed earlier about how to proceed in the interpretation of other cultures. In his interpretation of Javanese, Balinese and Moroccan cultures, he outlines how the language and symbolic systems available in each culture delimit and express different possibilities of the self. Much of his argument is aimed at showing that we can neither simply shed our language and see things exactly as the natives do, nor is it appropriate to impose our own 'peculiar idea' of the self on the Javanese, etc. To understand others' expressions of the concept and practices of the self requires an interplay of what Geertz calls experience-near and experience-distant concepts. This interplay is the dialectical oscillation between the particular, the 'exotic minutiae' of other forms of life and the general, more theoretical terms and characterizations of experience-distant concepts. This continued back-and-forth movement between the 'whole conceived through the parts that actualize it and the parts conceived through the whole that motivates them' is what is commonly referred to as the hermeneutic circle.

Geertz's argument also illustrates another point, a characteristic of interpretation that follows from the expressivist concern with levels of meaning beyond subjective intentions. Specifically, Geertz exemplifies what a depth hermeneutics consists of, one that connects individual activities and meaning to broader, deeper symbolic systems and networks of meaning.

William Connolly's article demonstrates another potential of expressivist interpretive theory, that is, its ability to explain the complexities of the relationship between appearance and reality. A complete account of political life must go beyond what Connolly calls pure interpretation (and what I have here described as the hermeneutics of recovery). Pure interpretation (most closely characterized by Winch), Connolly insists, is unable to account for deep inconsistencies between appearance and reality. At the same time, interpretive theory must avoid the tendency of structuralist theories to treat intersubjective and subjective understanding as merely a set of effects, the epiphenomena or consequences of underlying reality. More precisely, an interpretive account of appearance and reality will show how the realities themselves are partly constituted by the appearances. Consequently, changes in the appearance will in some important respects alter the underlying reality. To demonstrate this connection Connolly advances an interpretation of the predicament of white, married, blue-collar workers in the United States. What explains their willingness to submit to a variety of rigid routines and authoritarian controls at work is what Connolly calls 'the 'ideology of sacrifice', i.e. what they interpret as a voluntary sacrifice made now to provide security for their family and opportunity for their progeny to enjoy the promise of American life that has in fact escaped the blue-collar worker. Though his work life may be devoid of dignity, the sacrifice that the blue-collar worker makes for his family provides dignity and respect for him.

Connolly then introduces a series of revisions to that self-understanding to demonstrate how changes at the level of appearance would affect the underlying reality and the possible descriptions of it. Connolly's argument is winding and tightly packed but it speaks to several issues in the politics of interpretation. First, it shows how the self-understanding of social actors both constitutes and misrepresents their relationships within what he calls the civilization of productivity. Secondly, he shows how changes in that self-understanding modify and alter the nature of the constraints that participants face. Thirdly, he shows how changes in their self-understanding might be undermined and reversed as a consequence of the force of structural and institutional constraints even as those constraints become more visible to the participants. To put it another way, in response to criticisms such as that made by Fay that interpretive theory is incapable of explaining resistance by participants to explanations of social life at odds with their own self-understanding, Connolly claims that the self-identity of participants is linked to the institutional and structural constraints and consequently explains why new interpretations at odds with that self-understanding might meet considerable resistance. Finally, it shows that Fay's account of the relationship between theory and practice in interpretive theory is flawed. If Connolly's argument about the interpretive account of appearance and reality is correct, then interpretive theory does not encourage the political conservativism that Fay attributes to it.

Another way of putting this is to say that expressivist interpretive theory is able to explain the reality of appearance. It demonstrates how the subjective and intersubjective understanding and practices of a way of life themselves contribute to the constraints on that understanding, contribute to the creation and continuation of political relationships that remain invisible to political actors. The problem that remains here, however, is still serious. If, as Connolly argues, interpretation with a structural dimension is inherently contestable – if more than one defensible reading can be offered of the scenario under examination – how is it possible to say that interpretation delineates the complex relationship that appearance bears to reality? In other words, as we proceed from one level of interpretation to the next, the issues posed by Lukes and Fay reemerge in subtly different forms.

Habermas addresses this issue as it is developed by Hans-Georg Gadamer, and represented in this volume by Taylor's essay. Our understanding is conditioned and enabled by our linguistic tradition and prejudices and prejudgements it embodies; there is no Archimedean point from which we can objectively, neutrally examine our historical situation. This implies, Gadamer claims, that the authority of tradition is not simply the dogmatic antithesis of reason that the Enlightenment and its heirs (for example, Habermas) have assumed it to be. And indeed, Taylor's essay can be read as emphasizing the possibilities of reflective awareness that our language enables. According to Habermas, Gadamer's work goes a long way towards correcting and self-understanding of objectivist social science and discerning the possibilities for self-reflection lodged in our language. But there are problems that issue from the inflated claims of Gadamer's philosophical hermeneutics, problems that typify the expressivist claim that our everyday language and linguistic competence form the foundation upon which all understanding and experience must ultimately rest.

Habermas identifies two limitations to the hermeneutic claim to universality. The first consists of the possibilities of human understanding that are non-linguistic. The importance of this lies not only in the undermining of the universal claims of philosophical hermeneutics; it also challenges Taylor's claim that the expressivist dimension to language is more fundamental than the instrumental, designative dimension to a language.

The second set of limitations, conditioned by the first, lies in the possibility of theoretical understanding of the process and distortions of communication that are not available to participants. Habermas poses the question in this way:

> Can there be an understanding of meaning in relation to symbolic structures formulated in everyday language that is not tied to the hermeneutic presuppositions of context dependent processes of understanding that in this sense by-passes natural language as a last meta-language?

Habermas argues that there can. Both psychoanalysis and the critique of ideology identify the existence of systematically distorted communications, that is, structural limits to understanding that can be neither identified, nor explained, nor overcome by the communicative competence, however keenly developed and skilfully deployed, of everyday life. Habermas's essay then presents an example of a psychoanalytic explanation that offers an account of pathological, distorted communicative action.

Gadamer's response, one that flows from expressivism, is that this new understanding provided by psychoanalysis, though it may methodologically examine in detail very specific distortions in everyday understanding, none the less takes place against a background of shared understanding and meaning. In addition, the new understanding provided by psychoanalysis, or the critique of ideology for that matter, must be assimilated by everyday understanding and therefore must be translatable into the language of everyday life. Hence, our everyday language is the last metalanguage of theoretical understanding for social and political theory that seeks to have the practical import that both expressivists and Habermas desire. Consequently, theoretically established critique does in fact rely on everyday linguistic understanding, and this in part because it presupposes a background of linguistic tradition that we inherit.

The problem with this response from Habermas's point of view is that it seems to commit us to the supposition that our linguistic tradition is itself the embodiment of legitimate consensus, i.e. that our inherited linguistic tradition is itself the locus of truth and undistorted agreement. But clearly this is not the case, argues Habermas. It ignores the fact that the exercise of power, often in the form of dogmatic authority, results in the deformation of intersubjective communication. 'A critically enlightened hermeneutics that differentiates between insight and delusion', on the other hand, 'incorporates the meta-hermeneutic awareness of the conditions for the possibility of systematically distorted communication. It connects the process of understanding to the principle of rational discourse, according to which truth would only be guaranteed by that kind of consensus which was achieved under the idealized conditions of unlimited communication free from domination'.

To ignore or downplay the importance of coercion, force and power in establishing the acceptance of our traditions is to sink into a dogmatic recognition of tradition. Habermas argues that it leads Gadamar to deny the opposition between reason and authority and to place unreasonable restrictions on the project of enlightenment.

On the other hand, clearly Habermas's own recent (1978) attempt to identify the formal, pragmatic requirements of communication does not escape the historicity of understanding that expressivism emphasizes. For example, among the conditions of undistorted communication that Habermas identifies are the validity claims of truth, appropriateness and sincerity.[11] But of course what the criteria are for determining what is to count as truth or appropriateness, or sincerity, will vary from historical tradition to historical tradition.[12]

There are several ways of looking at this debate between Gadamer (and expressivism in general) on the one hand and Habermas on the other. One way, not particularly helpful, is to see it as a debate between interpretive theory and unreconstructed rationalism. But such a reading would have to de-emphasize Habermas's own appreciation of interpretive theory as well as his criticism of much of contemporary rationalism.

A second perspective would see it as a debate between the hermeneutics of recovery and the hermeneutics of suspicion. This interpretation is encouraged by the use of terms such as the 'hermeneutics of everydayness' and 'depth hermeneutics'. It is also encouraged by Habermas's examples of psychoanalysis and the critique of ideology as examples of the limits to philosophical hermeneutics. But this interpretation would elide Gadamer's emphasis on the creation of new meaning through the appropriation of tradition.

There is still a third interpretation. The debate between Habermas and Gadamer can be seen as a debate within expressivist interpretive theory, one in which each thinker accepts the general tenets of expressivism but at the same time each emphasizes different implications of that expressivism. Gadamer can be understood as emphasizing the limitations to methodologically informed reason that the expressivist dimension to language poses while Habermas can be seen as emphasizing the critical capacity of methodologically informed understanding. The advantage of this interpretation is that it would make sense of Habermas's own recognition that the problem of modern understanding is not one of consciousness but one of language[13] and his admission that ultimately we cannot locate a point outside history, removed from the language and tradition that we inherit from which we can explain and evaluate our political life. In Habermas's words:

> It is, of course, true that criticism is always tied to the context of tradition which it reflects. Gadamer's hermeneutic reservations are

> justified against monological self-certainty which merely arrogates to itself the title of critique. There is no validation of depth-hermeneutical interpretation outside of the self-reflection of all participants that is successfully achieved in a dialogue. . . . In present conditions it may be more urgent to indicate the limits of the false claim to universality made by criticism rather than that of the hermeneutic claim to universality. Where the dispute about the grounds for justification is concerned, however, it is necessary to critically examine the latter claim, too.

This last reading would also make sense of Gadamer's admission that an unreflective acceptance of the prejudices that constitute our background understanding, including our own acceptance of the Enlightenment and the prejudices of technologism, leads to misunderstanding the possibilities of tradition: 'It is the tyranny of hidden prejudices that makes us deaf to the language that speaks to us in tradition'.[14] The similarities between Habermas and Gadamer are further underscored by Habermas's conception of the role of philosophy in post-foundationalism.Once philosophy abandons the attempt to provide an ultimate (objective) foundation for all claims to knowledge, it still plays a pivotal role in the modern world, argues Habermas. This role is similar to what Gadamer attributes to philosophical hermeneutics:

> In everyday communication cognitive interpretations, moral expectations, expressions and evaluations cannot help overlapping and interpenetrating. Reaching understanding in the lifeworld requires a cultural tradition that ranges across the *whole spectrum*, not just the fruits of science and technology. As far as philosophy is concerned, it might do well to refurbish its link with the totality by taking on the role of interpreter on behalf of the lifeworld. It might then be able to help set in motion the interplay between the cognitive–instrumental, moral–practical, and aesthetic–expressive dimensions that has come to a standstill today, like a tangled mobile.[15]

In short, the critical appropriation of tradition which both thinkers endorse requires both a Gadamerian and a Habermasian moment. In sum, each thinker requires more of the other's position than is expressed in the exchange between the two.[16]

But this last reading must be careful not to de-emphasize the challenge Habermas poses to Gadamer's philosphical hermeneutics and to interpretation in general. A 'critically enlightened hermeneutics' emphasizes the extent to which reason and established political practices are potentially at odds with one another. In this respect there are similarities between Habermas's challenge to Gadamer on the one hand and Lukes's and Fay's challenges to Winch on the other that require careful consideration.

EXPRESSIVISM, PRAGMATISM AND GENEALOGY

The essays by Dreyfus, Foucault and Rorty introduce a different set of issues and challenges to interpretive theory which emerge from the 'deconstructionist' or genealogical and pragmatist perspectives. Dreyfus's article is particularly important at this point. He identifies some of the important differences within interpretation, identifies points of agreement between interpretation and genealogy and ultimately the differences between them.

He begins by tracing the shifting emphasis of Heidegger's original conception of hermeneutics within *Being and Time*. Division I of *Being and Time* addresses itself to the hermeneutics of everydayness. Our everyday practices involve an often unnoticed understanding of the world and our place in it. This interpretation is not a cognitively acquired belief system which we can separate from the practices it is located in. Rather, the meanings are embedded in the practices themselves. As Dreyfus points out, this primordial understanding is similar to what Taylor has elsewhere called 'intersubjective meanings'.[17] Through the hermeneutics of everydayness, this primordial understanding is revealed.

But there is a deeper truth to be revealed in Heidegger's existential analysis, which in Division II of *Being and Time* takes the form of the hermeneutics of suspicion, argues Dreyfus. The interpretation embedded in our everyday practice is a cover-up. It hides from us the fact that it is itself an interpretation, that it has no grounding other than the practices themselves. Moreover, this rootlessness is vaguely felt by human beings, which often leads to greater resistance to acknowledging it; as Dreyfus puts it: 'Thus, transcendental hermeneutic phenomenology does not simply seek to lay out the general structure of self-interpreting being; rather it claims to force a substantive truth about human beings. The truth, hidden by all cultures at all times, is that man can never be at home in the world.'

After what has become known as the 'turning' in Heidegger's thought, he changes his conception of the possibilities of hermeneutics and interpretation. Dreyfus describes those changes and we cannot discuss all of them. But Dreyfus brings our attention to several that are of significance for us in outlining the issues between expressivism and genealogy.[18]

First, the rootlessness that Heidegger originally characterized as a transcendental, existential condition of mankind is now seen as a condition of modernity, a response to our technological practices and understanding of the world. Secondly, he historicizes the hermeneutics of everydayness, showing that each interpretation is both a revealing and a concealing; each opens up some possibilities of being and eclipses others. The subsequent questions, as Dreyfus points out, are how has any particular understanding come about; to what extent does any particular understanding involve greater dangers than advantages; does it close off more than it makes manifest; and what are the possibilities of change? Thirdly, it is now important to examine previous epochs, according to Heidegger, for they throw into relief the pecularities of our own technological understanding and the costs of its control. Finally, according to the Dreyfus reading, Heidegger posits the possibility of a new rootedness, an attunement if you will, with the world. Perhaps man can overcome the alienation that characterizes modern anxiety. Perhaps there is an articulation of the possibilities of being that embodies an understanding that enables a hospitality between the self and society and between our public understanding and the world.

Foucault thinks not. Foucault's original critique of interpretation, or what he calls commentary, was focused at the epistemological level. Commentary, he argues, attempts to reveal the truth of what it interprets when in fact there is no truth, no hidden meaning to be had. Consequently, it results in a proliferation of exegesis but not much more. But as Foucault moved away from archaeology to geneology his critique of hermeneutic–interpretive theory as a form of modern thought shifted. The Foucault essay included here represents that point at which the shift from archaeology to genealogy takes place.[19]

From this genealogical perspective Foucault argues that we should not think of knowledge simply as reflecting or representing the world, 'that we should not imagine that the world presents us with a legible face, leaving us merely to decipher it, . . . there is no prediscursive fate disposing the world in our favor. We must conceive discourse as a violence that we do to things, or, at all events as a practice we impose upon them'.[20] What does explain the success of any particular discourse of knowledge is its connection with networks of power. In all societies power-knowledge functions to produce some forms of truth and to disqualify others. In modern society the production of truth, the function of power-knowledge, has taken a disciplinary, normalizing form that requires the production of man as both the subject and object of power-knowledge.

The task of genealogy is to link the unities of any particular epoch to specific networks of power-knowledge in which they are entangled.The unities of the self, between self and society and of society, are not just conventions, but are conventions that reproduce practices of the self, sexual conduct, citizenship, madness and health, consistent with and sustained by existing patterns of power-knowledge. To force the realization of the disparity between accepted conceptions of the self, reason, truth etc. and their possibilities of existence, genealogy will reveal that they are merely 'historical coagulations'.[21] In other words, genealogy shows that our practices of the self are the result of accidents, contingent developments that are presented to us as necessities: 'A genealogy of values, morality, asceticism and knowledge will never neglect as inaccessible the vicissitudes of history. On the contrary, it will cultivate the details and accidents that accompany every beginning.'

Because the modern episteme operates through the production of subjects, one task of genealogy will be to show how the episteme's practices of the self are productions and conventions. One tactic to be deployed toward this end is to show that the body is inscribed by practices of power-knowledge; to show how it is organized, arranged, directed, mobilized; in short, how it is made a disciplined instrument to create the modern subject. It will show that the 'body is the prison of the soul'.[22] For genealogy, the patient erudition typified by much of Foucault's work, is aimed at unsettling the consoling play of recognition; it is aimed at 'the destruction of the subject who seeks knowledge in the endless deployment of the will to knowledge' which closes us off from the hetereogeneity of human life.

In short, genealogy will look to explode and dissipate the unities that our discursive practices encourage. It will deploy the parodical, the farcical, reversals of meaning and strategic exemplars to encourage the play of discordance between the self and the social identities that our discourse produces. It will provide a multiplication of possibilities of the self that reveal what is excluded, what is disqualified, what is subjugated and what is compromised by our production of the truth of our selves that characterizes modern thought and the expressivist reaction to it.

As Dreyfus points out, there are a number of similarities between genealogy and what here is referred to as expressivist interpretive theory. First, both problematize the modern conception of the subject. For both, the idea of a knowing subject with a transparent relationship to the world, removed from history, is an obstacle to understanding the possibilities of human knowledge and social life. Secondly, both deny that either the conscious self-understanding or the deeper self-understanding of participants reveals *the* truth about the self. Because practices of the self are largely articulations of the possibilities of the self, (expressivism) or the medium of webs of power-knowledge (genealogy), there is no underlying reality to which practices of the self can appeal, or for that matter distort. Thirdly, and flowing from the above, any set of social practices will be both a revealing and a concealing; any set of social practices will encourage some possibilities of the self, some possibilities between one self and society and some possibilities between the self and the other while denying others. In the vocabulary of genealogy, any set of power-knowledge relations will produce some forms of truth while disqualifying others. Consequently, it will be important to show how each came into being, the costs it imposes, and the possibilities of resistance. Fourthly, Foucault and many expressivists agree that modern technological forms of understanding pose particularly significant problems for the variation of human experience, although they disagree over just what those distorting effects are. Finally, there are similarities, as Dreyfus points out, between Heidegger's and Foucault's respective uses of strategic examples (e.g. the hydroelectric plant and the prison) to illuminate the nature of modernity.

If the expressivist and the genealogist agree that conceptions of the self, reason, truth, the relationship between the self and society and the possibilities of social life are largely interpretations embedded in social practices, how do they differ? One primary disagreement lies in their respective views of what interpretation amounts to.

Whereas for expressivism the self-interpreting character of human being represents an articulation of possible meaning that can be determined to be better or worse than others, that one can, upon reflection, determine whether it does or does not embody the type of existence that one would reflectively endorse, Foucault sees the ultimate nature of interpretation in radically different terms. In his words 'if interpretation is the violent or surreptitious appropriation of a system of rules, which in itself has no essential meaning, in order to impose a direction, to bend it to a new will, to force its participation in a different game, and subject it to secondary rules, then the development of humanity is a series of interpretations. The role of genealogy is to record its history.'[23]

Rorty's account of the proper role and limitations of hermeneutics exhibits several affinities to Foucault's. The problems for hermeneutics begin with its acceptance of the Galilean conception of natural science, i.e., that science somehow provides 'an absolute conception of reality',[24] that somehow the language of science is nature's own language. Unfortunately for science, the language most appropriate for the explanation of human action, according to interpretive theory, is not the language of causal laws and quantifiable variables. Rather, argues the expressivist, it is the language that embodies the self-understanding of the participants within a way of life. The method appropriate to the study of social and political life is one that has access to that vocabulary. Consequently the social sciences must be interpretive or hermeneutical sciences.

There are two difficulties with this position, according to Rorty. First, it is a mistake to accept the Galilean conception of natural science. Science does not give us a more objective account of nature; it does not more accurately describe the natural world. The value and success of scientific theories lies in their pragmatic results; they are simply better or worse ways of fulfilling some purpose. This leads to the second mistake. Interpretive theorists have not really rejected the model of understanding involved in the Galilean conception of knowledge, argues Rorty. They simply deny that it is the vocabulary of causal science that has this special access. In effect they attempt to legitimize an interpretive approach to the study of politics by means of a meta-narrative that does for social science what philosophy has tried (and failed) to do for science.[25] But just as the language of science is not the true language of nature, the language and self-understanding of political actors is not the foundational or true language of politics: 'Objects are not "more objectively" described in any vocabulary than in any other. Vocabularies are useful or useless, good or bad, helpful or misleading, sensitive or coarse, and so on; but they are not "more objective" or "less objective" nor more or less "scientific".'

The upshot of this is that hermeneutics does not reveal the intrinsic nature of political life any more than behaviourist social science. Though the self-understanding of actors might have heuristic value or be morally privileged, there is no reason to assume it is epistemologically privileged.[26]

Having rejected the modernist conception of knowledge, method, truth, reason and rationality, Rorty sees two possibilities. One option, the genealogist's, is to see practices of knowledge and the social sciences in particular as simply the instruments of the disciplinary society, the will to truth that excludes, infiltrates, disciplines, transforms and normalizes that which does not fit neatly into its discrete categories or that challenges the concepts and practices that a discourse of power-knowledge seeks to establish. Such an alternative sees little hope for moral action. Foucault puts it this way:

> Humanity does not gradually progress from combat to combat until it arrives at universal reciprocity, where the rule of law finally replaces warfare; humanity installs each of its violences in a system of rules and thus proceeds from domination to domination. . . . Rules are empty in themselves, violent and unfinalized; they are impersonal and can be bent to any purpose. The success of history belongs to those who are capable of seizing these rules . . .

What hope there is lies in unravelling the web of disciplinary discourse that binds, limits and constrains our lives, perhaps by treating our lives as a work of art.[27]

The second alternative is to emphasize the 'moral importance of the social sciences – their role in widening and deepening our sense of community and of the possibilities of community.' Rorty claims this latter alternative, one that encourages hope, is provided by Dewey. But it is also to be found in Taylor, Connolly, Winch, Geertz and certainly in Heidegger, even if in terms unacceptable to Rorty.

The advantage of following Dewey over Foucault, from Rorty's perspective, lies in the fact that he has accomplished the deconstruction of the Galilean conception of science and social science while providing us with hope, with 'a vital sense of human solidarity'. The advantage of Dewey with respect to Taylor (and other expressivists) consists of the fact that Dewey, unlike Taylor, does not think that hope is or needs to be grounded in some truth about the nature of human beings.

One expressivist response to Rorty's objections to interpretive theory is that Rorty oversimplifies the expressivist position. Taylor, Connolly, Geertz and Winch would all insist that we can (in fact may need) to go beyond the self-description of social actors. Moreover the essays by Connolly and Geertz presented here make convincing cases that any additional, deeper explanation needs to take account of that first hand understanding. To make his case against an interpretive social science stick, I think Rorty must address these claims that any deeper structural or experience-distant explanation is necessary but that it is made available by the participants' self-understanding.

From another perspective, Rorty's argument seems to beg the question. One of the primary concerns of interpretive theory has been to identify the possibilities for community. The problem, however, is how to recognize better and worse forms of community. In part this question can be answered by examining the extent to which the self-understanding of political actors is reflected in the social arrangements they commit themselves to. The issue is to what extent the social and political identity made available to political actors is consistent with the social and personal identities individuals would endorse if they had the opportunity to evaluate alternatives. These are questions concerning the connections between appearance and reality, about how we can identify communities that are the result more of consensus than of force; and they are among the questions that concern claims to knowledge and truth. Though the expressivist would agree that there is no single truth about these questions, we must be able to expect that we can have provisional answers, a certain amount of knowledge about what constitutes better and worse communities, more genuine and less coerced consensus. Moreover, if in fact the establishment of a moral community is, as Rorty claims here and elsewhere, one of the concerns for social science, and if we can assume the importance of the self-understanding of actors in questions of morality as he also claims in this essay, it would seem that on his own account social science must be in some sense interpretive (i.e., hermeneutic), and for reasons that ultimately resemble those of expressivism. Foucault's response is that the very attempt to provide alternative conceptions of community, including the expressivist and pragmatic versions, is precisely the trap that modern political thought must escape.

In response to Foucault, one rejoinder available to expressivism is to point out that the practice of social theory as a carnival or treating one's life as a work of art, two of Foucault's strategies, only have critical import in contrast to a settled, somewhat more conventional style of life. The carnival and the dandy depend for their affect on the everyday life they define themselves against. This in turn leads to the argument, advanced elsewhere by Taylor, that Foucault's conception of genealogy leaves open and does not fully address the issue of whether or not there can ever be discursive practices or disciplines which political actors can be said to autonomously endorse and that are informed by notions of truth and freedom similar to those articulated by interpretive theory. Alternatively, there remains the possibility, as Connolly has argued, of treating Foucault's work as a double, an other that will not disappear, that cannot be completely enclosed within interpretation.[28]

One can summarize this debate amongst expressivism, genealogy and pragmatism in the following way. Protagonists of each perspective agree that the conception of knowledge as representation (of objective reality) and the positivist conceptions of truth, rationality, method and social science are wrong. Moreover, each agrees that human social and political life is largely an interpretation of the possibilities of the self, society and the other and the relationship amongst the three. But from this each draws different conclusions. The expressivist insists that from this we can expect both knowledge about social life, a certain amount of truth and the hope that knowledge can support the possibility of a moral community. The pragmatist agrees it is reasonable to emphasize the hope and possibility of moral community but is less sanguine about how much knowledge or truth we might expect. The genealogist insists that at best we can expect neither truth nor hope and at worst whatever truth or hope emerges from this contemporary situation is unlikely to be identical to what proponents want and more dangerous than they recognize.

It is tempting to try to provide closure to this debate amongst expressivism, genealogy, and pragmatism, perhaps to show that one mode of thought can capture or colonize the others. But instead of trying to enclose the debate between interpretation and its dialogical partners, I think it is helpful to examine how the presence of such challenges provides the opportunity to draw out tacit, inchoate or imperfectly understood dimensions of interpretation. To put it another way, it might be helpful to draw out how these challenges contribute to the edification of interpretive theory itself.

Let us consider two possibilities, two idealized conceptions, perhaps two limiting cases, two models of dialogue. The direction or purpose of the first type of dialogue is to come to an agreement about an issue or course of action. Because the participants in the dialogue are trying to persuade (as opposed to manipulate or coerce) each other, each will offer reasons, evidence, arguments as to why his or her own conclusion or position is that which the other ought to adopt. Ideally, the result is a consensus amongst those implicated in the dialogue. Though this idealized dialogue is seldom found in practice, its ideal does have implications for even imperfect approximations of it or those social relations that are informed by it. For example, when this ideal is operative, those implicated in the dialogue will feel compelled to try sincerely and honestly to meet the objections of others. When practical constraints require closure on the debate, participants holding a minority position may agree to consent to action and policies endorsed by other points of view if in the future they are afforded the opportunity for dissent and continued discussion of the policies at issue. But certainly here the integration of the other into a rational community, one that embodies non-coercive forms of identification with the common good, remains the primary ideal. This is the model of dialogue, of communicative action, that informs the work of Taylor and Habermas. Here a politics of attunement is celebrated.

The point behind the second model of a dialogue is different. Here the end is not a rational consensus. Rather, in this second model each participant, recognizing that his or her discourse is likely to be incomplete or open to challenge seeks out and cultivates opposition of the other as a challenge to the closure of one's own discourse, way of life, or theoretical perspective. Indeed, here the continuation of otherness is so important that when the other is persuaded, convinced or eclipsed, the search begins again for new challenges to this provisional order. Or as one set of issues is resolved, the conversation issues in a new set of challenges from a different other. On this model if the dialogue were ever to issue in quiet consensus, the suspicion would be that the agreement was actually an enforced silence. From this perspective it is crucial that we consult and confront ourselves with the other. Within this model of dialogue we might locate the work of Winch, Geertz and Connolly. Here, the politics of discordance, of otherness, is celebrated.

Two points need to be made about these two models of dialogue. First, and most obviously, neither is likely to be realized and sustained in its ideal form for any length of time. More likely, actual social and political relationships can be located between the two models or as imperfect variations of one or the other. Secondly, I would like to suggest that when informed by expressivist interpretive theory, each model, even in its idealized form, presupposes the alternative, that neither could exist if not informed by the possibility of the other.

The politics of attunement and the politics of discordance are two possibilities, two moments made possible by expressivist political theory. The interconnectedness of these two moments within expressivist interpretive theory are its strength. It encourages a more complex understanding of the relationship between appearance and reality and amongst the self, politics and the other than is available to either the hermeneutics of recovery or suspicion. It provides us with a critique of technological practices and conceptions of knowledge while at the same time providing us with hope that recognizes the dangers, the dark side of our aspirations for community. It opens interpretive theory to a dialogue with competing accounts of modernity and political life, with pragmatism and genealogy and perhaps with others yet to be articulated. In short, it seeks the possibility of community, of consensual discipline to use Foucault's term, while at the same time it resists the coerciveness of totalizing political discourse and practice.[29]

NOTES

1 In this essay I use the terms 'hermeneutics', 'interpretive theory' and 'interpretive social science' interchangeably.

2 Charles Taylor, 'Interpretation and the Sciences of Man', *Review of Metaphysics*, Volume XXV, no. 1 (September 1971), p. 24. It is appropriate to point out that empiricists often admit the language of everyday life is that which is most useful in explaining politics and that operationalized concepts should remain as close to everyday use as operationalization admits. They also often admit the undetermination of theory by evidence. But in practice this has had little impact on the structure or nature of empirical explanation. Interpretive theorists argue that the internal connections between language and political life and the undetermination of theory by evidence mean that the nature of explanation in the social sciences is radically different from what empiricists insist. Empirical and quantitative techniques can still be considered useful tools. But the explanation of social and political life is at rock bottom an interpretation.

3 Georg Herman von Wright, *Explanation and Understanding* (Ithaca: Cornell University Press, 1971).

4 For example, see A. R. Louch's interpretation of Peter Winch in Louch, *Explanation and Human Action* (Berkeley: University of California Press, 1969), pp. 174–81.

5 See Paul Ricoeur, *Freud and Philosophy* (New Haven: Yale University Press, 1970).

6 I am borrowing from Richard Bernstein's use of the terms 'objectivist' and 'objectivism'. Briefly it refers to the claim that there can be a single set of criteria that can define a concept or practice. See Bernstein, *Beyond Objectivism and Relativism* (Philadelphia: University of Pennsylvania Press, 1983).

7 Lukes discusses the role that a concept of real interests plays in the analysis of power in Lukes, *Power* (London: Macmillan, 1974).

8 Charles Taylor, 'Interpretation and the Sciences of Man', pp. 3–51.

9 Hans-Georg Gadamer, *Philosophical Hermeneutics* (Berkeley: University of California, 1976), p. 3.

10 Charles Taylor, 'What is Human Agency?' *Philosophical Papers, Volume I: Human Agency and Language* (Cambridge: Cambridge University Press, 1985), pp. 15–44; and Stuart Hampshire, *Freedom of the Individual* (Princeton NJ: Princeton University Press, 1971).

11 Jürgen Habermas, *Communication and the Evolution of Society* (Boston, Mass: Beacon Press, 1978).

12 In addition, as Habermas himself points out, when the validity claims are not met barriers to the fulfilment of each can be made the object of critical inquiry but only while the fulfilment of others is temporarily presumed. Thomas McCarthy has put it this way: 'the lifeworld is represented as a "culturally transmitted and linguistically organized stock of interpretive patterns". In the form of "language" and "culture" this reservoir of implicit knowledge supplies actors with unproblematic background convictions upon which they draw in the negotiation of common definitions of situations. Individuals cannot "step out" of their lifeworlds; nor can they objectify them in a supreme act of reflection. Particular segments of the lifeworld relevant to given action situations can, of course be problematized; but this always takes place against an indeterminate and inexhaustible background of other unquestioned presuppositions, a shared global preunderstanding that is prior to any problems or disagreements. . . . This is not altered by modern reflexivity and the development of a critical tradition. What does change is that fewer elements of the cultural tradition are exempted from problematization and that this problematization increasingly takes place in methodological and reflective form within specialized cultural spheres.' McCarthy, 'Translator's Introduction' to Habermas, *The Theory of Communicative Action,* vol I: *Reason and the Rationalization of Society* (Boston, Mass.: Beacon Press, 1984), pp. xxiv, 406. This passage could just as easily be used to describe Gadamer (and the expressivist view in general) on the importance of language and the possibility of reflection. Critics of this claim might argue that I am downplaying the Kantian or cognitivist dimension to Habermas's thought. I am, but I do so for virtuous, if not innocent, reasons; not to deny that cognitivism but to emphasize what I believe is a more fundamental aspect of Habermas's thought that ultimately limits the importance of that cognitivist moment.

13 Jürgen Habermas, 'Postscript', *Knowledge and Human Interests* (Boston, Mass.: Beacon Press, 1971).

14 Hans-Georg Gadamer, *Truth and Method* (New York: Seabury Press, 1976), p. 239.
15 Habermas, 'Philosophy as Stand-in and Interpreter', in Kenneth Baynes, Janice Bohman, and Thomas McCarthy (eds), *After Philosophy* (Cambridge, Mass: MIT Press, 1987), p. 313.
16 Compare to Paul Ricouer, *Hermeneutics and the Human Sciences* (New York: Cambridge University Press, 1978).
17 Taylor, 'Interpretation and the Sciences of Man'.
18 One significant change which we cannot examine here is Heidegger's claim to have gone beyond the hermeneutic circle. An issue remains as to whether or not something like the hermeneutic circle is not still required in the elucidation of everyday understanding.
19 It would be incorrect, of course, to claim that Foucault completely abandoned the method of archaeology.
20 Michel Foucault, 'Discourse on Language', in *The Archaeology of Knowledge* (New York: Harper and Row, 1969), p. 229.
21 Hubert Dreyfus and Paul Rabinow, *Michel Foucault: Beyond Structuralism and Hermeneutics* (Chicago: University of Chicago Press, 1983), p. 236.
22 Michel Foucault, *Discipline and Punish* (New York: Pantheon Books, 1977), p. 30.
23 I should emphasize that despite the intentionalist language Foucault employs here, the discursive practices are not at any one particular individual's or group's complete disposal. A strategy emerges with the appropriation of discursive practices, but no strategist.
24 Rorty borrows this term from Bernard Williams, *Descartes* (New York: Penguin Books, 1977).
25 Richard Rorty, *Philosophy and the Mirror of Nature* (Princeton, NJ: Princeton University Press, 1979). It is perhaps appropriate to point out here that Rorty does believe that there is a place for the practice of hermeneutics. Hermeneutics is that activity we engage in when we are critically examining competing theories; it resembles Kuhn's notion of revolutionary science, and is a process of edification. But this is considerably different from what Taylor and other expressivists have in mind.
26 There may be more agreement here between Rorty and expressivism than at first meets the eye. A complete account of the debate between expressivism and pragmatism would explore this question of how each addresses the problem of moral community.
27 Michel Foucault, 'On the Genealogy of Ethics', in Dreyfus and Rabinow, *Foucault*, pp. 236–7.
28 See the debate between Connolly and Taylor concerning the comportment of expressivism towards genealogy in Taylor, 'Foucault on Freedom and Truth', in *Philosophical Papers, Volume II: Philosophy and the Human Sciences* (Cambridge: Cambridge University Press, 1985), pp. 152–84; Connolly, 'Taylor, Foucault and Otherness', *Political Theory* 13 (August 1985), pp. 365–76; Taylor, 'Connolly, Foucault and Truth', *Political Theory*, 13 (August 1985), pp. 377–85; Connolly, *Politics and Ambiguity*, (Madison: University of Wisconsin Press, 1987).

29 I am borrowing the terms 'attunement' and 'discordance' from William Connolly, *Politics and Ambiguity* (Madison: University of Wisconsin Press, 1987). These issues are further explored in the debates among pragmatism, expressivism and genealogy, and within expressivism itself. See the following: Charles Taylor, *Philosophical Papers,* vols I and II (Cambridge: Cambridge University Press, 1985); Connolly, 'Taylor, Foucault and Otherness', *Political Theory*, 13 (August 1985), pp. 365–76 and *Politics and Modernity* (Madison: University of Wisconsin Press, 1986); Jürgen Habermas, 'The French Path to Postmodernity', *New German Critique* (Fall 1984), pp. 79–102; 'Modernity vs. Postmodernity', *NGC* (Winter 1981), pp. 3–14; and several essays in Richard Bernstein, ed., *Habermas and Modernity* (Cambridge, Mass.: MIT Press, 1985) and Richard Rorty, 'Habermas and Lyotard on Postmodernity', in Bernstein, ed., ibid., and Foucault, *The Foucault Reader*, Paul Rabinow ed. (New York: Pantheon Books, 1984).

1
Understanding a Primitive Society

PETER WINCH

This essay will pursue further some questions raised in my book, *The Idea of a Social Science*.[1] That book was a general discussion of what is involved in the understanding of human social life. I shall here be concerned more specifically with certain issues connected with social anthropology. In the first part I raise certain difficulties about Professor E. E. Evans-Pritchard's approach in his classic, *Witchcraft, Oracles and Magic among the Azande*.[2] In the second part, I attempt to refute criticisms made by Alasdair MacIntyre of Evans-Pritchard and myself, to criticize in their turn MacIntyre's positive remarks, and to offer some further reflections of my own on the concept of learning from the study of a primitive society.

I

THE REALITY OF MAGIC

Like many other primitive people, the African Azande hold beliefs that we cannot possible share and engage in practices which it is peculiarly difficult for us to comprehend. They believe that certain of their members are witches, exercising a malignant occult influence on the lives of their fellows. They engage in rites to counteract witchcraft; they consult oracles and use magic medicines to protect themselves from harm.

An anthropologist studying such a people wishes to make those beliefs and practices intelligible to himself and his readers. This means presenting an account of them that will somehow satisfy the criteria of rationality demanded by the culture to which he and his readers belong: a culture whose conception of rationality is deeply affected by the achievements and methods of the sciences, and one which treats such

Reprinted by permission of the author and *American Philosophical Quarterly* from Peter Winch, 'Understanding a Primitive Society', *American Philosophical Quarterly*, XLVIII (October 1964), pp. 307–24. This article reappeared in Peter Winch, *Ethics and Action* (London: Routledge and Kegan Paul, 1972).

things as a belief in magic or the practice of consulting oracles as almost a paradigm of the irrational. The strains inherent in this situation are very likely to lead to the anthropologist to adopt the following posture: *We* know that Zande beliefs in the influence of witchcraft, the efficacy of magic medicines, the role of oracles in revealing what is going on and what is going to happen, are mistaken, illusory. Scientific methods of investigation have shown conclusively that there are no relations of cause and effect such as are implied by these beliefs and practices. All we can do then is to show how such a system of mistaken beliefs and inefficacious practices can maintain itself in the face of objections that seem to us so obvious.[3]

Now although Evans-Pritchard goes a very great deal further than most of his predecessors in trying to present the sense of the institutions he is discussing as it presents itself to the Azande themselves, still, the last paragraph does, I believe, pretty fairly describe the attitude he himself took at the time of writing this book. There is more than one remark to the effect that 'obviously there are no witches'; and he writes of the difficulty he found, during his field work with the Azande, in shaking off the 'unreason' on which Zande life is based and returning to a clear view of how things really are. This attitude is not an unsophisticated one but is based on a philosophical position ably developed in a series of papers published in the 1930s in the unhappily rather inaccessible *Bulletin of the Faculty of Arts* of the University of Egypt. Arguing against Lévy-Bruhl, Evans-Pritchard here rejects the idea that the scientific understanding of causes and effects which leads us to reject magical ideas is evidence of any superior intelligence on our part. Our scientific approach, he points out, is as much a function of our culture as is the magical approch of the 'savage' a function of his:

> The fact that we attribute rain to meteorological causes alone while savages believe that Gods or ghosts or magic can influence the rainfall is no evidence that our brains function differently from their brains. It does not show that we 'think more logically' than savages, at least not if this expression suggests some kind of hereditary psychic superiority. It is no sign of superior intelligence on my part that I attribute rain to physical causes. I did not come to this conclusion myself by observation and inference and have, in fact, little knowledge of the meteorological process that leads to rain, I merely accept what everybody else in my society accepts, namely that rain is due to natural causes. This particular idea formed part of my culture long before I was born into it and little more was required of me than sufficient linguistic ability to learn it. Likewise a savage who believes that under suitable natural and

> ritual conditions the rainfall can be influenced by use of appropriate magic is not on account of this belief to be considered of inferior intelligence. He did not build up this belief from his own observations and inferences but adopted it in the same way as he adopted the rest of his cultural heritage, namely, by being born into it. He and I are both thinking in patterns of thought provided for us by the societies in which we live.
>
> It would be absurd to say that the savage is thinking mystically and that we are thinking scientifically about rainfall. In either case like mental processes are involved and, moreover, the content of thought is similarly derived. But we can say that the social content of our thought about rainfall is scientific, is in accord with the objective facts, whereas the social content of savage thought about rainfall is unscientific since it is not in accord with reality and may also be mystical where it assumes the existence of supra-sensible forces.[4]

In a subsequent article on Pareto, Evans Pritchard distinguishes between 'logical' and 'scientific'.

> Scientific notions are those which accord with objective reality both with regard to the validity of their premisses and to the inferences drawn from their propositions. . . . Logical notions are those in which according to the rules of thought inferences would be true were the premisses true, the truth of the premisses being irrelevant . . .
>
> A pot has broken during firing. This is probably due to grit. Let us examine the pot and see if this is the cause. That is logical and scientific thought. Sickness is due to witchcraft. A man is sick. Let us consult the oracles to discover who is the witch responsible. That is logical and unscientific thought.[5]

I think that Evans-Pritchard is right in a great deal of what he says here, but wrong, and crucially wrong, in his attempt to characterize the scientific in terms of that which is 'in accord with objective reality'. Despite differences of emphasis and phraseology, Evans-Pritchard is in fact hereby put into the same metaphysical camp as Pareto: for both of them the conception of 'reality' must be regarded as intelligible and applicable *outside* the context of scientific reasoning itself, since it is that to which scientific notions do, and unscientific notions do not, have a relation. Evans-Pritchard, although he emphasizes that a member of scientific culture has a different conception of reality from that of a Zande believer in magic, wants to go beyond merely registering this fact and making the differences explicit, and to say, finally, that the scientific conception agrees with what reality actually is like, whereas the magical conception does not.

It would be easy, at this point, to say simply that the difficulty arises from the use of unwieldy and misleadingly comprehensive expression 'agreement with reality'; and in a sense this is true. But we should not lose sight of the fact that the idea that men's ideas and beliefs must be checkable by reference to something independent – some reality – is an important one. To abandon it is to plunge straight into an extreme Protagorean relativism, with all the paradoxes that involves. On the other hand great care is certainly necessary in fixing the precise role that this conception of the independently real does play in men's thought. There are two related points that I should like to make about it at this stage.

In the first place we should notice that the check of the independently real is not peculiar to science. The trouble is that the fascination science has for us makes it easy for us to adopt its scientific form as a paradigm against which to measure the intellectual respectability of other modes of discourse. Consider what God says to Job out of the whirlwind: 'Who is this that darkeneth counsel by words without knowledge? . . . Where wast thou when I laid the foundations of the earth? declare, if thou hast understanding . Who hath laid the measures thereof, if thou knowest? or who hath stretched the line upon it . . . Shall he that contendeth with the Almighty instruct him? he that reproveth God, let him answer it.' Job is taken to task for having gone astray by having lost sight of the reality of God; this does not, of course, mean that Job has made any sort of theoretical mistake, which could be put right, perhaps, by means of an experiment.[6] God's reality is certainly independent of what any man may care to think, but what that reality amounts to can only be seen from the religious tradition in which the concept of God is used, and this use is very unlike the use of scientific concepts, say of theoretical entities. The point is that it is *within* the religious use of language that the conception of God's reality has its place, though, I repeat, this does not mean that it is at the mercy of what anyone cares to say; if this were so, God would have no reality.

My second point follows from the first. Reality is not what gives language sense. What is real and what is unreal shows itself *in* the sense that language has. Further, both the distinction between the real and the unreal and the concept of agreement with reality themselves belong to our language. I will not say that they are concepts of the language like any other, since it is clear that they occupy a commanding, and in a sense limiting, position there. We can imagine a language with no concept, of, say, wetness, but hardly one in which there is no way of distinguishing the real from the unreal. Nevertheless we could not in fact distinguish the real from the unreal without understanding the way this distinction operates in the language. If we wish then to understand the significance of these concepts, we must examine the use they actually do have – *in* the language.

Evans-Pritchard, on the contrary, is trying to work with a conception of reality which is *not* determined by its actual use in language. He wants something against which that use can itself be appraised. But this is not possible; and no more possible in the case of scientific discourse than it is in any other. We may ask whether a particular scientific hypothesis agrees with reality and test this by observation and experiment. Given the experimental methods, and the established use of the theoretical terms entering into the hypothesis, then the question whether it holds or not is settled by reference to something independent of what I or anybody else, care to think. But the general nature of the data revealed by the experiment can only be specificed in terms of criteria built into the methods of experiment employed and these, in turn, make sense only to someone who is conversant with the kind of scientific activity within which they are employed. A scientific illiterate, asked to describe the results of an experiment which he 'observes' in an advanced physics laboratory, could not do so in terms relevant to the hypothesis being tested; and it is really only in such terms that we can sensibly speak of the 'results of the experiment' at all. What Evans-Pritchard wants to be able to say is that the criteria applied in scientific experimentation constitute a true link between our ideas and an independent reality, whereas those characteristics of other systems of thought – in particular, magical methods of thought – do not. It is evident that the expressions 'true link' and 'independent reality' in the previous sentence cannot themselves be explained by reference to the scientific universe of discourse, as this would beg the question. We have then to ask how, by reference to what established universe of discourse, the use of those expressions *is* to be explained; and it is clear that Evans-Pritchard has not answered the question.

Two questions arise out of what I have been saying. First, is it in fact the case that a primitive system of magic, like that of the Azande, constitutes a coherent universe of discourse like science, in terms of which an intellilgible conception of reality and clear ways of deciding what beliefs are and are not in agreement with this reality can be discerned! Second, what are we to make of the possibility of understanding primitive social institutions, like Zande magic, if the situation is as I have outlined? I do not claim to be able to give a satisfactory answer to the second question. It raises some very important and fundamental issues about the nature of human social life, which require conceptions different from, and harder to elucidate than, those I have hitherto introduced. I shall offer some tentative remarks about these issues in the second part of this essay. At present I shall address myself to the first question.

It ought to be remarked here that an affirmative answer to my first question would not commit me to accepting as rational all beliefs couched in magical concepts or all procedures practised in the name of such beliefs. This is no more necessary than is the corresponding proposition that all procedures 'justified' in the name of science are immune from rational criticism. A remark of Collingwood's is apposite here:

> Savages are no more exempt from human folly than civilized men, and are no doubt equally liable to the error of thinking that they, or the persons they regard as their superiors, can do what in fact cannot be done. But this error is not the essence of magic; it is a perversion of magic. And we should be careful how we attribute it to the people we call savages, who will one day rise up and testify against us.[7]

It is important to distinguish a system of magical beliefs and practices like that of the Azande, which is one of the principal foundations of their whole social life and, on the other hand, magical beliefs that might be held, and magical rites that might be practised, by persons belonging to our own culture. These have to be understood rather differently. Evans-Pritchard is himself alluding to the difference in the following passage:

> When a Zande speaks of witchcraft he does not speak of it as we speak of the weird witchcraft of our own history. Witchcraft is to him a commonplace happening and he seldom passes a day without mentioning it. . . . To us witchcraft is something which haunted and disgusted our credulous forefathers. But the Zande expects to come across witchcraft at any time of the day or night. He would be just as surprised if he were not brought into daily contact with it as we would be if confronted by its appearance. To him there is nothing miraculous about it.[8]

The difference is not merely one of degree of familiarity, however, although, perhaps, even this has more importance than might at first appear. Concepts of witchcraft and magic in our culture, at least since the advent of Christianity, have been parasitic on, and a perversion of other orthodox concepts, both religious and, increasingly, scientific. To take an obvious example, you could not understand what was involved in conducting a Black Mass, unless you were familiar with the conduct of a proper Mass and, therefore, with the whole complex of religious ideas from which the Mass draws its sense. Neither would you understand the relation between these without taking account of the fact that the Black practices are rejected as *irrational* (in the sense proper to religion) in the system of beliefs on which these practices are thus parasitic. Perhaps a similar relation holds between the contemporary practice of astrology and astronomy and technology. It is impossible to keep a discussion of the rationality of Black Magic or of astrology within the bounds of concepts peculiar to them; they have an essential reference to something outside themselves. The position is like that which Socrates, in Plato's *Gorgias*, showed to be true of the Sophists' conception of rhetoric: namely, that it is parasitic on rational discourse in such a way that its irrational character can be shown in terms of this dependence. Hence, when we speak of such practices as 'superstitious', 'illusory', 'irrational', we have the weight of our culture behind us; and this is not just a matter of being on the side of the big battalions, because those beliefs and practices belong to, and derive such sense as they seem to have, from that same culture. this enables us to show that the sense is only apparent, in terms which are culturally relevant.

It is evident that our relation to Zande magic is quite different. If we wish to understand it, we must seek a foothold elsewhere. And while there may well be room for the use of such critical expressions as 'superstition' and 'irrationality', the kind of rationality with which such terms might be used to point a contrast remains to be elucidated. The remarks I shall make in Part II will have a more positive bearing on this issue. In the rest of this Part, I shall develop in more detail my criticisms of Evans-Pritchard's approach to the Azande.

Early in this book he defines certain categories in terms of which his descriptions of Zande customs are couched.

> *Mystical Notions* . . . are patterns of thought that attribute to phenomena supra-sensible qualities which, or part of which, are not derived from observation or cannot be logically inferred from it, *and which they do not possess.*[9] *Common-sense Notions* . . . attribute to phenomena only what men observe in them or what can logically be inferred from observation. So long as a notion does not assert something which has not been observed, it is not classed as mystical even though it is mistaken on account of incomplete observation. . . .
>
> *Scientific Notions*. Science has developed out of common sense but it is far more methodical and has better techniques of observation and reasoning. Common sense uses experience and rules of

> thumb. Science uses experiment and rules of Logic. . . . *Our body of scientific knowledge and Logic are the sole arbiters of what are mystical, common sense, and scientific notions*. Their judgements are never absolute.
>
> *Ritual Behaviour*. Any behaviour that is accounted for by mystical notions. *There is no objective nexus* between the behaviour and the event it is intended to cause. Such behaviour is usually intelligible to us only when we know the mystical notions associated with it.
>
> *Empirical Behaviour*. Any behaviour that is accounted for by common-sense notions.[10]

It will be seen from the phrases which I have italicized that Evans-Pritchard is doing more here than just defining certain terms for his own use. Certain metaphysical claims are embodied in the definitions: identical in substance with the claims embodied in Pareto's way of distinguishing between 'logical' and 'non-logical' conduct.[11] There is a very clear implication that those who use mystical notions and perform ritual behaviour are making some sort of mistake, detectable with the aid of science and logic. I shall now examine more closely some of the institutions described by Evans-Pritchard to determine how far his claims are justified.

Witchcraft is a power possessed by certain individuals to harm other individuals by 'mystical' means. Its basis is an inherited organic condition, 'witchcraft-substance' and it does not involve any special magical ritual or medicine. It is constantly appealed to by Azande when they are afflicted by misfortune, not so as to exclude explanation in terms of natural causes, which Azande are perfectly able to offer themselves within the limits of their not inconsiderable natural knowledge, but so as to supplement such explanations. 'Witchcraft explains *why* events are harmful to man and not *how*[12] they happen. A Zande perceives how they happen just as we do. He does not see a witch charge a man but an elephant. He does not see a witch push over the granary, but termites gnawing at its supports. He does not see a psychical flame igniting thatch, but an ordinary lighted bundle of straw. His perception of how events occur is as clear as our own.'[13]

The most important way of detecting the influence of witchcraft and of identifying witches is by the revelations of oracles, of which in turn the most important is the 'poison oracle'. This name, though convenient, is significantly misleading in so far as, according to Evans-Pritchard, Azande do not have our concept of a poison and do not think of, or behave towards, *benge* – the substance administered in the consultation of the oracle – as we do of and towards poisons. The gathering, preparation, and administering of *benge* is hedged with ritual and strict taboos. At an oracular consultation *benge* is administered to a fowl, while a question is asked in a form permitting a yes or no answer. The fowl's death or survival is specified beforehand as giving the answer 'yes' or 'no'. The answer is then checked by administering *benge* to another fowl and asking the question the other way round. 'Is Prince Ndoruma responsible for placing bad medicines in the roof of my hut? The fowl DIES giving the answer "Yes". . . . Did the oracle speak truly when it said that Ndoruma was responsible? The fowl SURVIVES giving the answer "Yes".' The poison oracle is all-pervasive in Zande life and all steps of any importance in a person's life are settled by reference to it.

A Zande would be utterly lost and bewildered without his oracle. The mainstay of his life would be lacking. It is rather as if an engineer, in our society, were to be asked to build a bridge without mathematical calculation, or a military commander to mount an extensive coordinated attack without the use of clocks. These analogies are mine, but a reader may well think that they beg the question at issue. For, he may argue, the Zande practice of consulting the oracle, unlike my technological or military examples, is completely unintelligible and rests on an obvious illusion. I shall now consider this objection.

First I must emphasize that I have so far done little more than note the *fact*, conclusively established by Evans-Pritchard, that the Azande *do* in fact conduct their affairs to their own satisfaction in this way and are at a loss when forced to abandon the practice – when, for instance, they fall into the hands of European courts. It is worth remarking too that Evans-Pritchard himself ran his household in the same way during his field researches and says: 'I found this as satisfactory a way of running my home and affairs as any other I know of.'

Further, I would ask in turn: *to whom* is the practice alleged to be unintelligible? Certainly it is difficult for us to understand what the Azande are about when they consult their oracles; but it might seem just as incredible to them that the engineer's motions with his slide rule could have any connection with the stability of his bridge. But this riposte of course misses the intention behind the objection, which was not directed to the question whether anyone in fact understands, or claims to understand, what is going on, but rather whether what is going on actually does make sense: i.e., in itself. And it may seem obvious that Zande beliefs in witchcraft and oracles cannot make any sense, however satisfied the Azande may be with them.

What criteria have we for saying that something does, or does not, make sense? A partial answer is that a set of beliefs and practices cannot make sense in so far as they involve contradictions. Now it appears that contradictions are bound to arise in at least two ways in the consultation of the oracle. On the one hand two oracular pronouncements may contradict each other; and on the other hand a self-consistent oracular pronouncement may be contradicted by future experience. I shall examine each of these apparent possibilities in turn.

Of course, it does happen often that the oracle first says 'yes' and then 'no' to the same question. This does not convince a Zande of the futility of the whole operation of consulting oracles: obviously, it cannot, since otherwise the practice could hardly have developed and maintained itself at all. Various explanations may be offered, whose possibility, it is important to notice, is built into the whole network of Zande beliefs and may, therefore, be regarded as belonging to the concept of an oracle. It may be said, for instance, that bad *benge* is being used; that the operator of the oracle is ritually unclean; that the oracle is being itself influenced by witchcraft or sorcery; or it may be that the oracle is showing that the question cannot be answered straightforwardly in its present form, as with 'Have you stopped beating your wife yet?' There are various ways in which the behaviour of the fowl under the influence of *benge* may be ingeniously interpreted by those wise in the ways of the poison oracle. We might compare this situation perhaps with the interpretation of dreams.

In the other type of case: where an internally consistent oracular revelation is apparently contradicted by subsequent experience, the situation may be dealt with in a similar way, by references to the influence of witchcraft, ritual uncleanliness, and so on. But there is another important consideration we must take into account here too. The chief function of oracles is to reveal the presence of 'mystical' forces – I use Evans-Pritchard's term without committing myself to his denial that such forces really exist. Now though there are indeed ways of determining whether or not mystical forces are operating, these ways do not correspond to what we understand by 'empirical' confirmation or refutation. This indeed is a tautology, since such differences in 'confirmatory' procedures are the main criteria for classifying something as a mystical force in the first place. Here we have one reason why the possibilities of 'refutation by experience' are very much fewer than might at first sight be supposed.

There is also another closely connected reason. The spirit in which oracles are consulted is very unlike that in which a scientist makes experiments. Oracular revelations are not treated as hypotheses and, since their sense derives from the way they are treated in their context, they therefore *are not* hypotheses. They are not a matter of intellectual interest but the main way in which Azande decide how they should act. If the oracle reveals that a proposed course of action is fraught with mystical dangers from witchcraft or sorcery, that course of action will not be carried out; and then the question of refutation or confirmation just does not arise. We might say that the revelation has the logical status of an unfulfilled hypothetical, were it not that the context in which this logical term is generally used may again suggest a misleadingly close analogy with scientific hypotheses.

I do not think that Evans-Pritchard would have disagreed with what I have said so far. Indeed, the following comment is on very similar lines:

> Azande observe the action of the poison oracle as we observe it, but their observations are always subordinated to their beliefs and are incorporated into their beliefs and made to explain them and justify them. Let the reader consider any argument that would utterly demolish all Zande claims for the power of the oracle. If it were translated into Zande modes of thought it would serve to support their entire structure of belief. For their mystical notions are eminently coherent, being interrelated by a network of logical ties, and are so ordered that they never too crudely contradict sensory experiences but, instead, experience seems to justify them. The Zande is immersed in a sea of mystical notions, and if he speaks about his poison oracle he must speak in a mystical idiom.[14]

To locate the point at which the important philosophical issue does arise, I shall offer a parody, composed by changing round one or two expressions in the foregoing quotation.

> Europeans observe the action of the poison oracle just as Azande observe it, but their observations are always subordinated to their beliefs and are incorporated into their beliefs and made to explain them and justify them. Let a Zande consider any argument that would utterly refute all European scepticism about the power of the oracle. If it were translated into European modes of thought it would serve to support their entire structure of belief. For their scientific notions are eminently coherent, being interrelated by a network of logical ties, and are so ordered that they never too crudely contradict mystical experience but, instead, experience seems to justify them. The European is immersed in a sea of scientific notions, and if he speaks about the Zande poison oracle he must speak in a scientific idiom.

Perhaps this too would be acceptable to Evans-Pritchard. But it is clear from other remarks in the book to which I have alluded, that at the time of writing it he would have wished to add: and the European is right and the Zande wrong. This addition I regard as illegitimate and my reasons for so thinking take us to the heart of the matter.

It may be illuminating at this point to compare the disagreement between Evans-Pritchard and me to that between the Wittgenstein of the *Philosophical Investigations* and his earlier *alter ego* of the *Tractatus Logico-Philosophicus*. In the *Tractatus* Wittgenstein sought 'the general form of propositions': what made propositions possible. He said that this general form is: 'This is how things are'; the proposition was an articulated model, consisting of elements standing in a definite relation to each other. The proposition was true when there existed a corresponding arrangement of elements in reality. The proposition was capable of saying something because of the identity of structure, of logical form, in the proposition and in reality.

By the time Wittgenstein composed the *Investigations* he had come to reject the whole idea that there must be a general form of propositions. He emphasized the indefinite number of different uses that language may have and tried to show that these different uses neither need, nor in fact do, all have something in common, in the sense intended in the *Tractatus*. He also tried to show that what counts as 'agreement or disagreement with reality' takes on as many different forms as there are different uses of language and cannot, therefore, be taken as given *prior* to the detailed investigation of the use that is in question.

The *Tractatus* contains a remark strikingly like something that Evans-Pritchard says:

> *The limits of my language mean the limits of my world*. Logic fills the world: the limits of the world are also its limits. We cannot therefore say in logic: This and this there is in the world, and that there is not.
>
> For that would apparently presuppose that we exclude certain possibilities, and this cannot be the case since otherwise logic must get outside the limits of the world: that is, if it could consider these limits from the other side also.[15]

Evans-Pritchard discusses the phenomena of belief and scepticism, as they appear in Zande life. There *is* certainly widespread scepticism about certain things, for instance, about some of the powers claimed by witchdoctors or about the efficacy of certain magic medicines. But, he points out, such scepticism does not begin to overturn the mystical way of thinking, since it is necessarily expressed in terms belonging to that way of thinking.

> In this web of belief every strand depends on every other strand, and a Zande cannot get outside its meshes because this is the only world he knows. The web is not an external structure in which he is enclosed. It is the texture of his thought and he cannot think that his thought is wrong.[16]

Wittgenstein and Evans-Pritchard are concerned here with much the same problem, though the difference in the directions from which they approach it is important too. Wittgenstein, at the time of the *Tractatus*, spoke of 'language', as if all language is fundamentally of the same kind and must have the same kind of 'relation to reality'; but Evans-Pritchard is confronted by two languages which he recognizes as fundamentally different in kind, such that much of what may be expressed in the one has no possible counterpart in the other. One might, therefore, have expected this to lead to a position closer to that of the *Philosophical Investigations* than to that of the *Tractatus*. Evans-Pritchard is not content with elucidating the differences in the two concepts of reality involved; he wants to go further and say: our concept of reality is the correct one, the Azande are mistaken. But the difficulty is to see what 'correct' and 'mistaken' can mean in this context.

Let me return to the subject of contradictions. I have already noted that many contradictions we might expect to appear in fact do not in the context of Zande thought, where provision is made for avoiding them. But there are some situations of which this does not seem to be true, where what appear to us as obvious contradictions are left where they are, apparently unresolved. Perhaps this may be the foothold we are looking for, from which we can appraise the 'correctness' of the Zande system.[17]

Consider Zande notions about the inheritance of witchcraft. I have spoken so far only of the role of oracles in establishing whether or not someone is a witch. But there is a further and, as we might think, more 'direct' method of doing this, namely by post-mortem examination of a suspect's intestines for 'witchcraft-substance'. This may be arranged by his family after his death in an attempt to clear the family name of the imputation of witchcraft. Evans-Pritchard remarks: 'To our minds it appears evident that if a man is proven a witch the whole of his clan are *ipso facto* witches, since the Zande clan is a group of persons related biologically to one another through the male line. Azande see the sense of this argument but they do not accept its conclusions, and it would involve the whole notion of witchcraft in contradiction were they to do so.'[18] Contradiction would presumably arise because a few positive results of post-mortem examinations, scattered among all the clans, would very soon prove that everybody was a witch, and a few negative results, scattered among the same clans, would prove that nobody was a witch. Though, in particular situations, individual Azande may avoid personal implications arising out of the presence of witchcraft-substance in deceased relatives, by imputations of bastardy and similar devices, this would not be enough to save the generally contradictory situation I have sketched. Evans-Pritchard comments; 'Azande do not perceive the contradiction as we perceive it because they have no theoretical interest in the subject, and those situations in which they express their belief in witchcraft do not force the problem upon them.'[19]

It might now appear as though we had clear grounds for speaking of the superior rationality of European over Zande thought, in so far as the latter involves a contradiction which it makes no attempt to remove and does not even recognize: one, however, which is recognizable as such in the context of European ways of thinking. But does Zande thought on this matter really involve a contradiction? It appears from Evans-Pritchard's account that Azande do not press their ways of thinking about witches to a point at which they would be involved in contradictions.

Someone may not want to say that the irrationality of the Azande in relation to witchcraft shows itself in the fact that they do not press their thought about it 'to its logical conclusion'. To appraise this point we must consider whether the conclusion we are trying to force on them is indeed a logical one; or perhaps better, whether someone who does press this conclusion is being more rational than the Azande, who do not. Some light is thrown on this question by Wittgenstein's discussion of a game,

> such that whoever begins can always win by a particular simple trick. But this has not been realized – so it is a game. Now someone draws our attention to it – and it stops being a game.
>
> What turn can I give this, to make it clear to myself? – For I want to say: 'and it stops being a game' – not: 'and now we see that it wasn't a game'.
>
> That means, I want to say, it can also be taken like this: the other man did not *draw our attention* to anything; he taught us a different game in place of our own. But how can the new game have made the old one obsolete? We now see something different, and can no longer naïvely go on playing.
>
> On the one hand the game consisted in our actions (our play) on the board; and these actions I could perform as well now as before. But on the other hand it was essential to the game that I blindly tried to win; and now I can no longer do that.[20]

There are obviously considerable analogies between Wittgenstein's example and the situation we are considering. But there is an equally important difference. Both Wittgenstein's games: the old one without the trick that enables the starter to win and the new one with the trick, are in an important sense on the same level. They are both *games*, in the form of a contest where the aim of a player is to beat his opponent by the exercise of skill. The new trick makes this situation impossible and this is why it makes the old game obsolete. To be sure, the situation could be saved in a way by introducing a new rule, forbidding the use by the starter of the trick which would ensure his victory. But our intellectual habits are such as to make us unhappy about the artificiality of such a device, rather as logicians have been unhappy about the introduction of a Theory of Types as a device for avoiding Russell's paradoxes. It is noteworthy in my last quotation from Evans-Pritchard, however, that the Azande, when the possibility of this contradiction about the inheritance of witchcraft is pointed out to them, do *not* then come to regard their old beliefs about witchcraft as obsolete. 'They have no theoretical interest in the subject.' This suggests strongly that the context from which the suggestion about the contradiction is made, the context of our scientific culture, is not on the same level as the context in which the beliefs about witchcraft operate. Zande notions of witchcraft do not constitute a theoretical system in terms of which Azande try to gain a quasi-scientific understanding of the world.[21] This in its turn suggests that it is the European, obsessed with pressing Zande thought where it would not naturally go – to a contradiction – who is guilty of misunderstanding, not the Zande. The European is in fact committing a category-mistake.

Something else is also suggested by this discussion: the forms in which rationality expresses itself in the culture of a human society cannot be elucidated *simply* in terms of the logical coherence of the rules according to which activities are carried out in that society. For, as we have seen, there comes a point where we are not even in a position to determine what is and what is not coherent in such a context of rules, without raising questions about the point which following those rules has in the society. No doubt it was a realization of this fact which led Evans-Pritchard to appeal to a residual 'correspondence with reality' in distinguishing between 'mystical' and 'scientific' notions. The conception of reality is indeed indispensable to any understanding of the point of a way of life. But it is not a conception which can be explicated as Evans-Pritchard tries to explicate it, in terms of what science reveals to be the case; for a form of the conception of reality must already be presupposed before we can make any sense of the expression 'what science reveals to be the case'.

II

OUR STANDARDS AND THEIRS

In Part I, I attempted, by analysing a particular case, to criticize by implication a particular view of how we can understand a primitive institution. In this second Part I shall have two aims. First, I shall examine in a more formal way a general philosophical argument, which attempts to show that the approach I have been criticizing is in principle the right one. This argument has been advanced by Alasdair MacIntyre in two places: (a) in a paper entitled *Is Understanding Religion Compatible with Believing?* Read to the Sesquicentennial Seminar of the Princeton Theological Seminar in 1962;[22] (b) in a contribution to *Philosophy, Politics and Society* (*Second Series*),[23] entitled *A Mistake about Causality in Social Science*. Next, I shall make some slightly more positive suggestions about how to overcome the difficulty from which I started: how to make intelligible in our terms institutions belonging to a primitive culture, whose standards of rationality and intelligibility are apparently quite at odds with our own.

The relation between MacIntyre, Evans-Pritchard and myself is a complicated one. MacIntyre takes Evans-Pritchard's later book, *Neur Religion*, as an application of a point of view like mine in *The Idea of a Social Science*; he regards it as an object lesson in the absurd results to which such a position leads, when applied in practice. My own criticisms of Evans-Pritchard, on the other hand, have come from precisely the opposite direction. I have tried to show that Evans-Pritchard did not at the time of writing *The Azande* agree with me *enough*; that he did not take seriously enough the idea that the concepts used by primitive peoples can only be interpreted in the context of the way of life of those peoples. Thus I have in effect argued that Evans-Pritchard's account of the Azande is unsatisfactory precisely to the extent that he agrees with MacIntyre and not me.

The best point at which to start considering MacIntyre's position is that at which he agrees with me – in emphasizing the importance of possibilities of *description* for the concept of human action. An agent's action 'is identified fundamentally as what it is by the description under which he deems it to fall'. Since, further, descriptions must be intelligible to other people, an action 'must fall under some description which is socially recognizable as the description of an action'.[24] 'To identify the limits of social action in a given period', therefore, 'is to identify the stock of descriptions current in that age'.[25] MacIntyre correctly points out that descriptions do not exist in isolation, but occur 'as constituents of beliefs, speculations and projects'. As these in turn 'are continually criticized, modified, rejected, or improved, the stock of descriptions changes. The changes in human action are thus ultimately linked to the threat of rational criticism in human history.'

This notion of rational criticism, MacIntyre points out, requires the notion of choice between alternatives, to explain which 'is a matter of making clear what the agent's criterion was and why he made use of this criterion rather than another and to explain why the use of this criterion appears rational to those who invoke it'.[26] Hence 'in explaining the rules and conventions to which action in a given social order conform [*sic*] we cannot omit reference to the rationality or otherwise of those rules and conventions'. Further, 'the beginning of an explanation of why certain criteria are taken to be rational in some societies is that they *are* rational. And since this has to enter into our explanation we cannot explain social behaviour independently of our own norms of rationality.'

I turn now to criticism of this argument. Consider first MacIntyre's account of changes in an existing 'stock' of available descriptions of actions. How does a candidate for inclusion *qualify* for admission to the stock? Unless there are limits, all MacIntyre's talk about possibilities of description circumscribing possibilities of action becomes nugatory, for there would be nothing to stop anybody inventing some arbitrary verbal expressions, applying it to some arbitrary bodily movement, and thus adding that expression to the stock of available descriptions. But of course the new description must be an *intelligible* one. Certainly, its intelligibility cannot be decided by whether or not it belongs to an *existing* stock of descriptions, since this would rule out precisely what is being discussed: the addition of *new* descriptions to the stock. 'What can intelligibly be said' is not equivalent to 'what has been intelligibly said', or it would never be possible to say anything new. *Mutatis mutandis* it would never be possible to *do* anyting new. Nevertheless the intelligibility of anything new said or done does depend in a certain way on what already has been said or done and understood. The crux of this problem lies in how we are to understand that 'in a certain way'.

In *Is Understanding Religion Compatible with Believing?* MacIntyre asserts that the development through criticism of the standards of intelligibility current in society is ruled out by my earlier account (in *The Idea of a Social Science*) of the origin in social institutions themselves of such standards. I shall not now repeat my earlier argument, but simply point out that I did, in various passages,[27] emphasize the *open* character of the 'rules' which I spoke of in connection with social institutions: i.e. the fact that in changing social situations, reasoned decisions have to be made about what is to count as 'going on in the same way'. MacIntyre's failure to come to terms with this point creates difficulties for him precisely analogous to those which he mistakenly attributes to my account.

It is a corollary of his argument up to this point, as well as being intrinsically evident, that a new description of action must be intelligible to the members of the society in which it is introduced. On my view the point is that what determines this is the further development of rules and principles already implicit in the previous ways of acting and talking. To be emphasized are not the actual members of any 'stock' of descriptions; but the *grammar* which they express. It is through this that we understand their structure and sense, their mutual relations, and the sense of new ways of talking and acting that may be introduced. These new ways of talking and acting may very well at the same time involve modifications in the grammar, but we can only speak thus if the new grammar is (to its users) intellgibly related to the old.

But what of the intelligibility of such changes to observers from another society with a different culture and different standards of intelligibility? MacIntyre urges that such observers must make clear 'what the agent's criterion was and why he made use of this criterion rather than another and why the use of this criterion appears rational to those who invoke it'. Since what is at issue is the precise relation between the concepts of rationality current in these different societies it is obviously of first importance to be clear about *whose* concept of rationality is being alluded to in this quotation. It seems that it must be that which is current in the society in which the criterion is invoked. Something can appear rational to someone only in terms of *his* understanding of what is and is not rational. If *our* concept of rationality is a different one from his, then it makes no sense to say that anything either does or does not appear rational to *him* in *our* sense.

When MacIntyre goes on to say that the observer 'cannot omit reference to the rationality or otherwise of those rules and conventions' followed by the alien agent, whose concept of rationality is now in question: ours or the agent's? Since the observer must be understood now as addressing himself to members of his own society, it seems that the reference must here be to the concept of rationality current in the observer's society. Thus there is a *non sequitur* in the movement from the first to the second of the passages just quoted.

MacIntyre's thought here and in what immediately follows, seems to be this. The explanation of why, in Society *S*, certain actions are taken to be rational, has got to be an explanation for *us*; so it must be in terms of concepts intelligible to us. If then, in the explanation, we say that in fact those criteria *are* rational, we must be using the word '*rational*' in *our* sense. For this explanation would require that we had previously carried out an independent investigation into the actual rationality or otherwise of those criteria, and we could do this only in terms of an understood concept of rationality – *our* understood concept of rationality. The explanation would run: members of Society *S* have seen to be the case something that we know to be the case. If 'what is seen to be the case' is common to us and them, it must be referred to under the same concept for each of us.

But obviously this explanation is not open to us. For we start from the position that standards of rationality in different societies do not always coincide; from the possibility, therefore, that the standards of rationality current in *S* are different from our own. So we cannot assume that it will make sense to speak of members of *S* as discovering something which we have also discovered; such discovery presupposes initial conceptual agreement.

Part of the trouble lies in MacIntyre's use of the expression, 'the rationality of criteria', which he does not explain. In the present context to speak thus is to cloak the real problem, since what we are concerned with are differences in *criteria of rationality*. MacIntyre seems to be saying that certain standards are taken as criteria of rationality because they *are* criteria of rationality. But whose?

There are similar confusions in MacIntyre's other paper: *Is Understanding Religion Compatible with Believing?* There he argues that when we detect an internal incoherence in the standards of intelligibility current in an alien society and try to show why this does not appear, or is made tolerable to that society's members, 'we have already invoked our standards'. In what sense is this true? In so far as *we* 'detect' and 'show' something, obviously we do so in a sense intelligible to us; so we are limited by what *counts* (for us) as 'detecting', 'showing' something. Further, it may well be that the interest in showing and detecting such things is peculiar to our society – that we are doing something in which members of the studied society exhibit no interest, because the institutions in which such an interest could develop are lacking. Perhaps too the pursuit of that interest in our society has led to the development of techniques of inquiry and modes of argument which again are not to be found in the life of the studied society. But it cannot be guaranteed in advance that the methods and techniques we have used in the past – e.g., in elucidating the logical structure of arguments in our own language and culture – are going to be equally fruitful in this new context. They will perhaps need to be extended and modified. No doubt, if they are to have a logical relation to our previous forms of investigation, the new techniques will have to be recognizably continuous with previously used ones. But they must also so extend our conceptions of intelligibility as to make it possible for us to see what intelligibility amounts to in the life of the society we are investigating.

The task MacIntyre says we must undertake is to make intelligible (a) (to us) why it is that members of *S* think that certain of their practices are intelligible (b) (to them), when in fact they are not. I have introduced differentiating letters into my two uses of 'intelligible', to mark the complexity that MacIntyre's way of stating the position does not bring out: the fact that we are dealing with two different senses of the word 'intelligible'. The relation between these is precisely the question at issue. MacIntyre's task is not like that of making intelligible a natural phenomenon, where we are limited only by what counts as intelligibility for us. We must somehow bring *S*'s conception of intelligibility (b) into (intelligible!) relation with our own conception of intelligibility (a). That is, we have to create a new unity for the concept of intelligibility, having a certain relation to our old one and perhaps requiring a considerable realignment of our categories. We are not seeking a state in which things will appear to us as they do to members of *S*, and perhaps such a state is unattainable anyway. But we *are* seeking a way of looking at things which goes beyond our previous way in that it has in some way taken account of and incorporated the other way that members of *S* have of looking at things. Seriously to study another way of life is necessarily to seek to extend our own – not simply to bring the other way within the already existing boundaries of our own, because the point about the latter in their present form, is that they *ex hypothesi* exclude that other.

There is a dimension to the notions of rationality and intelligibility which may make it easier to grasp the possibility of such an extension. I do not think that MacIntyre takes sufficient account of this dimension and, indeed, the way he talks about 'norms of rationality' obscures it. Rationality is not *just* a concept *in* a language like any other; it is this too, for, like any other concept it must be circumscribed by an established use: a use, that is, established in the language. But I think it is not a concept which a language may, as a matter of fact, have and eqally well may not have, as is, for instance, the concept of politeness. It is a concept necessary to the existence of any language: to say of a society that it has a language[28] is also to say that that it has a concept of rationality. There need not perhaps be any *word* functioning in its language as 'rational' does in ours, but at least there must be features of its members' use of language analogous to those features of *our* use of language which are connected with our use of the word 'rational'. Where there is language it must make a difference what is said and this is only possible where the saying of one thing rules out, on pain of failure to communicate, the saying of something else. So in one sense MacIntyre is right in saying that we have already invoked our concept of rationality in saying of a collection of people that they constitute a society with a language: in the sense, namely, that we imply formal analogies between their behaviour and that behaviour in our society which we refer to in distinguishing between rationality and irrationality. This, however, is so far to say nothing about what in particular constitutes rational behaviour in that society; that would require more particular knowledge about the norms they appeal to in living their lives. In other words, it is not so much a matter of invoking 'our own norms of rationality' as of invoking our notion of rationality in speaking of their behaviour in terms of 'conformity to norms'. But how precisely this notion is to be applied to them will depend on our reading of their conformity to norms – what counts for them as conformity and what does not.

Earlier I criticized MacIntyre's conception of a 'stock of available descriptions'. Similar criticisms apply to his talk about 'our norms of rationality', if these norms are taken as forming some finite set. Certainly we learn to think, speak, and act rationally *through* being trained to adhere to particular norms. But having learned to speak, etc., rationally does not *consist* in having been trained to follow those norms; to suppose that would be to overlook the importance of the phrase 'and so on' in any description of what someone who follows norms does. We must, if you like, be open to new possibilities of what could be invoked and accepted under the rubric of 'rationality' – possibilities which are perhaps suggested and limited by what we have hitherto so accepted, but not uniquely determined thereby.

This point can be applied to the possibilities of our grasping forms of rationality different from ours in an alien culture. First, as I have indicated, these possibilities are limited by certain formal requirements centering around the demand for consistency. But these formal requirements tell us nothing about what in particular is to *count* as consistency, just as the rules of the propositional calculus limit, but do not themselves determine what are to be proper values of p, q, etc. We can only determine this by investigating the wider context of the life in which the activities in question are carried on. This investigation will take us beyond merely specifying the rules governing the carrying out of those activities. For, as MacIntyre quite rightly says, to note that certain rules are followed is so far to say nothing about the *point* of the rules; it is not even to decide whether or not they have a point at all.

MacIntyre's recipe for deciding this is that 'in bringing out this feature of the case one shows also whether the use of this concept is or is not a possible one for people who have the standards of intelligibility in speech and action which we have'.[29] It is important to notice that his argument, contrary to what he supposes, does not in fact show that our *own* standards of rationality occupy a peculiarly central position. The appearance to the contrary is an optical illusion engendered by the fact that MacIntyre's case has been advanced in the English language and in the context of twentieth century European culture. But a formally similar argument could be advanced in *any* language containing concepts playing a similar role in that language to those of 'intelligibility' and 'rationality' in ours. This shows that, so far from overcoming relativism, as he claims, MacIntyre himself falls into an extreme form of it. He disguises this from himself by committing the very error of which, wrongly as I have tried to show, he accuses me: the error of overlooking the fact that 'criteria and concepts have a history'. While he emphasizes this point when he is dealing with the concepts and criteria governing action in particular social contexts, he forgets it when he comes to talk of the *criticism* of such criteria. Do not the criteria appealed to in the criticism of existing institutions equally have a history? And in whose society do they have that history? MacIntyre's implicit answer is that it is in ours; but if we are to speak of difficulties and incoherencies appearing and being detected in the way certain practices have hitherto been carried on in society, surely this can only be understood in connection with problems arising *in* the carrying on of the activity. Outside that context we could not begin to grasp what was problematical.

Let me return to the Azande and consider something which MacIntyre says about them, intended to support the position I am criticizing.

> The Azande believe that the performance of certain rites in due form affects their common welfare; this belief cannot in fact be refuted. For they also believe that if the rites are ineffective it is because someone present at them had evil thoughts. Since this is always possible, there is never a year when it is unavoidable for them to admit that the rites were duly performed, but they did not thrive. Now the belief of the Azande is not unfalsifiable in principle (we know perfectly well what would falsify it – the conjunction of the rite, no evil thoughts and disasters). But in fact it cannot be falsified. Does this belief stand in need of rational criticism? And if so by what standards? It seems to me that one could not hold the belief of the Azande rational *in the absence of* any practice of science and technology in which criteria of effectiveness, ineffectiveness and kindred notions had been built up. But to say this is to recognize the appropriateness of scientific criteria of judgement from our standpoint. The Azande do not intend their belief either as a piece of science or as a piece of non-science. They do not possess these categories. It is only *post eventum*, in the light of later and more sophisticated understanding that their belief and concepts can be classifed and evaluated at all.[30]

Now in one sense classification and evaluation of Zande beliefs and concepts does require 'a more sophisticated understanding' than is found in Zande culture; for the sort of classification and evaluation that are here in question are sophisticated philosophical activities. But this is not to say that Zande forms of life are to be classified and evaluated in the way MacIntyre asserts: in terms of certain specific forms of life to be found in our culture, according as they do or do not measure up to what is required within these. MacIntyre confuses the sophistication of the interest in classification with the sophistication of the concepts employed in our classificatory work. It is of interest to us to understand how Zande magic is related to science; the concepts of such a comparison is a very sophisticated one; but this does not mean that we have to see the unsophisticated Zande practice in the light of more sophisticated practices in our own culture, like science – as perhaps a more primitive form of it. MacIntyre criticizes, justly, Sir James Frazer for having imposed the image of his own culture on more primitive ones; but that is exactly what MacIntyre himself is doing here. It is extremely difficult for a sophisticated member of a sophisticated society to grasp a very simple and primitive form of life; in a way he must jettison his sophistication, a process which is itself perhaps the ultimate in sophistication and simplicitly becomes unhelpful at this point.

It may be true, as MacIntyre says, that the Azande do not have the categories of science and non-science. But Evans-Pritchard's account shows that they do have a fairly clear working distinction between the technical and the magical. It is neither here nor there that individual Azande may sometimes confuse the categories, for such confusions may take place in any culture. A much more important fact to emphasize is that *we* do not initially have a category that looks at all like the Zande category of magic. Since it is we who want to understand the Zande category, it appears that the onus is on us to extend our understanding so as to make room for the Zande category, rather than to insist on seeing it in terms of our own ready-made distinction between science and non-science. Certainly the sort of understanding we seek requires that we see the Zande category in relation to our own already understood categories. But this neither means that it is right to 'evaluate' magic in terms of criteria belonging to those other categories; nor does it give any clue as to *which* of our existing categories of thought will provide the best point of reference from which we can understand the point of the Zande practices.

MacIntyre has no difficulty in showing that *if* the rites which the Azande perform in connection with their harvests are 'classified and evaluated' by reference to the criteria and standards of science or technology, then they are subject to serious criticism. He thinks that the

Zande 'belief' is a sort of *hypothesis* like, e.g., an Englishman's belief that all the heavy rain we have been having is due to atomic explosions.[31] MacIntyre believes that he is applying as it were a neutral concept of '*A* affecting *B*', equally applicable to Zande magic and western science. In fact, however, he is applying the concept with which *he* is familiar, one which draws its significance from its use in scientific and technological contexts. There is no reason to suppose that the Zande magical concept of '*A* affecting B' has anything like the same significance. On the contrary, since the Azande do, in the course of their practical affairs, apply something very like our technical concept – though perhaps in a more primitive form – and since their attitude to and thought about their magical rites are quite different from those concerning their technological measures, there is every reason to think that their concept of magical 'influence' is quite different. This may be easier to accept if it is remembered that, even in our own culture, the concept of causal influence is by no means monolithic: when we speak, for example, of 'what made Jones get married', we are not saying the same kind of thing as when we speak of 'what made the aeroplane crash'; I do not mean simply that the events of which we speak are different in kind but that the relation between events is different also. It should not then be difficult to accept that in a society with quite different institutions and ways of life from our own, there may be concepts of 'causal influence' which behave even more differently.

But I do not want to say that we are quite powerless to find ways of thinking in our own society that will help us to see the Zande institution in a clearer light. I only think that the direction in which we should look is quite different from what MacIntyre suggests. Clearly the nature of Zande life is such that it is of very great importance to them that their crops should thrive. Clearly too they take all kinds of practical 'technological' steps, within their capabilities, to ensure that they *do* thrive. But that is no reason to see their magical rites as a further, misguided such step. A man's sense of the importance of something to him shows itself in all sorts of ways: not merely in precautions to safeguard that thing. He may want to come to terms with its importance to him in quite a different way: to contemplate it, to gain some sense of his life in relation to it. He may wish thereby, in a certain sense, to *free* himself from dependence on it. I do not mean by making sure that it does not let him down, because the point is that, *whatever* he does, he may still be let down. The important thing is that he should understand *that* and come to terms with it. Of course, merely to understand that is not to come to terms with it, though perhaps it is a necessary condition for so doing, for a man may equally well be transfixed and terrorized by the contemplation of such a possibility. He must see that he can still go on even if he is let down by what is vitally important to him; and he must so order his life that he still *can* go on in such circumstances. I stress once again that I do not mean this in the sense of becoming 'technologically independent', because from the present point of view technological independence is yet another form of dependence. Technology destroys some dependencies but always creates new ones, which may be fiercer – because harder to understand – than the old. This should be particularly apparent to *us*.[32]

In Judaeo–Christian cultures the conception of 'If it be Thy Will', as developed in the story of Job, is clearly central to the matter I am discussing. Because this conception is central to Christian prayers of supplication, they may be regarded from one point of view as freeing the believer from dependence on what he is supplicating for.[33] Prayers cannot play this role if they are regarded as a means of influencing the outcome for in that case the one who prays is still dependent on the outcome. He frees himself from this by acknowledging his complete dependence on God; and this is totally unlike any dependence on the outcome precisely because God is eternal and the outcome contingent.

I do not say that Zande magical rites are at all like Christian prayers of supplication in the positive attitude to contingencies which they express. What I do suggest is that they are alike in that they do, or may, express an attitude to contingencies; one, that is, which involves recognition that one's life is subject to contingencies, rather than an attempt to control these. To characterize this attitude more specifically one should note how Zande rites emphasize the importance of certain fundamental features of their life which MacIntyre ignores. MacIntyre concentrates implicitly on the relation of the rites to consumption, but of course they are also fundamental to social relations and this seems to be emphasized in Zande notions of witchcraft. We have a drama of resentments, evil-doing, revenge, expiation, in which there are ways of dealing (symbolically) with misfortunes and their disruptive effects on a man's relations with his fellows, with ways in which life can go on despite such disruptions.

How is my treatment of this example related to the general criticisms I was making of MacIntyre's account of what it is for us to see the *point* of the rules and conventions followed in an alien form of life? MacIntyre speaks as though our own rules and conventions are somehow a paradigm of what it is for rules and conventions to have a point, so that the only problem that arises is an accounting for the point of the rules and conventions in some other society. But in fact, of course, the problem is the same in relation to our own society as it is in relation to any other; no more than anyone else's are *our* rules and conventions immune from the dantger of being or becoming pointless. So an account of this matter cannot be given simply in terms of any set of rules and conventions at all:

our own or anyone else's; it requires us to consider the relations of a set of rules and conventions to something else. In my discussion of Zande magical rites just now what I tried to relate the magical rites to was a sense of the significance of human life. This notion is, I think, indispensable to any account of what is involved in understanding and learning from an alien culture; I must now try to say more about it.

In a discussion of Wittgenstein's philosophical use of language games[34] Rush Rhees points out that to try to account for the meaningfulness of language solely in terms of isolated language games is to omit the important fact that ways of speaking are not insulated from each other in mutually exclusive systems of rules. What can be said in one context by the use of a certain expression depends for its sense on the uses of that expression in other contexts (different language games). Language games are played by men who have lives to live – lives involving a wide variety of different interests, which have all kinds of different bearings on each other. Because of this, what a man says or does may make a difference not merely to the performance of the activity upon which he is at present engaged, but to his *life* and to the lives of other people. Whether a man sees point in what he is doing will then depend on whether he is able to see any unity in his multifarious interests, activities, and relations with other men; what sort of sense he sees in his life will depend on the nature of this unity. The ability to see this sort of sense in life depends not merely on the individual concerned, though this is not to say it does not depend on him at all; it depends also on the possibilities for making such sense which the culture in which he lives does, or does not, provide.

What we may learn by studying other cultures are not merely possibilities of different ways of doing things, other techniques. More importantly we may learn different possibilities of making sense of human life, different ideas about the possible importance that the carrying out of certain activities may take on for a man, trying to contemplate the sense of his life as a whole. This dimension of the matter is precisely what MacIntyre misses in his treatment of Zande magic; he can see in it only a (misguided) technique for producing consumer goods. But a Zande's crops are not just potential objects of consumption: the life he lives, his relations with his fellows, his chances for acting decently or doing evil, may all spring from his relation to his crops. Magical rites constitute a form of expression in which these possibilities and dangers may be contemplated and reflected on – and perhaps also thereby transformed and deepened. The difficulty we find in understanding this is not merely its remoteness from science, but an aspect of the general difficulty we find, illustrated by MacIntyre's procedure, of thinking about such matters at all except in terms of 'efficiency of production' – production, that is, for consumption. This again is a symptom of what Marx called the 'alienation' characteristic of man in industrial society, though Marx's own confusions about the relations between production and consumption are further symptoms of that same alienation. Our blindness to the point of primitive modes of life is a corollary of the pointlessness of much of our own life.

I have now explicitly linked my discussion of the 'point' of a system of conventions with conceptions of good and evil. My aim is not to engage in moralizing, but to suggest that the concept of *learning from* which is involved in the study of other cultures is closely linked with the concept of *wisdom*. We are confronted not just with different techniques, but with new possibilities of good and evil, in relation to which men may come to terms with life. An investigation into this dimension of a society may indeed require a quite detailed inquiry into alternative techniques (e.g., production), but an inquiry conducted for the light it throws on those possibilities of good and evil. A very good example of the kind of thing I mean is Simon Weil's analysis of the techniques of modern factory production in *Oppression and Liberty*, which is not a contribution to business management, but part of an inquiry into the peculiar form which the evil of oppression takes in our culture.

In saying this, however, I may seem merely to have lifted to a new level the difficulty raised by MacIntyre of how to relate our own conceptions of rationality to those of other societies. Here the difficulty concerns the relation between our own conceptions of good and evil and those of other societies. A full investigation would thus require a discussion of ethical relativism at this point. I have tried to show some of the limitations of relativism in an earlier paper.[35] I shall close the present essay with some remarks which are supplementary to that.

I wish to point out that the very conception of human life involves certain fundamental notions – which I shall call 'limiting notions' – which have an obvious ethical dimension, and which indeed in a sense determine the 'ethical space', within which the possibilities of good and evil in human life can be exercised. The notions which I shall discuss very briefly here correspond closely to those which Vico made the foundation of his idea of natural law, on which he thought the possibility of understanding human history rested: birth, death, sexual relations. Their significance here is that they are inescapably involved in the life of all known human societies in a way which gives us a clue where to look, if we are puzzled about the point of an alien system of institutions. The specific forms which these concepts take, the particular institutions in which they are expressed, vary very considerably from one society to another; but their central position within a society's institutions is and must be a constant factor. In trying to understand the life of an alien society, then, it will be of the utmost important to be clear about the way in which these notions enter into it. The actual practice of social anthropologists bears this out, although I do not know how many of them would attach the same kind of importance to them as I do.

I speak of a 'limit' here because these notions, along no doubt with others, give shape to what we understand by 'human life'; and because a concern with questions posed in terms of them seems to me constitutive of what we understand by the 'morality' of a society. In saying this, I am of course, disagreeing with those moral philosophers who have made attitudes of approval and disapproval, or something similar, fundamental in ethics, and who have held that the *objects* of such attitudes were conceptually irrelevant to the conception of morality. On that view, there might be a society where the sorts of attitudes taken up in *our* society to questions about relations between the sexes were reserved, say, for questions about the length people wear their hair, and *vice versa*. This seems to me incoherent. In the first place, there would be a confusion in *calling* a concern of that sort a 'moral' concern, however passionately felt. The story of Samson in the Old Testament confirms rather than refutes this point, for the interdict on the cutting of Samson's hair is, of course, connected there with much else: and pre-eminently, it should be noted, with questions about sexual relations. But secondly, if that is thought to be merely verbal quibbling, I will say that it does not seem to me a merely conventional matter that T. S. Eliot's trinity of 'birth, copulation and death' happen to be such deep objects of human concern. I do not mean that they are made such by fundamental psychological and sociological forces, though that is no doubt true. But I want to say further that the very notion of human life is limited by these conceptions.

Unlike beasts, men do not merely live but also have a conception of life. This is not something that is simply added to their life; rather, it changes the very sense which the word 'life' has, when applied to men. It is no longer equivalent to 'animate existence'. When we are speaking of the life of man, we can ask questions about what is the right way to live, what things are most important in life, whether life has any significance, and if so what.

To have a conception of life is also to have a conception of death. But just as the 'life' that is here in question is not the same as animate existence, so the 'death' that is here in question is not the same as the end of animate existence. My conception of the death of an animal is of an event that will take place in the world; perhaps I shall observe it – and my life will go on. But when I speak of 'my death', I am not speaking of a future event in my life;[36] I am not even speaking of an event in anyone else's life. I am speaking of the cessation of my world. That is also a cessation of my ability to do good or evil. It is not just that *as a matter of fact* I shall no longer be able to do good or evil after I am dead; the point is that my very *concept* of what it is to be able to do good or evil is deeply bound up with my concept of my life as ending in death. If ethics is a concern with the right way to live, then clearly the nature of this concern must be deeply affected by the concept of life as ending in death. One's attitude to one's life is at the same time an attitude to one's death.

This point is very well illustrated in an anthropological datum which MacIntyre confesses himself unable to make any sense of.

> According to Spencer and Gillen some aborigines carry about a stick or stone which is treated *as if* it is or embodies the soul of the individual who carries it. If the stick or stone is lost, the individual anoints himself as the dead are anointed. Does the concept of 'carrying one's soul about with one' make sense? Of course we can redescribe what the aborigines are doing and transform it into sense, and perhaps Spencer and Gillen (and Durkheim who follows them) misdescribe what occurs. But if their reports are not erroneous, we confront a blank wall here, so far as meaning is concerned, although it is easy to give the rules for the use of the concept.[37]

MacIntyre does not say why he regards the concept of carrying one's soul about with one in a stick 'thoroughly incoherent'. He is presumably influenced by the fact that it would be hard to make sense of an action like this if performed by a twentieth-century Englishman or American; and by the fact that the soul is not a material object like a piece of paper and cannot, therefore, be carried about in a stick as a piece of paper might be. But it does not seem to me as hard to see sense in the practice, even from the little we are told about it. Consider that a lover in our society may carry about a picture or lock of hair of the beloved; and this may symbolize for him his relation to the beloved and may, indeed, change the relation in all sorts of ways: for example, strengthening or perverting it. Suppose that when the lover loses the locket he feels guilty and asks his beloved for her forgiveness; there might be a parallel to the aboriginal's practice of anointing himself when he 'loses his soul'. And is there necessarily anything irrational about either of these practices? Why should the lover not regard his carelessness in losing the locket as a sort of betrayal of the beloved? Remember how husbands and wives feel about the loss of a wedding ring. The aborigine is clearly expressing a concern with his life as a whole in this practice; the anointing shows the close connection between such a concern and contemplation of death. Perhaps it is precisely this practice which makes such a concern possible for him, as religious sacraments make certain sorts of concern possible. The point is that a concern with one's life as a whole, involving as it does the limiting conception of one's death, if it is to be expressed *within* a person's life, can necessarily only be expressed quasi-sacramentally. The form of the concern shows itself in the form of the sacrament.

The sense in which I spoke also of sex as a 'limiting concept' again has to do with the concept of a human life. The life of a man is a man's life and the life of a woman is a woman's life: the masculinity or the femininity are not just *components* in the life, they are its mode. Adapting Wittgenstein's remark about death, I might say that my masculinity is not an experience in the world, but my way of experiencing the world. Now the concepts of masculinity and femininity obviously require each other. A man is a man in relation to women; and a woman is a woman in relation to men.[38] Thus the form taken by man's relation to women is of quite fundamental importance for the significance he can attach to his own life. The vulgar identification of morality with sexual morality certainly *is* vulgar; but it is a vulgarization of an important truth.

The limiting character of the concept of birth is obviously related to the points I have sketched regarding death and sex. On the one hand, my birth is no more an event in my life than is my death; and through my birth ethical limits are set for my life quite independently of my will: I am, from the outset, in specific relations to other people, from which obligations spring which cannot but be ethically fundamental.[39] On the other hand, the concept of birth is fundamentally linked to that of relations between the sexes. This remains true, however much or little may be known in a society about the contribution of males and females to procreation; for it remains true that man is born of woman, not of man. This, then, adds a new dimension to the ethical institutions in which relations between the sexes are expressed.

I have tried to do no more, in these last brief remarks, than to focus attention in a certain direction. I have wanted to indicate that forms of these limiting concepts will necessarily be an important feature of any human society and that conceptions of good and evil in human life will necessarily be connected with such concepts. In any attempt to understand the life of another society, therefore, an investigation of the forms taken by such concepts – their role in the life of the society – must always take a central place and provide a basis on which understanding may be built.

> Now since the world of nations has been made by men, let us see in what institutions men agree and always have agreed. For these institutions will be able to give us the universal and eternal

principles (such as every science must have) on which all nations were founded and still preserve themselves.

We observe that all nations, barbarous as well as civilized, though separately founded because remote from each other in time and space, keep these three human customs: all have some religion, all contract solemn marriages, all bury their dead. And in no nation, however savage and crude, are any human actions performed with more elaborate ceremonies and more sacred solemnity than the rites of religion, marriage and burial. For by the axiom that 'uniform ideas, born among peoples unknown to each other, must have a common ground of truth', it must have been dictated to all nations that from these institutions humanity began among them all, and therefore they must be most devoutly guarded by them all, so that the world should not again become a bestial wilderness. For this reason we have taken these three eternal and universal customs as the first principles of this Science.[40]

NOTES

1 London and New York, 1958.
2 Oxford, 1937.
3 At this point the anthropologist is very likely to start speaking of the 'social function' of the institution under examination. There are many important questions that should be raised about functional explanations and their relations to the issues discussed in this essay; but these questions cannot be pursued further here.
4 E. E. Evans-Pritchard, 'Lévy-Bruhl's Theory of Primitive Mentality', *Bulletin of the Faculty of Arts*, University of Egypt, 1934.
5 'Science and Sentiment', *Bulletin of the Faculty of Arts*. University of Egypt, 1935.
6 Indeed, one way of expressing the point of the story of Job is to say that in it Job is shown as going astray by being induced to make the reality of goodness of God contingent on what happens.
7 R. G. Collingwood, *Principles of Art* (Oxford, 1958), p. 67.
8 Evans-Pritchard, *Witchcraft, Oracles and Magic among the Azande* (Oxford, 1937), p. 64.
9 The italics are mine throughout this quotation.
10 Evans-Pritchard, *Witchcraft*, p. 12.
11 For further criticism of Pareto see Peter Winch, *The Idea of a Social Science* (London and New York, 1958), pp. 95–111.
12 Evans-Pritchard's italics.
13 Evans-Pritchard, *Witchcraft*, p. 72.
14 Ibid., p. 319.
15 Ludwig Wittgenstein, *Tractatus Logico-Philosophicus*, 5.6–5.61.
16 Evans-Pritchard, *Witchcraft*, p. 194.

17 I shall discuss this point in a more general way in Part II.
18 Ibid., p. 24.
19 Ibid., p. 25.
20 L. Wittgenstein, *Remarks on the Foundations of Mathematics*, Pt II, Para. 77. Wittgenstein's whole discussion of 'contradiction' in mathematics is directly relevant to the point I am discussing.
21 Notice that I have *not* said that Azande conceptions of witchcraft have nothing to do with understanding the world at all. The point is that a different form of the concept of understanding is involved here.
22 Published along with other papers in John Hick, ed., *Faith and the Philosophers* (London, 1964).
23 Edited by Peter Laslett and W. G. Runciman (Oxford, 1962).
24 Ibid., p. 58.
25 Ibid., p. 60.
26 Ibid., p. 61.
27 *The Idea of a Social Science* (London and New York, 1958), pp. 57–65; 91–4; 121–3.
28 I shall not discuss here what justifies us in saying *this* in the first place.
29 'Is Understanding Religion Compatible with Believing?' Brian Wilson (ed.), *Rationality* (New York, 1971), p. 69.
30 Ibid., p. 67.
31 In what follows I have been helped indirectly, but greatly, by some unpublished notes made by Wittgenstein on Frazer, which Mr Rush Rhees was kind enough to show me; and also by various scattered remarks on folklore in *The Notebooks* of Simone Weil (London, 1963).
32 The point is beautifully developed by Simone Weil in her essay on 'The Analysis of Oppression' in *Oppression and Liberty* (London, 1958).
33 I have been helped to see this point by D. Z. Phillips, *The Concept of Prayer* (London and New York, 1965).
34 Rush Rhees, 'Wittgenstein's Builders', *Proceedings of the Aristotelian Society*, 20 (1960), pp. 171–86.
35 Peter Winch, 'Nature and Convention', *Proceedings of the Aristotelian Society*, 20 (1960), pp. 231–52.
36 Cf. Wittgenstein, *Tractatus Logico-Philosophicus*, 6.431–6.4311.
37 'Is Understanding Religion Compatible with Believing?' p. 68.
38 These relations, however, are not simple converses. See Georg Simmel, 'Das Relative und das Absolute im Geschlechter-Problem' in *Philosophische Kultur* (Leipzig, 1911).
39 For this reason, among others, I think A. I. Melden is wrong to say that parent-child obligations and rights have nothing directly to do with physical genealogy. Cf. Melden, *Rights and Right Conduct* (Oxford, 1959).
40 Giambattista Vico, *The New Science*, paras 332–3.

2
On the Social Determination of Truth

STEVEN LUKES

> I think that I gained some understanding of communist Russia by studying witchcraft among the Azande.
>
> E. E. Evans-Pritchard, *Social Anthropology*

The argument of this chapter may be stated abstractly as follows: (1) there are no good reasons for supposing that all criteria of truth and validity are (as many as have been tempted to suppose) context-dependent and variable; (2) there are good reasons for maintaining that some are not, that these are universal and fundamental, and that those criteria which *are* context-dependent are parasitic upon them; (3) it is only by assuming such universal and fundamental criteria that a number of crucial sociological questions about beliefs can be asked, among them questions about differences between 'traditional' and 'modern' or 'pre-scientific and 'scientific' modes of thought; and therefore (4) despite many possible difficulties and pitfalls, the sociologist or anthropologist need not prohibit, indeed he should be ready to make, cognitive and logical judgements (however provisional) with respect to the beliefs he studies.

It will be seen that this argument has four distinct stages: critical, philosophical, sociological and prescriptive. None of these is conclusive in itself, but hopefully they are more effective in combination than any of them taken singly. I take them to apply quite generally to the sociology of belief, and to be as relevant (see the quotation above) to the study of primitive religion and magic as to the study of ideology in contemporary industrial societies.

Reprinted by permission of Faber and Faber Ltd from Steven Lukes, 'On the Social Determination of Truth', in *Modes of Thought: Essays on Thinking in Western and Non-Western Societies*, R. Horton and R. Finnegan (eds) (London: Faber and Faber, 1973), pp. 230–48.

CRITICAL

A wide range of thinkers in various traditions of thought have been tempted by the view that criteria of truth, or logic, or both, arise out of different contexts and are themselves variable. The temptation consists in an urge to see the rules specifying what counts as true and/or what counts as valid reasoning as themselves relative to particular groups, cultures or communities. (I shall leave aside purely philosophical attempts to establish relativism.)[1] Among those who have succumbed to the temptation in varying degrees have been a number of sociologists of knowledge (especially Mannheim), as well as philosophically minded social anthropologists and philosphers interested in the social sciences (from Lévy-Bruhl to Winch), linguists (most notably Whorf) and, most recently, historians and philosophers of science (notably Kuhn). Among those who have successfully resisted it are other sociologists of knowledge (including Durkheim), Marxist theorists (from Marx onwards), other social anthropologists (from Frazer and Tylor to Evans-Pritchard) and other philosophers of science (such as Popper). What forms has the temptation taken?

The various forms it has taken really amount to different ways of taking seriously Pascal's observation that what is truth on one side of the Pyreneses is error on the other.[2]

Thus Mannheim writes of revising 'the thesis that the genesis of a proposition is under all circumstances irrelevant to its truth'. For him the sociology of knowledge is an attempt to analyse the 'perspectives' associated with different social positions, to study the 'orientation towards certain meanings and values which inheres in a given social position (the outlook and attitude conditioned by the collective purposes of a group), and the concrete reasons for the different perspectives which the same situation presents to the different positions in it'. He holds that social or 'existential' factors are relevant, 'not only to the genesis of ideas, but penetrate into their forms and content and . . . decisively determine [*sic*] the scope and intensity of our experience and observation'. This, he claims, has decisive implications for epistemology:

> The next task of epistemology, in our opinion, is to overcome its partial nature by incorporating into itself the multiplicity of relationships between existence and validity as discovered by the sociology of knowledge; and to give attention to the types of knowledge operating in a region of being which is full of meaning and which affects the truth value of the assertions.

Yet he also writes, as though trying to resist temptation, that it 'is, of course, true that in the social sciences, as elsewhere, the ultimate criterion of truth or falsity is to be found in the investigation of the object, and the sociology of knowledge is no substitute for this'.[3]

Likewise, Lévy-Bruhl, who followed Durkheim in many respects, diverged from him in this, arguing that primitive thought violates 'our most deeply rooted mental habits, without which, it seems to us, we could no longer think': it is 'mystical, that is oriented at every moment towards occult forces . . . pre-logical, that is indifferent for most of the time to contradiction' and committed to a view of causality 'of a type other than that familiar to us'. For Lévy-Bruhl (above all in his earlier writings), primitives literally 'live, think, feel, move and act in a world which at a number of points does not coincide with ours'[4] and 'the reality in which primitives move is itself mystical'.[5] Furthermore, he began from the hypothesis that societies with different structures had different logics;[6] what he came to call 'pre-logical' thinking might violate 'our' rules but it had its own 'structure', albeit 'strange and even hostile' to 'our conceptual and logical thought'.[7] But, in his latest writings, Lévy-Bruhl too struggled to resist the temptations of this position, acknowledging that the 'mystical mentality' only defined part of the primitives' world and that 'the logical structure of the mind is the same in all known human societies'.[8]

Winch gives a general philosophical rationale for giving in to temptation. For him 'our idea of what belongs to the realm of reality is given for us in the language that we use',[9] so that '[w]hat is real and what is unreal shows itself in the sense that language has. Further, both the distinction between the real and the unreal and the concept of agreement with reality themselves belong to our language.'[10] Similarly, 'criteria of logic . . . arise out of, and are only intelligible in the context of, ways of living and modes of social life': in fact, 'logical relations between propositions themselves depend on social relations between men'.[11] Indeed, for Winch, 'standards of rationality in different societies do not always coincide' and rationality itself comes down in the end to 'conformity to norms'.[12] Yet Winch too goes some way to qualifying this position, at least with respect to logic, when he speaks of 'certain [which?] formal requirements centering round the demand for consistency' – though he (mysteriously) thinks that these 'tell us nothing about what in particular is to *count* as consistency'.[13]

Whorf's linguistic relativity principle represents a relatively unqualified form of the view we are considering. For Whorf, 'all observers are not led by the same physical evidence to the same picture of the universe, unless their linguistic backgrounds are similar, or can in some way be calibrated'. We 'dissect nature along lines laid down by our native languages'; we 'cut up and organise the spread and flow of events as we do, largely because, through our mother tongue, we are parties to an agreement to do so, not because nature itself is segmented in exactly that way for all to see'. Whorf also speaks of 'possible new types of logic' and even claims that 'science CAN have a rational or logical basis even though it be a relativistic one', which 'may vary with each tongue'. Indeed,

> when anyone, as a natural logician, is talking about reason, logic, and the laws of correct thinking, he is apt to be simply marching in step with purely grammatical facts that have somewhat of a background character in his own language or family of languages but are by no means universal in all languages and in no sense a common substratum of reason.[14]

Finally, it is worth citing some of the statements of Kuhn, who has been strongly tempted by this view in relation to scientific paradigms, whose 'incommensurability' he stresses:

> Examining the record of past research from the vantage of contemporary historiography, the historian of science may be tempted to exclaim that when paradigms change, the world itself changes with them . . . paradigm changes do cause scientists to see the world of their research-engagement differently. In so far as their only recourse to that world is through what they see and do, we may want to say that after a revolution scientists are responding to a different world.[15]

From wanting to say it, Kuhn gradually induces himself to say it. Thus he writes that at 'the very least, as a result of discovering oxygen, Lavoisier saw nature differently' and 'in the absence of some recourse to that hypothetical fixed nature that he "saw differently", the principle of economy will urge us to say that after discovering oxygen Lavoisier worked in a different world'.[16] Then, more boldly, he expresses his conviction that 'we must learn to make sense of statements that at least resemble these'; and finally, he claims that in 'a sense that I am unabe to explicate further, the proponents of competing paradigms practise their trades in different worlds'. Kuhn explicitly suggests that we may need to revise the traditional 'epistemological viewpoint that has most often guided Western philosophy for three centuries; as well as our conception of scientific progress; we may 'have to relinquish the notion, explicit or implicit, that changes of paradigm carry scientists and those who learn from them closer and closer to the truth'. In paradigm choice 'there is no standard higher than the assent of the relevant community'; in fact, the 'very existence of science depends upon vesting the power to choose between paradigms in the members of a special kind of community'.[17]

So far as I have tried to show how a number of thinkers with an acute sense of the diversity of human thought (whether linked to social position, as in Mannheim, or culture, as in Lévy-Bruhl and Winch, or language, as in Winch and Whorf, or changing scientific paradigms, as in Kuhn) have allowed themselves to advance the further, crucial claim that truth and validity are similarly diverse. Do they advance any good arguments to support that claim?

Briefly, they appear, with varying degrees of explicitness, to offer two sorts of argument. The first is that since men's perception and understanding of the world is ineradicably theory-dependent, there is no theory-independent reference for terms like 'the world', 'nature', 'reality', and so on,[18] and therefore no theory-independent criterion of truth; and since theories differ, as between social positions, cultures, languages or scientific communities, standards of truth likewise differ. Similarly, since men's notion of what constitutes a valid move from *p* to *q* is theory-dependent, there is no theory-independent logic, and so, for parallel reasons, canons of validity are variable. The second sort of argument, found most explicitly in Mannheim, rests on a denial of the so-called genetic fallacy and asserts that identifying the social determinants of beliefs is not irrelevant to their truth and validity – on the ground that canons of truth and validity can thereby be shown to be socially variable.

The first argument is implausible for two reasons. In the first place, no reason is given for passing from the first step to the second. The influence, however deep, of theories upon men's perceptions and understanding is one thing; the claim that there are no theory-independent objects of perception and understanding is another. Similarly, the influence of theories upon what men may count as valid or consistent is one thing; the claim that validity and consistency are theory-dependent is another. In the second place, it does not follow from the diversity of theories, or indeed from the existence of different concepts of criteria of truth and validity in different contexts, that there may not be some such criteria which are invariable because universal and fundamental (see pp. below).

As for the second argument, to assess it fully would require a detailed analysis of the possible interpretations of 'social', 'determination' and 'belief' (not to mention 'truth' and 'validity'). Let us, briefly, assume a range of definitions of 'social' extending from the purely material or morphological (for example physical size or spatial arrangement of groups) to the purely ideational or cultural.[19] Let us take 'determination' to mean any form of explanatory relation – whether causes; or reasons, motives, desires, purposes, aspirations or interests;[20] or structural identities or correspondences.[21] Let us take 'belief' to mean a proposition accepted as true. One can now ask: if beliefs are socially determined, are there any good reasons for seeing truth and validity as variable?

First, suppose a causal relation can be established between a social factor and a belief or set of beliefs: a certain social factor is shown to have a causal influence (whether weak or strong, partial or total) on the appearance or the adoption or the maintenance of a belief or set of beliefs or on their content or their form. This provides absolutely no ground for concluding that their truth or validity are relative – a point on which Marxists, maintaining that 'social being determines consciousness', have always been clear (since they count their own theories as non-relatively true). This is true even if all beliefs are causally determined – since some men may be lucky enough to be caused to believe what is true.[22] Causation may operate on both sides of the Pyrenees, but that does not commit us to French and Spanish truths and logics.

Second, it might be shown that a certain group of persons have certain good reasons or motives to adopt or adhere to certain beliefs because such beliefs accord with their desires, purposes, aspirations or interests: beliefs are imputed to them as expressing, whether in a transparent or distorted form, their aims or interests in a particular historical situation. They believe their beliefs because they have intelligible reasons for doing so, which can be explicated by an analysis of their situation. This might be shown for all beliefs, but still nothing would follow concerning the truth or consistency of what is believed by any particular category of persons (though, again, it might be shown, as Marx thought was the case, that a certain class of men had no good reason not to believe, and every good reason to believe, what is true).

Finally, the identification of structual identities or instances of conceptual fit between beliefs on the one hand and other social factors (including beliefs) on the other can show how these beliefs cohere with other beliefs and with other features of social life, but it will not in itself have any bearing on their truth or validity.

I conclude that, among the writers we have considered, no satisfactory reason has been given for supposing that there are no invariable and context-independent criteria of truth and valid reasoning.

PHILOSOPHICAL

Are there, then, any good reasons for supposing that there are such criteria? I have argued elsewhere that there are,[23] and will merely summarise those arguments here. Of course, any really hard-boiled relativist could just reject these arguments as themselves relative, but to do so he must realise the full implications of the pluralistic social solipsism his position entails; thus, he cannot speak, as Mannheim does, of 'perspectives' (on what?) or, as Whorf and Kuhn do, of different ways of dissecting nature and seeing the world. The consistent relativist must always take the theory-dependence of his worlds seriously.

Let us suppose we are considering the beliefs of a group of persons *G* (which may be identified in any way – as occupying a partial social position, as sharing a culture or a language, as a scientific community, and so on). Are the truth of their beliefs and the validity of their reasoning simply up to them, a function of the norms to which they conform?

I maintain that the answer to this question is no – or at least that we could never know if it were yes; indeed, that we could not even conceive what it could *be* for it to be yes. For, in the first place, the existence of a common reality is a necessary precondition of our understanding *G*'s language. Though we need not agree about all 'the facts', the members of *G* must have our distinction between truth and falsity as applied to a shared reality if we are not to understand their language, for if, *per impossibile*, they did not, we and they would be unable even to agree about the successful identification of public, spatio-temporally located objects. Moreover, any group which engages in successful prediction must presuppose a given reality, since there must be (independent) events to predict. Thus, if we can in principle learn *G*'s language (and they ours) and we know that they engage in successful prediction, then we and they share a common and independent reality.

Second, *G*'s language must have operable logical rules and not all of these can be pure matters of convention. Winch states that 'logical relations between propositions . . . depend on social relations between men'. Does this imply that the concept of negation and the laws of identity and non-contradiction need not operate in *G*'s language? If so, then it must be mistaken, for if the members of *G* do not possess even these, how could we ever understand their thought, their inferences and their arguments? Could they even be credited with the possibility of inferring, arguing or even thinking? (Lévy-Bruhl came perilously near to maintaining this.)[24] If, for example, they were unable to see that the truth of *p* excludes the truth of its denial, how could they ever communicate truths to one another or reason from them to other truths?

I conclude that if *G* has a language in which it expresses its beliefs, it must, minimally, possess criteria of truth (as correspondence to a common and independent reality)[25] and logic – which are not and cannot be context-dependent. Suppose that *G*'s language and belief-system operated according to quite different critiera. But then, if the members of *G* really did not have our criteria of truth and logic, we would have no adequate grounds for attributing to them a language expressing beliefs and would *a fortiori* be unable to make any statements about these.

The argument sketched here does not, however, entail that the members of *G* might not, against the background of what I claim are universal criteria of truth and logic, adhere systematically to beliefs which violate those criteria. This may happen unconsciously. Thus, according to Spiro, following Frazer and Roth, the Tully River Blacks 'are ignorant of physiological paternity, believing rather that conception is the result of four kinds of "magical" causation'.[26] Again, as Evans-Pritchard reports, Azande do not perceive contradictions in their beliefs, 'because they have no theoretical interest in the subject, and those situations in which they express their beliefs in witchcraft do not force the problem upon them'; indeed, 'it would involve the whole notion of witchcraft in contradiction' were they to pursue some arguments to their conclusions.[27] On the other hand, the violation of criteria of truth and logic may be quite conscious, as when contemporary theologians explain 'seeming' contradictions as mysteries. Again, it may be relatively harmless and socially insignificant, as when a religious sect engages in fantasy and inconsistency of thought; or it may be of the greatest social and political importance, as when the ideological controls over a society involve the systematic propagation of falsehoods and incompatible beliefs.

If, as I have claimed, there are universal criteria of truth and logic, why do I wish to call these criteria fundamental? I think it can be shown that they are fundamental in at least two senses. In the first place, they specify the ultimate constraints to which all thought is subject. Thus all societies, with languages expressing beliefs, must apply them in general (though they may violate them in particular); indeed, it could be argued that they represent basic adaptive mechanisms for any human society. But they are also, I think, fundamental in a second sense: namely, that it can probably be shown that those criteria of truth and validity which are at variance with them and *are* context-dependent are in fact parasitic upon them. That is, where there are second-order native beliefs about what counts as 'true' or 'valid' which are at odds with the basic criteria, those beliefs can only be rendered fully intelligible as operating against the background of such criteria.

For example, according to Franz Steiner,[28] the Chagga have a concept of 'truth' which is 'connected with the institution of the oath', and oath, vow and swearing are 'concerned in the formation of jural relationships and in legal procedure'. Steiner attempts to sketch 'an analysis of truth concepts and their relation to structural situations' among the Chagga. Their words *lohi* or *loi* mean 'a completely reliable statement'; *Ki lohi* means 'this is true' and *Kja lohi* means 'to speak true'. Witnesses, instead of acting as instruments of verification, are 'persons who, under oath, declare their solidarity with one of the parties' and his statements'. The 'story to which they finally bind themselves is *lohi*' and a 'witness in court merely agrees to the words of the party under oath. He speaks *lohi*.' But Steiner's analysis shows that among the Chagga certain structural situations require *alternative* ways of guaranteeing the reliability of statements than verification (which is the basic way); as he says, the witness 'helps to establish a "truth" because no "verification" is possible'.[29] Again, it is clearly a parasitic notion of truth which is presupposed by Stalin's favourite ideological slogan during the last two decades of his rule: that in the dialectical unity of theory and practice, theory guides practice, but practice is the criterion of theoretical truth.[30] Here practice, as officially interpreted, served as a substitute for, and functional equivalent of, verification.

This last is, clearly, an empirical question. All I claim is that, while, as Steiner says, anthropologists (and sociologists) 'are interested in the social reality of "truth" rather than it its logical connexion with verification',[31] verification is likely to provide the basic paradigm against which other criteria of truth gain their sense.

SOCIOLOGICAL

What consequences does the assumption of universal and fundamental criteria of truth and validity have for the sociology of belief? There are, I think, at least four sorts of questions which such an assumption opens up, and which denying it closes off.

In the first place, there are questions about the content and structure of a belief-system itself. A belief-system may consist in a number of ideas, theories and doctrines that are held to be plausible and naturally related partly because a number of distinctions have not been made or conclusions drawn. The good historian of ideas does not seek merely to reproduce a belief-system; he also aims to analyse it and thereby reveal its inner structure – a structure that may not have been perceptible to the believers. In order to do this, he must apply external and critical standards – not just the standards of his own culture or period, but the closest approximation he can make to standards of rational criticism.

Thus Lovejoy describes the first task of the historian of ideas as one of 'logical analysis – the discrimination *in* the texts, and the segretating *out* of the texts, of each of . . . the basic or germinal ideas, the identification of each of them so that it can be recognized wherever it appears, in different contexts, under different labels or phrasings, and in diverse provinces of thought'. And his next task, according to Lovejoy, is 'to examine the relations between these ideas . . . logical, psychological and historical – and, especially, under the latter, genetic – relations'. By 'logical relations' Lovejoy says he means

> relations of implications or opposition between categories, or tacit presuppositions, or express beliefs or doctrines. When he has ascertained the currency and influence of a given idea in this period, the historian does well to ask himself, what does this idea logically presuppose, what does it imply, and with what other ideas is it implicitly incompatible – whether or not these logical relations were recognized by those who embraced the idea. For if it should turn out that some of its implications were not recognised, this may become a highly important, though negative, historical fact. Negative facts are of much more significance for the intellectual historian than is usually appreciated. The things that a writer, given his premises, might be expected to say, but doesn't say – the consequences which legitimately and fairly evidently follow from his theses, but which he never sees, or persistently refuses to draw – these may be even more noteworthy than the things he does say or the consequences he does deduce. For they may throw light upon peculiarities of his mind, especially upon his biases and the non-rational elements in his thinking – may disclose to the historian specific points at which intellectual processes have been checked, or diverted, or perverted, by emotive factors. Negative facts of this kind are thus often indicia of positive but unexplicit or subconscious facts. So, again, the determination of not-immediately-obvious *in*compatibilities between ideas may lead to the recognition of the historically instructive fact that one or another writer, or a whole age, has held together, in closed compartments of the mind, contradictory preconceptions of beliefs. Such a fact – like the failure to see necessary positive implications of accepted premises – calls for psychological explanation, if possible; the historian must at least seek for a hypothesis to account for it.

This leads directly to the second sort of question, intimately related to the first, that assuming non-context-dependent criteria makes possible – namely, why certain beliefs continue to be believed, or cease to be. It is only through the critical application of rational standards that one can identify the mechanisms that prevent men from perceiving the falsity or inconsistency of their beliefs, or the reasons which might lead some men at certain junctures to modify or reject accepted beliefs.

Only thus can one ask, as Evans-Pritchard does, why it is that Azande 'do not perceive the futility of their magic', or how ideological consensus may be maintained in the face of disconfirming evidence and internal coherence. Only thus, for instance, can one identify the whole network of 'secondary elaborations' which protect 'sacred' beliefs against predictive failure and falsification. Such procedures are quite obviously not confined to primitive magic and witchcraft; they are part of the stock-in-trade of the professional ideologist (and Kuhn's work suggests that they are not absent from the practice of 'normal science'); it is, for example, highly instructive to examine critically the precise ways in which the seeming closure and internal coherence of Soviet ideology is maintained, how *a priori* assertions are substituted for, and hence preclude, empirical inquiry, and incompatibilities between different assertions are concealed.[33] And, finally, change in, and rejection of, prevailing ideas cannot be entirely explicable in terms of context-dependent criteria, above all where the criteria themselves are questioned or rejected. Only by assuming rational criteria applicable to all contexts can one fully explain why men abandon religious or magical beliefs, or scientific paradigms in the face of intolerable anomalies (what makes an anomaly intolerable? The answer to this question cannot be internal to the paradigm), or why intellectuals come to reject official myths.

This, in turn, leads to the third set of questions that assuming non-context-dependent criteria makes possible – namely, questions about the social role of ideology and false consciousness. These arise wherever men's beliefs about their own or other societies can be characterised as to some degree distorted or false and where, in virtue of this feature, such beliefs have significant social consequences. It is only by assuming that one has reliable, non-relative means of identifying a disjunction between social consciousness or collective representations on the one hand and social realities on the other that one can raise certain questions about the ways in which belief-systems prevent or promote social change.

Only such an assumption, for instance, can enable an anthropologist to distinguish between, say, the 'conscious model' of a tribe's marriage-system and its actual structure,[34] or between 'real Kachin society' and its 'ideal structure'.[35] Only such an assumption could enable Marx to relate the 'insipid illusions of the eighteenth century', picturing society as made up of abstracted, isolated and 'natural' individuals, to '"bourgeois society", which had been in course of development since the sixteenth century and made gigantic strides towards development since the eighteenth':

> the period in which this view of the isolated individual becomes prevalent, is the very one in which the inter-relations of society (general from this point of view) have reached the highest state of development.[36]

Similarly, only such an assumption could enable Lukács to speak of the 'incapacity' of 'bourgeois thought' to 'understand its own social bases' and of 'unmasking' the 'illusion of the reified fixity' of social phenomena.[37] And only this assumption could enable Ossowski to explore the consequences of certain conceptions of social structure in the social consciousness. Thus, in considering the concepts of non-egalitarian classlessness, he shows how

> the objective reality with which these ways of viewing are concerned may impose an interpretation which is very far from that which a classless society would require. But from the viewpoint of the interests of privileged and ruling groups the utility of presenting one's own society in terms of a non-egalitarian classless society is apparent. In the world of today, both in the *bourgeois* democracies and the people's democracies, such a presentation affords no bases for group solidarity amongst the underprivileged; it inclines them to endeavour to improve their fortunes, and to seek upward social mobility by means of personal effort and their own industry, and not by collective action.

It is on this assumption that Ossowski can observe (with truth) that 'Marxian methods – and in general all sociological methods that threaten stereotypes and social fictions – are rarely found suitable from the viewpoint of the ruling or privileged groups for the analysis of their own society'[38] The central point here is that to speak (non-rhetorically) of 'illusions' and 'social fictions' whose social functions one seeks to explain involves the critical application of criteria that are not merely relative to a particular social position.

Thus a student of Soviet ideology has recently observed, pursuing an argument interestingly parallel to that advanced here, that

> The only way to prove which ideological beliefs have performed what functions in the social process is to study the beliefs and the social process from the vantage point of genuine knowledge. Consider, for example, this belief, which was mandatory in the thirties: The land belongs to the people, and therefore collective farmers hold their land rent free. This . . . presents a specific, verifiable statement as a logical consequence of a vague but stirring principle.

The appropriate model for the historian of ideology should, it is argued, be

> not Voltaire's brilliant mocking of religious illogic, but the anthropologist's strenous effort to discover the social functions of various types of thought. As the student of primitive religion begins his analysis of rain-making ceremonies with the quiet assumption that they do not affect the weather, the student of Soviet ideology should begin his analysis with the observation that rent has existed in the Soviet Union, whether or not Soviet leaders have been aware of it.

Thus '[s]erious analysis begins when one asks how the system of agricultural procurement have been distributing rent from the twenties to the present, and how beliefs and systems have been interacting and changing each other'. In this way one can examine the latent functions of the denial of rent in the context of forcible collectivization – for example, 'to reassure "realistic" leaders that an insoluble problem, the result of their own wild action, did not exist'.[39]

Finally, the fourth set of questions which non-relative criteria open up relates to the differences between traditional or 'pre-scientific' and modern or 'science-orientated' modes of thought. Among the most central of such questions is: what factors have made possible the immensely superior cognitive powers of the latter? Another is: in what spheres are the former cognitively weak, or strong, and why? To see the matter in this way is not necessarily to make ethnocentric assumptions about 'the stupidity of savages'.[40] On the contrary, it is to acknowledge the underlying unity between pre-scientific and scientific world-views.

As Durkheim said, in criticism of Lévy-Bruhl, 'We believe . . . that these two forms of human mentality, however different they are, far from deriving from different sources, are born one from the other and are two moments of a single evolution.'[41] Both seek, among other things, to explain the natural and social world – so as 'not to leave the mind enslaved to visible appearances, but to induce it to master them and to connect what the senses separate'. Thus:

> The explanations of contemporary science are surer of being objective becuse they are more methodical and because they rest on more rigorously controlled observations, but they do not differ in nature from those which satisfy primitive thought. Today, as formerly, to explain is to show how one thing participates in one or several others. It has been said that the participations postulated by mythologies violate the principle of contradiction and are, for that reason, opposed to those implied by scientific explanations. Is not the statement that a man is a kangaroo, or that the sun is a bird, equal to identifying the two with each other? But our mode of

> thinking is no different when we characterize heat as movement, or light as a vibration of the ether, etc. Whenever we unite heterogeneous terms by an internal bond, we necessarily identify contraries. Of course the terms we unite in this way are not those which the Australian aborigine connects together; we select them according to other criteria and for other reasons; but there is no essential difference in the process and by which the mind relates them.[42]

From this standpoint, while conscious of the infinitely rich and various symbolic and expressive features of primitive and traditional thought and ritual (as Durkheim evidently was), one will be under no temptation to explain away false or inadequate attempts at explaining the world and reasoning about it as 'really' emotive, or expressive, or symbolic utterances, and thereby removed from the sphere of application of non-context-dependent criteria of truth and logic.

PRESCRIPTIVE

The final section of this chapter can be brief, since it merely draws the practical moral of the previous three. The sociology of belief need not prohibit a critical cognitive and logical stance *vis-à-vis* the beliefs it studies; indeed, such a prohibition precludes its raising a whole range of problems which are, on the face of it, both genuine and important. On the other hand, there is a real danger involved in adopting such a stance which needs to be appreciated.

The danger lies in confusing the *current content* of Western beliefs with universal and fundamental criteria of truth and validity and in then proceeding to use this current content as a yardstick for classifying other people's beliefs. The English 'intellectualist' school so castigated by Lévy-Bruhl – above all Frazer and Tylor – certainly erred in this direction. Thus Tylor could speak confidently of 'occult science' – 'one of the most pernicious delusions that ever vexed mankind' – as 'mistaking an ideal for a real connexion'.[43] It could be argued that Evans-Pritchard, despite his own excellent criticism of that school,[44] inherits the same tendency in his distinction between mystical and common-sense notions and his appeal to 'science' 'for a decision when the question arises whether a notion shall be classed as mystical or common-sense. Our body of scientifici knowledge and logic are the sole arbiters of what are mystical, common-sense, and scientific notions' – even though he adds that their 'judgements are never absolute'.[45]

Indeed they are not, and it can be dangerous for the social

anthropologist or sociologist to take his own assumptions for granted in classifying the beliefs of others. Above all is this so in the case of social and psychological matters, but it applies quite generally. A particularly striking instance of this is provided by Robin Horton in his discussion of the traditional African diagnosis of disease, which, though reference is made to spiritual agencies, usually identifies 'the human hatreds, jealousies, and misdeeds, that have brought such agencies into play'. Thus Victor Turner 'shows how, in diagnosing the causes of some bodily affliction, the Ndembu diviner not only refers to unseen spiritual forces, but also relates the patient's condition to a whole series of disturbances in his social field'. The idea of the social causation of disease, especially so-called 'organic' disease, was not scientifically respectable when Evans-Pritchard wrote his book on the Azande, and he accordingly classified such hypotheses as 'mystical'. Horton is surely right to urge 'the need to approach traditional religious theories of the social causation of sickness with respect'.[46]

Such respect is obviously methodologically sound and should be applied generally. It underlines the essential provisional nature of all cognitive judgements. Which is to say that, without embracing any form of epistemological or logical relativism, the sociologist of belief should be as critical of his own beliefs as of the beliefs of others.

NOTES

1 They have been interestingly made, and combated, within the Polish philosophical tradition and subsequently among Polish Marxists (for example Schaff and Kolakowski). See H. Skolimowski, *Polish Analytical Philosophy* (London: Routledge, 1967) and Z. Jordan, *Philosophy and Ideology* (Dordrecht: Reidel, 1963). Also relevant is the American pragmatist tradition, and especially, the work of Quine.

2 *Pensées*, v, 294, quoted in P. L. Berger and T. Luckman, *The Social Construction of Reality* (New York: Anchor Books, 1967), p. 5.

3 K. Mannheim, *Ideology and Utopia* (London: Routledge, 1960), pp. 262–3, 255–6, 240, 264, 4.

4 L. Lévy-Bruhl, *La Mentalité primitive* (Paris: Alcan, 1922), pp. 48, 85, 47.

5 L. Lévy-Bruhl, *Les Fonctions mentales dans les sociétés inférieures* (Paris: Alcan, 1910), p. 30.

6 See *Les Carnels de Lucien Lévy-Bruhl* (Paris: Presses Universitaires de France, 1949), p. 61.

7 *La Mentalité primitive*, p. 520.

8 *Les Carnets*, p. 62.

9 P. Winch, *The Idea of a Social Science and its Relation to Philosophy* (London: Routledge, 1958), p. 15.

10 P. Winch, 'Understanding a Primitive Society', *American Philosophical Quarterly*, 1, 4 (1964), p. 309; this volume, p. 000 above.
11 Winch, *The Idea of a Social Science*, pp. 100, 126.
12 'Understanding a Primitive Society', pp. 317, 318.
13 Ibid., p. 318.
14 *Language, Thought and Reality: Selected Writings of Benjamin Lee Whorf*, ed. with intro. by J. B. Carroll (MIT Press, 1964), pp. 214, 213, 240, 241, 239, 211.
15 T. S. Kuhn, *The Structure of Scientific Revolution* (University of Chicago Press, 1964), p. 110. For Kuhn's more recent statement concerning these issues, see his postscript to the second edition (1970), and his contributions to *Criticism and the Growth of Knowledge*, ed. I. Lakatos and A. Musgrave (Cambridge University Press, 1970).
16 Ibid., p. 117. I owe to Jerry Cohen the observation that it is an odd principle of economy which favours a policy of multiplying entire worlds.
17 Ibid., pp. 120, 149, 125, 169, 93, 166.
18 Thus, for example, for Kuhn, paradigms are 'constitutive of nature' (ibid., p. 109) and for Winch 'there is no way of getting outside the concepts in terms of which we think of the world': *The Idea of a Social Science*, p. 15.
19 For an interesting discussion of different definitions of 'social', see W. L. Wallace, *Sociological Theory* (London: Heinemann, 1969).
20 I leave aside the controversial question of whether, or to what extent, this set of relations can be regarded as causal.
21 The term 'structural identity' comes from Max Scheler. I have in mind a wide range of such relations, ranging from Durkheim's and Mauss's attempts to relate symbolic classification and social structure, on the one hand, to Sorokin's attempts to identify structural relations between particular ideas with a given *Weltanschauung*, on the other.
22 This is evidently Lukác's view: see G. Lukács, *Histoire et conscience de classe* (1923) trans. into French by K. Axelos and J. Bois (Paris: Editions de Minuit, 1960), esp. pp. 189–256. See also English translation by Rodney Livingstone (London: Merlin Press, 1971).
23 S. Lukes, 'Some Problems about Rationality', *European Journal of Sociology*, 8 (1967) reprinted in *Rationality*, ed. B. R. Wilson (Oxford: Blackwell, 1970).
24 For example: '[primitive thought] is not oriented, like our thought, towards knowledge properly so-called. It does not know the joys and the usefulness of knowledge. Its collective representations are always in large part of an emotional nature. Its thought and language remain scarcely conceptual': *La Mentalité primitive*, p. 50.
25 Cf. Russell's definition: 'when a sentence or belief is "true", it is so in virtue of some relation to one or more facts; but the relation is not always simple, and varies both according to the structure of the sentence concerned and according to the relation of what is asserted experience:' B. Russell, *My Philosophical Development* (London: Allen & Unwin, 1959), p. 189.
26 M. E. Spiro, 'Religion: Problems of Definition and Explanation', in *Anthropological Approaches to the Study of Religion*, ed. M. Banton

(London: Tavistock, 1966), p. 111. I do not see that E. Leach, 'Virgin Birth', *Proceedings of the Royal Anthropological Institute for 1966* (1967), has in any way cast doubt on this interpretation.

27 E. E. Evans-Pritchard, *Witchcraft, Oracles and Magic among the Azande* (Oxford: Clarendon Press, 1937), pp. 25, 24.

28 F. Steiner, 'Chagga Truth', *Africa*, 24 (1954).

29 Ibid., pp. 364, 368, 366, 365, 368, 367, 364.

30 See D. Joravsky, 'Soviet Ideology', *Soviet Studies*, 18, 1 (1966), pp. 2–19, esp. p. 10.

31 Steiner, 'Chagga Truth', p. 304.

32 A. O. Lovejoy, 'The Meaning of Romanticism for the Historian of Ideas', *Journal of the History of Ideas*, 2 (1941), pp. 262, 264–5.

33 See. G. Wetter, *Soviet Ideology Today*, trans. P. Heath (London: Heinemann, 1966); D. Bell. 'Soviet Ideology', *Slavic Review*, 24 (1965); and the present writer's review article about the former in *New Society* (16 June 1966).

34 See, for example, P. Rivière, *Marriage among the Trio* (Oxford: Clarendon Press, 1970).

35 E. Leach, *Political Systems of Highland Burma* (London: Bell, 1954, p. 106.

36 K. Marx, *Introduction to the Critique of Political Economy* (1857), in *A Contribution to the Critique of Political Economy*, trans. N. I. Stone (Chicago: Kerr, 1913), pp. 226–8.

37 Lukács, *Histoire et conscience de classe*, French edn., pp. 229, 253.

38 S. Ossowski, *Class Structure in the Social Consciousness*, trans. S. Patterson (London: Routledge, 1963), pp. 154, 116. Ossowski treated the 'official image of contemporary Soviet society' as in crucial ways at variance with social realities (he attempted the same for 'the American Creed') and he wrote optimistically of 'the Polish October of 1956' as leading to 'the destruction of the official myths which concealed our reality' (pp. 112, 193).

39 Joravsky, 'Soviet Ideology', pp. 11, 13, 14. 'The outside observer', Joravsky writes, 'has easily identified an illogical argument and an unverified belief by reference to his own genuine knowledge of logic and economics' (p. 12).

40 Leach, 'Virgin Birth', p. 46. This article constitutes something of a credo for the opposite view to that which I am advancing. For a splendid defence and application of the latter, see R. Horton, 'African Traditional Thought and Western Science', *Africa*, 37 (1967) and his earlier papers referred to therein.

41 E. Durkheim, 'Review of Lévy-Bruhl, *Les Fonctions mentales* . . . and his own *Formes élémentaires de la vie religieuse*', *Année sociologique*, 12 (1909–12), p. 35.

42 E. Durkheim, *Les Formes élémentaires de la vie religieuse* (Paris: Alcan, 1912), pp. 340, 340–1.

43 E. B. Tylor, *The Origins of Culture*, pt 1 of *Primitive Culture* (1871) (New York: Harper, 1958), pp. 112, 116.

44 E. E. Evans-Pritchard, 'The Intellectualist (English) Interpretation of

Magic', *Bulletin of the Faculty of Arts*, Egyptian University (Cairo), 1, 2 (1933).

45 Evans-Pritchard, *Witchcraft*, p. 12.

46 Horton, 'African Traditional Thought', pp. 53, 54, 56. The reference to Turner is to his *Ndembu Divination*, Rhodes-Livingstone Papers, 31 (1962) and 'An Ndembu Doctor in Practice', in *Magic, Faith and Healing*, ed. A. Kiev (London: Collier-Macmillan, 1964).

3
An Alternative View: Interpretive Social Science

BRIAN FAY

In this chapter I want to examine an alternative to the positivist theory. I will be able to provide only a brief description of it, partially because my purpose here is simply to offer a contrast, but also because the philosophical alternative is at an incomplete state at the present time.

Speaking of a philosophical exploration leads me to an important caveat regarding the account I shall give in this chapter and in the next, when I discuss the idea of a critical social science. It is that while I will be employing the names 'interpretive social science' and 'critical social science' I will not be simply reproducing the accounts that are given by many of the theorists who self-consciously identify themselves by means of these names. I will not, for example, be trying to elucidate Schutz's *The Phenomenology of the Social World* when I discuss 'interpretive theory'; or regurgitating Habermas's ideas when I examine 'critical theory'; indeed, in some respects I will be offering accounts which differ from theirs in important ways. My reasons for this are two-fold: in the first place I want to ground my accounts in a philosophical theory of meaning rather than in some other philosophical base (and thus my accounts develop out of the tradition of analytic philosophy rather than those of phenomenology or Marxist dialectics); and, in the second place, I think that what has been written in these other traditions is obscure or wrong-headed in some significant areas, and that it is because of this, among other reasons, that these other approaches have so often been dismissed. I hope that by proceeding in this manner my account will be lucid and plausible. Of course, and I want to emphasise this, such accounts are no substitute for the real and difficult work of systematically and vigorously pursuing a philosophical analysis of what it means to understand social behaviour; what I offer here is simply a brief sketch.

Reprinted by permission of Allen and Unwin from Brian Fay, 'An Alternative View: Interpretive Social Science', in *Social Theory and Political Practice* (London: Allen and Unwin, 1975), pp. 70–91.

In this chapter I will: first, give an exposition of the nature of interpretive social science; second, explicate the notion of theory and practice which is implied by, and which supports, this view of social science; and third, offer some fundamental criticisms of this approach.

THE IDEA OF AN INTERPRETIVE SOCIAL SCIENCE

The interpretive approach to social science, as constructed from the viewpoint of analytical philosophy, starts with the fact that a large part of the vocabulary of social science is comprised of *action concepts*, and it attempts to give an account of social science by examining the logical implications of employing this class of concepts. Action concepts are all those terms that are used to describe doings as opposed to happenings, so that 'jumping' is an action concept while 'falling' is not – jumping is something that someone does, whereas falling is something that happens to one. A way of understanding what an action concept is is to think of the difference between a leaf waving in the breeze and a person waving his hand. Action concepts are employed to describe behaviour which is done with a purpose such that one can ask, what is its point, aim or intent, or what was the person trying to do, desiring or meaning. Examples of action concepts are: buying, bribing, promising, hiking, voting, handshaking and speaking. It is these concepts which go to make up the data which the social scientist seeks to explain.

There is an immediately obvious and yet extremely important point regarding the use of action concepts, and this is that the criteria for the application of these terms involve more than the mere observation of physical movements; in fact, they require an *interpretation* on the part of the observer. The reason for this is that any action concept involves reference to either the subject's intentions, plans or desires (these are called 'intentional action concepts', and an example of one is the concept 'waiting'), or such things as the moral, legal or social rules in accordance with which the subject is acting (these are called 'conventional action concepts', and an example of one is the concept 'voting'), and neither of these two features can be identified simply by reference to physical movements. For no physical movement is ever a necessary condition for an action – think of the myriads of ways in which one can vote, for example – simply because the aims which an action is intended to achieve can always be accomplished in literally countless ways; moreover, no physical movement can ever be a sufficient condition for a specific action to be said to have occurred because it is only in certain circumstances that particular movements can count as an action of a certain sort – thus, for example, saying 'I do' in front of a priest and one's fiancé, may be an act of marriage and it may not, depending on the circumstances, for the participants may be pretending or acting in a movie or rehearsing the ceremony, and so on. What specific action is being undertaken depends upon the meanings that the bodily movements being performed have.

This point about the relationship between interpretation and the description of an action immediately raises the question as to how descriptions of actions are related to their explanation. For if any action is a physical movement performed for a purpose such that its description involves implicit reference to the *point* of the action, then it seems that such a description also contains an explanatory element within it. In describing actions we are also making clear the intentions of the actor, which is to say that we are revealing the meaning that the act had for the actor. However, this does not mean that by giving a single description of an act one has thereby explained it, such that one cannot ask, why did he *do* X?; any action may have many descriptions which place it in a wider and wider context of purposes, intentions and rules, so that one can ask, why did he do X?, and get an answer which consists of a 'higher-level' description. A man may be opening the window, but at the same time and with the same movements he may also be cooling the room, signalling to an accomplice outside, demonstrating a new sort of window, showing off his strength, and so on. Any action will have many consequences, some of which the agent may be intending to bring about, and it is for this reason that one can always seek to discover the *further intention* which the agent possessed beyond the one contained in the initial action description, and these further intentions will be expressed in the redescription of the act that one gives. It is these redescriptions which constitute explanations of the act described at a lower intentional level: 'why did he shoot the gun?' – to kill that man; 'why did he kill that man?' – to protect the president from an assassination.

One of the major tasks of an interpretive social science is to discover the intentions which actors have in doing whatever it is they are doing. This has historically been called a *verstehen* explanation, and this term would be fine except for the gross confusions that surround it. The term arose in the context of a rigid dualism in the philosophy of mind, in which intentions (and meanings, purposes, motives, desires, and so on) were taken to be mental acts in the minds of actors which caused the overt physical movements which the observers could see; as a result, it was thought the *verstehende* social scientist had to ferret out invisible causes and that he could only do this by a special method called 'empathy' in which he relived the lives of those whose acts he wished to explain. By 'reliving' or 'identifying with' his subjects, the social scientist was supposed to be able to discern their mental states and therefore reveal the (mental) causes of the actions he observed. Such an account of social scientific explanation has been rightly criticized,[1] but unfortunately this is not an accurate account of *verstehen* explanation, and therefore the traditional criticisms of it which assumed this account miss their mark. This notion of *verstehen* is in error because it is based on a misunderstanding of the ways in which concepts like 'intention', 'meaning', and 'motive' function in our language. These do not refer to occult processes hidden from the view of all but the individual person who is experiencing them and which cause the person's body to move in particular ways, but are rather ways of characterising the accounts that we observe. Intentional explanations, for example, make sense of a person's actions by fitting them into a purposeful pattern which reveals how the act was warranted, given the actor, his social and physical situation and his beliefs and wants. An intention is no more 'behind' the action than the meaning of the word is 'behind' the letters of which it is composed, and it is no more an 'invisible mental cause' of an act than is a melody the invisible cause of the pattern of notes that we hear at a concert.

The arguments supporting this contention would require a recapitulation of Wittgenstein's *Philosophical Investigations* and parts of his *Zettel*, and this is obviously much too difficult and complex to do here. Suffice it to say that the interpretive social scientist offers *verstehen* explanations, that these consist, at the level of individual actions, in demonstrating the *reasons* why a particular act was performed,[2] and that this is accomplished by setting the act within a larger context which includes the aims and cognitions of the actor and the circumstances in which he found himself, which is to say that it is accomplished by using *public* evidence.[3]

However, concentrating on the intentions etc., of individual actors, even at the level of individual psychology, leads to the mistake of omitting the fundamentally social element inherent in all action descriptions and explanations, and it is this which is of equal or even more interest to the interpretive social scientist. For an action is an action, and a specific action concept can be used only in the context of a certain set of social rules which provide the criteria in terms of which an actor can be said to be performing that action.[4] Thus, one can be described as 'stopping at the traffic light' only in a society which has certain traffic rules, or be described as 'striking out' only if the describer implicitly invokes the rules of baseball. The fact is true not only of conventional action concepts – where it is obviously true, since these concepts implicitly refer to the rules which underlie them – but also of intentional action concepts as well; it is so because one can employ an intentional action concept only by judging that a certain set of basic body actions falls within a definite range which counts as doing X, and it is the background of social rules of a particular society which provides the limits of this range, i.e. specifies what is to count as doing X. Thus it is only by reference to certain rules that one can know whether a man is 'horse-playing' as opposed to fighting, waiting instead of loitering. For an action to be of a certain kind it must fall under some description which is socially recognisable as the description of that action because it involves reference to certain social rules.

I want to make this point even more strongly. *These rules*[5] *logically constitute the very possibility of a particular action being said to occur*, which is to say that without the presence of certain rules there can be no action of a certain type. It is for this reason that to describe a person as 'doing X' is thereby to imply that there are rules present in his social order which define what it is to do X and when it is appropriate to do it. Thus, in the absence of certain economic rules one cannot be described as 'buying' or 'selling' in a certain instance (it is this which provides the reason why it would be a mistake to say that 'John *sold* his wife a gift of a watch at Christmas'); and conversely, to describe John as 'selling' is to imply that he is in a special rule-governed situation and is acting accordingly.

Now this set of social rules which is the framework implicitly referred to when one uses an action concept I want to call a *social practice*, so that, to sum up what I have said, action descriptions involve implicit reference to social practices. An example of a social practice is the set of rules referred to by the concept 'market-place', so that one might say that the concept 'buying' logically presupposes the existence of the social practice of the market-place. Moreover, just as certain action concepts implicitly contain within themselves a reference to an intention, and just as to understand an action one must understand its intention, so also to understand an action one must understand the practice which it embodies. Another task of the interpretive social scientist is, therefore, to discover the set of rules which underlies a given class of actions, to make these rules explicit, and to relate them to other rules in the society.[6]

But this is not the end of the matter. For if practices constitute the logical possibility of certain classes of actions, then *constitutive meanings* underlie social practices in the same way that practices underlie actions. By a 'constitutive meaning' I mean all those shared assumptions, definitions and conceptions which structure the world in certain definite ways (hence 'meanings'), and which constitute the logical possibility of the existence of a certain social practice, i.e. without them the practice as defined could not exist (hence 'constitutive'). It is only because actors share certain basic conceptions that there can be certain types of social action. For example, the social practice of the market-place can occur given the shared constitutive meanings of (say) some conceptions of private property, the notion that in the exchange of goods and services some form of maximising one's own resources is the appropriate course of action, some idea of being an independent agent, etc., etc. Moreover, it follows from this that when one employs a specific action concept in his description of a social activity he thereby, at least implicitly, invokes a set of constitutive meanings as a necessary backdrop in order for this action concept to be used in the first place.

Now constitutive meanings are even less accessible to the social actors involved than are the rules which underlie their actions, for *it is in terms of* these meanings that the actors speak and act. Thus, one cannot simply ask the particular actors what the relevant meanings are – as a social scientist might poll people about their beliefs, for example – precisely because it is these meanings which comprise the very language in terms of which people describe and explain themselves, reveal their beliefs and express their attitudes; in order for them to get at these meanings they would have to leave the framework of their ordinary language and experience and look at it 'from the outside', i.e. at least see the possibility of conceptualising themselves in a different way. Here the social scientist is not concerned with what would be the proper thing to do in some context – in which case an ideal informant's word would be privileged – but with understanding the concepts and presuppositions in terms of which something can be said to be what is appropriate. It is therefore a task for the social scientist to attempt to elucidate the meanings which inform specific social practices, and thereby to reveal the structure of intelligibility which accounts for the behaviour he witnesses.[7]

Furthermore, constitutive meanings are obviously not unrelated to one another, and an additional step in explaining a social practice is to relate the constitutive meanings which support it to the other constitutive meanings which underline the social world of which it is a part, and to see how these constitutive meanings are patterned in such a way as to form a world-view. The purpose in doing this is to discover the *point* a social practice has in a specific society, to see how it fosters the aims and satisfies the needs of the social actors as they themselves define them. Of course, this obviously requires that the social scientist come to terms with a culture's conception of human needs and purposes, which is to say that he must attempt to grasp the ideas which a certain culture has about the importance which carrying out certain activities may have for a man, its ideas about the sense of human life and what is significant for living it.

These sorts of considerations lead to the conclusion that attempting to set a social practice within the world-view of the social order of which it is a component involves elucidating the basic notions which a people share about the world, society and human nature. By 'basic notions' I mean such things as a social order's conception of masculinity and femininity; its understanding of the meaning and role of work; its views on nature; its distinctions between public and private; its conception of agency; its ideas about authority, the community, the family; its notion of sex; its beliefs about God and death and so on. In revealing these, the social scientist explains a given social order by articulating the conceptual scheme that defines reality in certain ways, and in terms of which the actions that he views make sense.

Now articulating conceptual schemes has always been regarded as a philosophical activity, and rightly so: for such an enterprise is a conceptual one, attempting to explain the basic presuppositions which underpin and make possible the basic distinctions, responses and categories of thought and action.[8] An interpretive social science at this level of analysis is a philosophical activity because it attempts to reveal the *a priori* conditions which make social experience in a given society what it is, and it is thus no surprise that the primary examples of this type of social analysis are to be found in political and social philosophy.[9] This is one of the reasons, though not the only one, why philosophy is essential to social analysis, so that the oft-expressed hope of separating out philosophy from social science is a misguided one; this is also one of the reasons why the classics of social thought continue to have a relevance qualitatively different from that enjoyed by the classics of natural science.

An interpretive social science is one which attempts to uncover the sense of a given action, practice or constitutive meaning; it does this by discovering the intentions and desires of particular actors, by uncovering the set of rules which give point to these sets of rules or practices, and by elucidating the basic conceptual scheme which orders experience in ways that the practices, actions and experiences which the social scientist observes are made intelligible, by seeing how they fit into a whole structure which defies the nature and purpose of human life. In each of these types of explanation, the social scientist is redescribing an act or experience by setting it into progressively larger contexts of purpose and intelligibility, he reveals *what* the agents are doing by seeing what they are up to and how and why they would be up to that.

ITS CONCEPTION OF THEORY AND PRACTICE

Just as a positivist social science contains within itself, and is sustained by, a view of theory and practice – the notion of technical control I discussed above – so also interpretive social science is conceptually linked to a notion of theory and practice and is, in fact, partially conceived in terms of this notion. In this section I will first examine its views as to how knowledge from social science is related to human action, and then I will show how these views are defining elements of what constitutes knowledge of social behaviour according to an interpretive social science.

It ought to be clear from the account that I have just given that an interpretive social science is one which reveals to people what it is that they and others are doing when they act and speak as they do. It does this by articulating the symbolic structures in accordance with which people in a particular social setting act, by making clear the criteria of rationality in virtue of which certain alternatives were chosen rather than others, and by revealing the basic assumptions which pattern the world in distinct ways. An interpretive social science uncovers the connections which exist between parts of people's lives, thereby allowing one to see these lives in the whole and enabling one to grasp the significance of particular behaviour in terms of this whole. The result of this sort of analysis is thus a kind of enlightenment in which the meanings of actions, both of one's own as well as of others, are made transparent.

Another way of saying this, and one which leads directly to a discussion of the practical consequences of such a social science, is to draw an analogy with learning a language. Such an analogy is not so far fetched, of course, because speech is itself the paradigm form of social action. Attempting to give an interpretation of social action is like trying to learn a language, for in both one is initially confronted with overt signs (sounds, movements) which are unintelligible and perhaps quite strange, and in both one can only come to understand these signs by learning the rules in accordance with which these signs are expressed, i.e. by relating them to other signs in a systematic and coherent way. Of course, engaging in an exercise of interpretation is even more difficult than simply learning to speak a language because it involves more than just knowing *how* to employ sounds or movements correctly; it also consists in being able to formulate and explain the rules which define what a correct sound or movement is, in being able to relate these rules to one another in a systematic way, and in being able to uncover the conceptual background which structures these formulated rules in a certain way. None the less, it is still true that an interpretation of social action reveals to us its grammar.

The practical upshot of this is that an interpretive social science thereby increases the *possibility of communication* between those who come into contact with the accounts of such a science and those whom it studies. For by revealing what it is that people are doing, i.e. by revealing the rules and assumptions upon which they are acting, it makes it possible for us to engage in a dialogue with them – we understand, as it were, the language of their social life. This is most obviously the case when we are confronted by a foreign culture which, just because we do not understand the rules which govern its peoples' actions or the point of these rules, is cut off from us – we cannot communicate with its members. An interpretive understanding, however, creates the possibility for discourse between us and them by showing us what 'is done' in that society and therefore how to speak and act there. And the same is true within our own culture as well. Coming to understand the ways of so-called deviants, learning the 'vocabulary' of children, 'entering the world' of neurotics in therapy, seeing the concerns, hopes and fears of those in different classes and thus grasping the reasons for their apparent odd behaviour, and even uncovering the assumptions by which we ourselves live and thereby perhaps seeing ourselves as related to types or groups of people which we might have thought were radically different from us – all of these are instances in which, by removing the appearance of irrationality or arbitrariness from particular actions, we arrive at a position in which we can speak and act with others.

Moreover, in all of this it is not just being able to communicate with others, but also thereby opening oneself up to their influence, which is significant. For the interpretive social scientist uses concepts to understand beings who define themselves by means of their use of concepts, so that to construct a theory in which one employs new concepts to grasp the sense of one's own or another's social behaviour is to afford people a new means of self-comprehension and thereby to interject new possibilities into their lives. New ways of living become real alternatives when one is able to see the sense of alternative life styles and different ways of looking at the world. At the least one's own assumptions are thrown into relief and therefore one becomes more fully self-conscious; at other times one may well come to redefine oneself and therefore to act differently. To make available a new form of language is to make available a new form of life.

Thus the knowledge gained from an interpretive social science is useful to men, and can be translated into social life, because it creates the conditions for mutual understanding between different members of the same social order or between members of different social orders, which is to say that it makes possible communication between them where none existed before, or where, if it did exist, such communication was distorted. Moreover, in so far as it opens channels of communication, such knowledge expands the horizons of those who are now able to discourse, because learning how to communicate is learning both new ways of characterising oneself as well as highlighting one's own presuppositions. The aim of an interpretive social theory is to make possible a successful dialogue in speaking and acting between different social actors or within oneself.[10]

Now this notion of theory and practice is not merely appended externally on to the idea of an interpretive social science as is sometimes thought; rather, the two are conceptually connected. For just as possible technical control constitutes the framework within which true knowledge of social behaviour is made possible according to the positivist conception of social science, so for an interpretive social science what can count as a truth is that which creates the possibility for increased communication.

In the first place, the experience which initially gives rise to an interpretive social science is the non-agreement of reciprocal explanations between two acting subjects, so that the aim of such a science is to interpret actions that have blocked communicative interaction in such a way that such interaction becomes possible again. In fact, the relationship between interpretation and communication is even stronger than this; for an interpretive social science only that which is validated as conceivable or likely by the object of study as a possibly true account of what he is doing can be counted as true, which means to say that *only when both the observer and the actor ultimately come to talk about the actions and beliefs of the actor in the same way is it possible to claim that a correct account has been given*. With regard to ascertaining an agent's purposes and intentions, this point is simply a truistic extension of the phrase 'his purpose'; with regard to the uncovering of social rules, this point is based on the fact that it is our ability to act in the expected and appropriate manner that determines whether we have understood the rules which establish the grounds for communication between socialised individuals; and with regard to constitutive meanings, this point is based on the fact that interpretation attempts to make sense of a particular practice by making explicit what is tacitly assumed by the practitioners, so that we can claim that we have succeeded in uncovering the constitutive meanings only when those who engage in this practice agree that it can be understood in this way – the meanings are meanings *for them*, and whether they are meanings for them can ultimately only be told by them. In each of these three cases, agreement in the concepts used to describe and explain actions and beliefs is a necessary, though obviously not a sufficient, condition for an account to be true,[11] *and this is to say that it is the ability to participate in a communicative interaction which defines what is to count as truth in an interpretive social science*.

I do not mean by this, of course, that the agent can explain his actions better than anyone else – I have already argued against this claim; what I mean is that what the agent does not allow as a reasonable or probable interpretation under the conditions of an uncoerced dialogue cannot be a correct interpretation of what he is doing. Putting it this way, in the context of a dialogue, immediately shows the connection between the criteria of truth in an interpretive social science and its views about how social theory is related to social practice.

SOME CRITICISMS OF THIS APPROACH

There are any number of criticisms which might be offered of the foregoing account of the nature of social science and its relation to social practice, but in this section I will confine myself to remarks offered in a positive spirit, i.e. to criticisms that accept the basic foundations that the interpretive model has established, but which argue that the model, taken by itself, is inadequate. For convenience sake I have divided my critical analysis into two main parts, the first dealing with the interpretive theory of social science, the second with its understanding of how theory is related to practice. Of course it ought to be clear by now that I think these two aspects are interrelated with one another, and that I thus make this division for expository reasons only.

The inadequacy of the interpretive model of social science as I have presented it can be seen in at least four different ways. In the first place, such a social science leaves no room for an examination of the conditions which give rise to the actions, rules and beliefs which it seeks to explicate, and, more particularly, it does not provide a means whereby one can study the relationships between the structural elements of a social order and the possible forms of behaviour and beliefs which such elements engender. A social scientist will want to investigate not only the meanings of particular types of actions, but those causal factors which give rise to and support the continuing existence of these meanings.

This particular type of analysis may take several different forms. The social sicentist may well wish to discover the causes of people adopting certain roles or rule-following activities by examining how a particular social structure constrains its members, delimiting the sorts of activity open to them.[12] Again, he may desire to explain how certain non-social conditions affect the form of social life, for example the ways in which social structure represents an adaptation to the natural environment and the level of technology.[13] Or again, the social scientist may want to uncover the causes of the particular reasons, motives, desires and beliefs which an actor or a group of actors possess, which is to say that he will search for the origins and particular mechanisms through which the surrounding economic, demographic, psychological, political, and religious factors influence the choices that actors make.

In each of these types of analysis the social scientist is attempting to provide *quasi-causal accounts* of the ways in which certain configurations of conditions give rise to certain forms of action, rules, and common meanings. I say 'quasi-causal' rather than causal[15] because, in these sorts of conditionship relations, consciousness functions as a mediator between the determining antecedent factors and the subsequent action; in other words, men act in terms of their interpretations of, and intentions towards, their external conditions, rather than by being governed directly by them, and therefore these conditions must be understood not as causes but as warranting conditions which make a particular action or belief more 'reasonable', 'justified', or 'appropriate', given the desires, beliefs, and expectations of the actors. Nevertheless, such quasi-causal accounts are a legitimate explanatory device without which a social science would be radically impoverished.

A second type of explanation which the interpretive model neglects is the explanation of *the pattern of unintended consequences of actions*, a feature of social life which, by definition, cannot be explained by referring to the intentions of the individuals concerned. Societies consist of ordered sets of relationships among their members, and it is this basic fact which accounts for the phenomenon that when an action is performed its results rebound throughout the society in ways that are relatively predictable, though the actors themselves might not have been aware of them nor exercise any control over them. It is one job of social science to explore these patterned unintended consequences.[16]

There is one important type of unintended consequence which deserves special mention, namely that which reinforces the actions, beliefs, and roles of the other members of the society such that it 'serves the purpose' of maintaining the structure of the group as a whole. The rules, practices and meanings of a society are structurally interrelated, often mutually reinforcing one another such that they seem to form what might be called a 'system'. This observation is strengthened by the fact that this structure remains relatively stable over time despite a constantly fluctuating membership. Because of these facts a social scientist will want to discuss the ways in which social wholes maintain themselves as ongoing systems which persist in an environment, and in this *functional explanations* are invaluable. For a functional explanation attempts to explain a given practice or institution, not by revealing how it arose, nor by disclosing the purposes it is thought to fulfil, but by explaining why it continues to exist, and it does this by demonstrating the contribution its effects make to the continued existence of the social whole which in turn sustains it. A functional analysis uncovers the ways in which the (unintended) consequences of an act or the (unforeseeen) effects of an institutional practice modify a host of other social factors, demonstrating how such effects reinforce and strengthen the complex of factors which comprises the social whole, and how, in turn, this complex of factors helps to maintain the original act or practice.[17]

A third way in which the interpretive model is inadequate is that it provides no way for the social scientist to understand structural conflict within a society, that is, it offers no method of analysing the contradictions which might exist between certain actions, rules, and common meanings, or between these and their causes or results. Indeed the problem is worse than this, for an interpretive social science not only fails to give the tools for analysing such situations, but it actually precludes the possibility of identifying such conflicts. The reason for this is that one of the criteria which a good interpretation must satisfy is the demonstration of the coherence with the initially unintelligible act, rule, or belief has in terms of the whole of which it is a part, and this means that, given this standard, the interpreter must assume that the meanings, beliefs, practices and actions which he encounters are congruent with one another in so far as they are understandable.

This is a fundamental shortcoming, for it means that whole areas of social experience are left out of analysis. What sort of social experience am I referring to? I mean those situations in which people's self-understanding are at variance with their actual social behaviour, so that the way people characterise their activity is in error;[18] in which an actor's ideas and feelings are joined in ways that he is not aware of, and which lead him to act in a pattern which he might not realise and would resent if he knew about;[19] in which a specific belief and action system is incompatible with other stated norms of the culture;[20] in which there are endemic conflicts as the result of conflicts in structural principles;[21] and in which there is a tension within the basic conceptual scheme of a society.[22] In these and other instances what the social scientist wishes to explain is how these discrepancies, incoherences and contradictions function.

But even more importantly, he will also seek to inquire why they can continue to exist in a given society, and this will lead him to explore the mechanisms which blind agents and thereby enable them to ignore these irrationalities. In this regard, both the ideas and beliefs which social actors have *about* society, as well as the ideas and conceptions which constitute their social reality, may be involved: on the one hand, their theories about society may actually be masking reality in some important way, particularly by obscuring a situation of rationalising it;[23] and on the other hand, particular constitutive meanings of a particular social practice may serve to obscure contradictions between them and other aspects of social life.[24] Here, if one simply tries to 'grasp the intelligibility' of these concepts one will miss the real role which they play in social life.[25]

There is a fourth area of concern to the social scientist, but one again which the interpretive model neglects, and this is the explanation of historical change. For it is also the job of the social scientist to show how a specific institution or social order came to be what it is, and how it will change in determinate ways. An interpretive social science, by methodologically assuming an internal coherence between the self-understandings of the actors, their common meanings, their social practices, and their actions is unable to explain why it is that a social order will develop – except in invoking external forces – and why it will develop in definite ways. In this regard, all of the types of questions that I have discussed so far will come into play: the actors might well act in a certain way, follow certain rules, and operate in terms of certain constitutive meanings; nevertheless, they might very well also be creating consequences which will in turn affect their needs, interests, and capacities in specific, though to them unknown, ways; they might also come to change their social behaviour as the result of conditions which they themselves have created, though unwittingly; they might be forced to adopt new practices and come to think of themselves in fundamentally new ways because of the contradictions which mark their social arrangements and belief systems, but about which they are unaware. In these and in a myriad of other similar events the social scientist will be interested, precisely because he is interested not only in social order but in social change.[26]

An interpretive social science is not only inadequate in its account of the nature of social theory, but in its notions of how this theory is related to practice; not surprisingly, these latter difficulties are related to the former ones. I intend here to discuss just two of them.

The interpretive model is inadequate as an account of how social theory is related to social practice because the undistorted communication, which it posits that an interpretive social science will elicit, will most often fail to occur, and this is because the social actors will experience *resistance* (to borrow a Freudian term which is directly applicable here) to the insights of such a science. In order to understand why, it is necessary to grasp the role which ideas about themselves, their social order and other societies play in men's intellectual and emotional lives, and, more specifically, the way in which these ideas are related to the social conditions in which men find themselves. Another way of saying this is that, while the interpretive model promises an increase in communication, it fails to take into account the conditions under which such communication would occur. And this is no accident, for, as I pointed out above, one of the major shortcomings of the interpretive model is its failure to provide a way of understanding the quasi-causal relationship which exists between men and their environment.

A person's ideas about himself and others[27] are never *merely* true or false, abstract statements which he is free to accept or reject simply on the basis of rational argumentation. The reason why this is the case is that these ideas are also ways of coping with the social and natural conditions of his life, they are action-guiding and role supporting. Such ideas are employed to justify to himself and others the particular way of life which he is engaged in living, which means that they make it possible for him to continue living as he does in the situation in which he finds himself. The ideas that he has are deeply ingrained in the way he lives, and the force that such ideas carry for him cannot be appreciated until it is understood exactly what forms this relationship takes.

Moreover, a person learns who and what he is through his early education as he acquires a language, internalises norms, beliefs, values and attitudes, as he becomes a member of a specific social group, and this means that his very identity as a person is tied up with the particular world-view of this group and the particular beliefs which are rooted in this world-view. The emotional power which ideas have stems from the fact that such ideas go to the core of what it means to be a person, and it is thus no accident that such ideas are avidly held on to, and that competing interpretations of what one is doing are seen as personally threatening or as ridiculous.

These are some of the reasons why people believe the way they do – and, ironically, these are the very same reasons why misunderstandings and distorted communication between people occur in the first place (because people are unable readily to adopt a 'different viewpoint'). Any political theory which fails to deal with these facts in some appropriate way, which thinks that the simple presentation of ideas will foster a change in social actors' self-conceptions, is naive. The network of communication will only be restored when the problem of resistance is squarely faced.

The second way in which the interpretive model of theory and practice can be criticised is its implicit conservativism. On a superficial level this conservativism manifests itself in the fact, already mentioned, that it assumes an inherent continuity in a particular society, i.e. it systematically ignores the possible structures of conflict within a society, structures which would generate change. This methodological assumption leads to a conservative political theory just because such a science cannot generate any standards of criticism of existing social reality – in fact, it leads one to view the attempt as constructing such standards on the basis of an internal criticism of a social order as misguided.

But the conservativism of the interpretive model is much deeper than this. For such a model makes it appear that all social tensions are rooted in the breakdown of communication between the relevant actors, a breakdown which is itself the result of mistaken ideas that they have about the meaning of their own or another's actions, practices, or beliefs. An interpretive social science promises to reveal to the social actors what they and others are doing, thereby restoring communication by correcting the ideas that they have about each other and themselves. But this makes it sound as if all conflict (or breakdown in communication, for that matter) is generated by mistaken ideas about social reality rather than by the tensions and incompatibilities inherent in this reality itself.

The upshot of this is profoundly conservative, because *it leads to reconciling people to their social order*, and it does this by demonstrating to them that, contrary to their initial beliefs which had caused the breakdown in communication in the first place, actual social practice is inherently rational. In a sitution of social conflict and disruption, the interpretive model asserts that the ensuing anxiety and suffering is the result of misunderstandings which, if cleared away, will restore the flow of discourse and hence order – as if such cleavage and breakdown in communication might not result from the irreconcilable demands, interests, needs, and beliefs of the conflicting parties. In a time of upheaval the interpretive model would lead people to seek *to change the way they think about what they are others are doing*, rather than provide them with a theory by means of which they could *change what they or others are doing*, and in this way it supports the *status quo*.

NOTES

Fay is interested in examining the implications that different approaches to social theory have for the practice of politics. In chapters preceding this excerpt he discusses positivist social theory, concluding that it issues in a technocratic approach to politics. In the chapter following this excerpt he sketches the foundations of his own version of critical theory which he argues contains emancipatory or liberating implications for political practice – Editor.

1 Cf. T. Abel, 'The Operation called *Verstehen*', and E. Nagel, *Structure of Science*, pp. 480–5.

2 Thus it is best to think of intentional etc. explanations as appraisal explanations constructed in the form of a practical syllogism. The sort of explanation appropriate to social science, according to the interpretive model is, therefore, not causal but teleological. For a brilliant philosophical discussion of this, cf. G. H. Von Wright, *Explanation and Understanding*, ch. 3. For an exposition of both the philosophical and methodological aspects of this, cf. R. Harré and P. Secord, *The Explanation of Social Behaviour*. A good example of this approach is H. S. Sullivan, *The Interpersonal Theory of Psychiatry*.

3 Perhaps the most damaging criticism of the view that intentions are private mental events is the fact that each person is not necessarily the best or sole judge of his own intentions. In discovering the intentions of an act there is no special mental event called an intention which one simply remembers

happening; even if one remembers saying to oneself, 'I now intend to do X' this does not guarantee that X was one's intention, for how does one know that one meant what one said except by reference to what one does and the circumstances in which one found oneself, i.e. except by reference to just those considerations which are also available to a third party. One can be deceived about one's intentions just because all intentional explanations involve retrospective interpretations about the point of an act.

4 Thus it is that all intentional explanations must be set within a given social context. A good example of this is Weber's *The Protestant Ethic and the Spirit of Capitalism*. Another more readily apparent example is the transactional role-analysis of action to be found in E. Goffman, *The Presentation of Self in Everyday Life*.

5 'Rules' refer to expectations of the members in a social group as to what performances are appropriate in certain situations which itself is definable by means of these rules. Rules refer, therefore, to all socially recognised procedures and standard identifications of situations.

6 This is particularly true of the anthropologist because he is immediately confronted with behaviour which is unintelligible until the rules underlying this behaviour are discovered and explicated. However, this is also an endeavour relevant to sociology and all those other disciplines which study the society of which the social scientist is a member, and this is because the rules by which men act are hardly ever made explicit to them as actors; on this point, cf. H. Garfinkel, *Studies in Ethnomethodology*. Examples of this type of study are the attempt to articulate the rules of price determination in a modern capitalist society (on this, cf. P. W. S. Andrews, *On Competition in Economic Theory*, especially Part 1 which is a review of modern theory), and the attempt to uncover the rules of legislative process in the US Government (on this, cf. the review book of Nelson Polsby, *Congress and the Presidency*). I think that this is also the proper way to view Weber's *Theory of Social and Economic Organisation*.

7 For examples of this sort of analysis in social science, cf. S. Beer, *Modern British Politics*; E. and L. Banfield, *The Moral Basis of a Backward Society*; J. Douglas, *The Social Meanings of Suicide*.

8 This does *not* mean that an interpretive social science is an armchair activity, foregoing empirical research: for even at this level one must be thoroughly aware of the character of social experience before one can reflect on the conditions which make such experience possible.

9 I have in mind, e.g. Aristotle's *Politics*; Arendt's *Human Condition*; de Tocqueville's *Democracy in America*; Marx's *Grundrisse* and *Economic and Philosophical Manuscripts*; Rousseau's *Second Discourse*; Smith's *Wealth of Nations* and so on. Once again this is an activity long practised in anthropology, cf. e.g. R. Redfield, *The Primitive World and its Transformations*, ch. 4.

10 One result of this would be to foster a tolerance and respect for others which is an essential prerequisite for a democratic social order; moreover, it would presumably lessen the attractiveness of violence as a way of dealing with those with whom one disagrees.

11 In other words, the actors' accepting the theorist's explanation as true is not a conclusive demonstration that the explanation *is* true; rather, it is a necessary prerequisite in order for it to qualify as possibly true.

12 Cf., for example, E. Goffman, *Asylums*; Meyer Fortes, *Kinship and the Social Order*.

13 Cf., for example, Lynn White, *Medieval Technology and Social Change*.

14 Cf., for example, G. W. Thompson, *The Twelve Days*. I take it that it is just this sort of inquiry which the sociology of knowledge undertakes. Cf. P. L. Berger and T. Luckman, *The Social Construction of Reality*.

15 I adopt this terminology from Von Wright, *Explanation and Understanding*, ch. 4. I do not mean to imply here that there are no conditionship relations which influence human behaviour and yet operate independently of human will, and which are vital to social scientific explanation. For example, the effect of nutrition on fertility and thus on age distribution levels, and the effect of chemicals on sexual activity, are both instances of genuinely causal explanations of social phenomena. However, the important point here is that in these instances the causal relationships are discovered by natural scientists, and are only employed by social scientists to explain breakdowns in performance or to set the limitations within which the actors must act. For a brilliant example of this, cf. H. Zinnser's *Rats, Lice and History*.

I also do not want to deny that within the class of quasi-causal explanations there may be important distinctions to be drawn, for example, between those changes in conditions which are directly perceived by the actors and those which are only indirectly perceived, or between those changes which lead to an alteration in perceptions and states of the persons and those which lead to an alteration in action without such 'internal' changes. I cannot discuss these subtleties here, unfortunately.

16 Cf. for example, R. C. O. Matthews, *The Trade Cycle*.

17 Cf. for example, E. E. Evans-Pritchard's discussion of the function of the blood feud among the Nuer in southern Sudan in *The Nuer*.

18 Cf. for example, R. Bendix and S. Lipset, *Social Mobility in Industrial Society*, which attempts to demonstrate, contrary to the ethos and beliefs of the whole society, that the USA does not have a rate of social mobility significantly higher than other industrial societies.

19 Cf. for example, V. Aubert, *Sociology of Law*, ch. 6 which attempts to show that judges' sentencing behaviour is affected by the social class of the accused, although this inconsistency with judicial principles is not recognised by the judges.

20 Cf. Chalmers Johnson, *Revolutionary Change*.

21 Cf. for example, Victor Turner, *Schism and Continuity in an African Society*.

22 Cf. for example, the article by W. Sellers, 'Philosophy and the Scientific Image of Man' in his *Science, Perception and Reality*, in which the tensions between our conception of man is expressed in our ordinary language and as expressed in our scientific language are explored and analysed in a brilliantly insightful way.

23 Cf. for example, C. B. Macpherson, *Possessive Individualism*.

24 For example, in *On the Jewish Question* part of what I take Marx to be claiming is that the universalist norms of the bourgeois legal system and the doctrine of rights in the capitalist political sphere – both of which are rooted in particular conceptions of man and society – function to obscure and rationalise contradictions in the socio-economic order between, on the one hand, the distribution of goods and conditions of work, and, on the other, the capitalist ideology regarding the equality of opportunity. Such constitutive meanings allow men in capitalist society to claim and to act as if a person's position is a function of his merit and energy (when in fact it is a function of where he started out), and it thereby makes just a situation which on other grounds the society would condemn.

25 It is interesting to note here how so-called 'ideology-critique' – which many social scientists eschew – is intimately related to the more generally recognised social scientific task of discovering and explaining structural contradictions which generate conflict.

26 The best example of this is, of course, Marxist historiography. Cf. E. Mandel, *Marxist Economic Theory*.

27 What I say here probably applies to our ideas about natural objects too.

4
Language and Human Nature

CHARLES TAYLOR

I

Language is a central area of concern in the twentieth century. This is evident on all sides. First, our century has seen the birth and explosive growth of the science of linguistics. And in a sense 'explosive' is the right word, because like the other sciences of man, linguistics is pursued in a number of mutually irreducible ways, according to mutually contradictory approaches, defended by warring schools. There are structuralists in the Bloomfield sense, there are proponents of transformational theories, there are formalists.

These schools and others have made a big impact. They are not just collections of obscure scholars working far from the public gaze. Names like Jakobson and Chomsky are known far outside the bounds of their discipline.

But what is even more striking is the partial hegemony, if one can put it this way, that linguistics has won over other disciplines. From Saussure and the formalists there has developed the whole formidable array of structuralisms, of which Lévi-Strauss is the pathfinder, which seek to explain a whole range of other things: kinship systems, mythologies, fashion (Barthes), the operations of the unconscious (Lacan), with theories drawn in the first place from the study of language. We find terms like 'paradigm', 'syntagm', 'metaphor', 'metonymy', used well beyond their original domain.

And then we have to add that some of the most influential philosophical movements of the century have given language a central place; they have not only been concerned with language as one of the problems of philosophy, but have also been *linguistic*, in that philosophical understanding is essentially bound up with the understanding of the

Reprinted by permission of Cambridge University Press from Charles Taylor, 'Language and Human Nature', in *Human Agency and Language: Philosophical Papers 1* (Cambridge: Cambridge University Press, 1985), pp. 215–47;

medium of language. This is true not only of logical positivism and what is often called 'linguistic analysis' in the Anglo-Saxon world, but also of the philosophy of Heidegger, for instance, in a very different way, as well as of the philosophies which have arisen out of structuralism, for example those of Derrida and Lacan.

The concern for language as a medium links up with the twentieth-century concern with meaning. What is it that makes speech meaningful, or indeed that makes meaningful any of the things that have meanings? For this question has been raised not just in connection with language, which is what philosophical theories of meaning have been concerned with. It has also been raised acutely for the arts, for instance music and painting. It is necessarily posed by the rise of non-representational painting, and of music which stepped outside the seemingly fixed code of the eight-tone scale. The revolutions of the beginning of the century, for instance, of Schönberg and cubism, put these questions on the agenda; and they have keen kept on it by all the revolutions we have seen since. They have taught us to ask the question, What is meaning?, in a broader context than simply that of language. They induce us to see language as one segment of that range of meaningful media that men can deploy. And this range comes to seem all the more problematic.

On top of this, the range of the meaningful has been further extended dramatically by Freudian psychoanalysis. Now not just speech and art objects, but also slips of the tongue, symptoms, affinities and tastes, can be 'analysed', that is, interpreted.

And 'interpretation' itself has become a key term. 'Hermeneutical' approaches have a wide audience in a number of fields, most strikingly in history and social science.

What emerges from this, I believe, is that the twentiety-century concern for language is a concern about meaning. And I believe that this concern reflects a largely inarticulate sense of ourselves which is very widespread in our century, and which I shall try to formulate in two related propositions: (1) that the question of language is somehow strategic for the question of human nature, that man is above all the language animal; (2) that language is very puzzling, even enigmatic – and all the more so, if we take it in a wide sense to include the whole range of meaningful media; something we seem bound to do once we see language as the defining character of man, for man is also characterized by the creation of music, art, dance, by the whole range of 'symbolic forms', to use Cassirer's phrase. The paradox involved in this is that in an age of great scientific advance, and after spectacular progress in so many fields, human language appears to us much more enigmatic than it did to men of the Enlightenment. But I recognize that this is a controversial point, and that my thumbnail sketch of our sense of our situation will be strongly resisted by all those who believe or who want to believe in the competence of the methods of natural science to explain human behaviour. Indeed, the trouble with the above sketch is that it is not neutral in one of the big debates of our civilization; so that some will find it banal and others tendentious.

What I ought to attempt now, therefore, is to make it less sketchy for the first group, and less implausible for the second. But this is something I find it hard to encompass by a direct assault. What I want to do instead is trace the origins and hence the growing shape of our intellectual landscape. In doing this, I hope to cast enough light on it to achieve my ends by indirection – to allay at least some doubts, and fill in at least some contour.

This will involve weaving together two themes: first, how did we get here? How did we come to see language as central and meaning as puzzling? This is the historical, diachronic theme. The second theme is problematic: what is the problem of meaning, and why is it puzzling?

A word about each to start.

On the first: our traditional view of man was of a rational animal. That is the definition according to the major philosophical tradition of our civilization, going back to the Greeks. How did we slide to the sense that the secret of human nature was to be found in man as a 'language animal' (to use George Steiner's phrase)?

The answer is that the slide was not that great. If we go back to the original formula in Aristotle, for instance, that man is a rational animal, we find that it reads 'zôon logon echon', which means 'animal possessing logos'. This 'logos' is a word we are already familiar with because it has entered our language in so many ways. It straddles speech and thought, because it means, inter alia, 'word', 'thought', 'reasoning', 'reasoned account', as well as being used for the words deployed in such an account. It incorporates in its range of meanings a sense of the relation of speech and thought.

If we wanted to translate Aristotle's formula directly from the Greek, instead of via the Latin 'animal rationale', and render it 'animal possessing logos', which means in fact leaving it partly untranslated in all its rich polysemy, then we do not have such a leap to make between the traditional formulation of the nature of man and the one that I want to claim underlies much twentieth-century thought and sensibility. There is a shift, but it is one within the complex thought/language, the displacement of its centre of gravity. A shift of this kind in our understanding of thought/language would explain the change from the old formula to the new. And in fact I want to claim, there has been such a shift. This is my historical theme.

On the second, problematic theme: what is the problem about

meaning? And what is it to find it puzzling – or for that matter, unpuzzling? What questions are we asking, when we are asking about meaning?

We are not asking about meaning in the sense that we may ask about the meaning of life, or in the sense of 'meaning' where we speak of a love or a job being meaningful. This is a related sense, but here we are talking about the significance things have for us in virtue of our goals, aspirations, purposes.

The question I am talking about here is the radical question: how is it that these segments of a medium that we deploy, when we talk, make music, paint, make signals, build symbolic objects, *how is it that these say something*? How is it that we can complete sentences of the form: 'What this means (to say) is . . .?' whereas we cannot say this of sticks, stones, stars, mountains, forests – in short, of the things we find in the world?

Or if we object to this way of putting it, because it seems to rule out one of the great traditional ways of understanding the world, as signs made by God, or embodiment of the Ideas – a view we will look at in a minute – we could equally ask: what is it that we see in things when we understand them as signs which we do not when we fail to apprehend them as such, but just as the furniture of a non-expressive universe?

There are two sides or dimensions of meaningful objects, which can each be taken up as the guiding thread of the answer. The first is what we could call the designative: we could explain a sign or word having meaning by pointing to what it designates, in a broader sense, that is, what it can be used to refer to in the world, and what it can be used to say about that thing. I say 'The book is on the table'; this is meaningful speech, and it is so because 'book' designates a particular kind of object and 'table' another, 'the' can be used to pick out a particular object in some context of reference, and the whole phrase puts together the two referring expressions in such a way as to assert that the designatum of one is placed on the designatum of the other. On this view, we give the meaning of a sign or a word by pointing to the things or relations that they can be used to refer to or talk about.

The second dimension we could call the expressive. The sentence 'The book is on the table' designates a book and a table in a certain relation; but it can be said to express my thought, or my perception, or my belief that the book is on the table. In a wider sense, it might be said to express my anxiety, if there is something particularly fateful about the book's being on the table, or perhaps my relief, if the book were lost.

What is meant by 'expression' here? I think it means roughly this: something is expressed, when it is embodied in such a way as to be made manifest. And 'manifest' must be taken here in a strong sense. Something is manifest when it is directly available for all to see. It is not manifest when there are just signs of its presence, from which we can infer that it is there, such as when I 'see' that you are in your office because of your car being parked outside. In this kind of case, there is an implied contrast with another kind of situation, in which I could see you directly.

Now we consider things expressions when they make things manifest in the stronger sense, one which cannot be contrasted with a more direct manner of presentation, one where things would be there before us 'in person', as it were.

Take the example of facial expressions. If you have an expressive face, I can see your joy and sorrow in your face. There is no inference here; I see your moods and feelings, they are manifest, in the only way they can be manifest in public space. Contrast this with your neighbour, who is very good at hiding his feelings; he has a 'poker face'. But I happen to know of him (because his mother told me) and whenever he feels very angry a muscle twitches just beside his ear. I observe the muscle, and see that he is angry.

But the muscle twitching does not amount to an angry expression. That is because it is like the case above where I see you are in your office from your car's being outside. In these cases, I infer to something that I am *not* seeing directly. Expressions, by contrast, make our feelings manifest; they put us in the presence of people's feelings.

Expression makes something manifest in embodying it. Of course, a given expression may reveal what it conveys in a partial, or enigmatic, or fragmentary fashion. But these are all manifestations in the above sense, that however imperfect we cannot contrast them with another, more direct, but non-expressive mode of presentation. What expression manifests can *only* be manifested in expression.

Now we can see much of what we say in both the designative and the expressive dimension, as we did with the sentence above. In each dimension we relate the sentence to something different: to the objects it is about, in one; and to the thought it expresses, in the other.

Each may seem to offer the more natural approach to the question of meaning in different contexts. In discussing the meaning of a sentence like 'The book is on the table', we are more naturally inclined to give an account in designative terms. When we are thinking about a poem, or a piece of music, on the other hand, we more naturally think of its meaning in the expressive dimension. Indeed, with a symphony or a sonata, it is hard to speak of designating. This dimension seems to disappear altogether.

But although each is more natural in a certain context, there seems no reason to see the expressive and the designative as rival modes of explanation wherever they both apply, as in ordinary speech. Rather they seem to answer different questions.

But there is an important dispute in the history of thought over the issue of which of these dimensions is more fundamental in the order of explanation. If 'The book is on the table' expresses my thought to this effect, is this because the words concerned have the designative meanings that they have? If this is so, then the fundamental phenomenon is that of designative meaning. This is what we need to understand in order to get to the root of things. The exprssive function of words will be dependent on this.

Or is there something about the expressive function which cannot be so understood? Is there a dimension of expressive meaning which is not simply determined by designative meaning? Are the tables even to be turned, and is expressive meaning in some way primary, providing the foundation or framework in which words can have designative meaning in the first place? If this is true, then the fundamental thing in language is expressive meaning.

These two approaches define very different ways of understanding the question, What is meaning? A long struggle between the two has led up to our present understanding of language. Before turning to look at this history, I would like to say something about the metaphysical motivations of the two types of theory.

Designative theories, those which make designation fundamental, make meaning something relatively unpuzzling, ummysterious. That is a great part of their appeal. The meaning of words or sentences is explained by their relation to things or states of affairs in the world. There need be nothing more mysterious about meaning than there is about these things or states of affairs themselves. Of course, there is the relation of meaning itself, between word and thing, whereby one signifies or points to the other. But this can be made to seem unmysterious enough. At the limit, if talk about signifying makes us nervous, we can think of this as a set of correlations which have been set up between noises we utter and certain world events or states. At the end of this road, we have behaviourist theories, like that of Skinner (followed by Quine, who has in turn been influential on Davidson).

But if we are not all that metaphysically fastidious, we can simply take the designating relation as primitive and hope to illuminate meaning by tracing the correlations between words and things – or, in more contemporary guise, between sentences and their truth conditions.

By contrast, expressive theories maintain some of the mystery surrounding language. Expressive meaning cannot be fully separated from the medium, because it is only manifest in it. The meaning of an expression cannot be explained by its being related to something else, but only by another expression. Consequently, the method of isolating terms and tracing correlations cannot work for expressive meaning. Moreover, our paradigm-expressive objects function as wholes. Take a face or a work of art. We cannot break either down into parts, and show the whole to be simply a function of the parts, if we want to show how it is expressive.

The sense that expression is mysterious can be formulated more exactly. The point is that expressive theories run counter to what is considered one of the fundamental features of scientific thought in the modern age, where designative theories do not. Scientific thought is meant to be objective; and this means it must given an account of the universe not in terms of what we could call subject-related properties, that is, properties that things have in the experience of subjects, and which would not exist if subjects of experience did not exist. The most notorious example of these in seventeenth-century discussion were the secondary properties, and it was an integral part of the great scientific revolution of that time that these were expelled from physics.

Now an expressive account of meaning cannot avoid subject-related properties. Expression is the power of a subject; and expressions *manifest* things, and hence essentially refer us to subjects for whom these things can be manifest. And as I said above, what expression manifests can only be made manifest in expression, so that expressive meaning cannot be accounted for independently of expression. If we make expression fundamental, it seems impossible to explain it in terms of something else; but it is itself a subject-related phenomenon, and hence does not allow of an objective science.

By contrast, a designative theory accounts for meaning by correlating signs to bits of the world, and these can in principle be identified objectively. It offers the promise of a theory of language which can fit within the canons of modern natural science. It is in this sense that they promise to make language unpuzzling and unmysterious.

On this terrain, expressive theories cannot follow.

II

I turn now to the historical account. If we trace the development of these rival theories of meaning, we can see that the preoccupation with *language* is a modern one. The actual doctrines about language, about words, were rather unimportant and marginal among the ancients. They were not that concerned about speech, they were concerned about thought.

But then how about the insight implicit in the many-meaninged word *logos*? *Logos* meant 'word'; and the root it came from, *legein*, meant 'to say'. What underpinned this connection between saying, words and reason was what one could call a discourse-modelled notion of thought. Thought was seen as like discourse; it revealed things as discourse can do. When we take something which is puzzling and we give an account of it in speech, we lay it out, articulate its different aspects, identify them and relate them. Because thinking was like discourse, we could use the same word, *logos*, for both. Plato says that you do not really know something unless you can give an account of it. Otherwise you have just opinion (*doxa*) and not real knowledge (*epistêmê*). *But* 'give an account' translates *logon didonai*.

The striking fact about the preponderant outlook of the ancients, which was bequeathed to the European Middle Ages, was their view about reality. It too was modelled on discourse-thought. In Plato's version, underlying reality, are the Ideas. Of course, it is we moderns who are tempted to put this by saying that reality was modelled on discourse-thought. For Plato this was no false projection, and we should better say that our discourse and thought ought to be modelled on reality. Reality itself, the ultimate reality of which empirical things are in a sense copies, was Idea; it articulated itself in its aspects which necessarily connected together according to its inner logic. It should be the aim of our thought to limp along after this and try to match it.

Now beside this powerful line-up of an ontic *logos*, or discourse-thought, which was followed by a *logos* in the thinking subject, words did not seem very important. They were the mere external clothing of thought. They could not aspire to more, not human words, for clearly they were not necessary to the ontic *logos*. So language plays a small and marginal role in the theories of the ancients.

But a powerful theory of meaning is in embryo here. The ancient view develops through several stages, notably through neo-Platonism, and then through the thought of the early Fathers, which owes so much to neo-Platonism: St Augustine in the West, and the Greek Fathers in the East.

In this amalgam of Christian theology and Greek philosophy, a notion is developed that Plato first adumbrated in the *Timaeus*. God in creating the world gives embodiment to his ideas. The Platonic Ideas are the thoughts of God.

And so we get an obvious analogy, which St Augustine makes explicit. Just as our thought is clothed externally in our words, so is the thought of God, the *Logos* the *Verbum*, for Augustine – deployed externally in the creation. This is, as it were, God's speech. That is why everything is a sign, if we can see it properly.

So the paradigm and model of our deploying signs is God's creation. But now God's creation is to be understood expressively. His creatures manifest his *logos* in embodying it; and they manifest the *logos* as fully as it can be manifest in the creaturely medium. There can be no more fundamental designative relation, precisely because everything is a sign. This notion is nonsense on a designative view. For words can only have designative meaning if there is something else, other than words or signs, which they designate. The notion that everything is a sign only makes sense on an expressive view.

So what we have in Augustine and his successors is an expressive theory of meaning embedded in their ontology. The originator of meaning, God, is an expressivist. This sets the framework for the theories of the Middle Ages and the early Renaissance, what one could call the semiological ontologies, which picture the world as a meaningful order, or a text. This kind of view of the world is dominant right up to the seventeenth century, when it was pulverized in the scientific revolution.

It was a view of this kind which understood the universe in terms of a series of correspondences, linking for instance the lion in the kingdom of animals, the eagle among birds, and the king in his realm, or linking the stars in the heavens to the shape of the human frame, or linking certain beasts and plants to certain planets. In all these cases, what is at stake is an expressive relation. These terms are linked because they embody/manifest the same ideas. To view the universe as a meaningful order is to see the world as shaped in each of its domains and levels in order to embody the ideas.

We have here a very powerful expressive theory of meaning, a theory of the divine language. But all this is compatible with the relative unimportance of human words. Indeed, it rather requires their taking marginal status; because the real thought, that of God or the Ideas, is quite independent of human expression. The theory of language is still in its infancy.

It was the rebellion against this semiological view of the universe, in nominalism, which began to make *language* important.

Medieval nominalism rejected the discourse-thought model of the real. It denied that there are real essences of things, or universals. True, we think in general terms. But this is not because the world exists in general terms, as it were; on the contrary, everything that is is a particular. The universal is not a feature of the world, but an effect of our language. We apply words to classes of objects, which we thus gather into units; that is what makes general terms.

Now this theory gives language a crucial role. The word is that whereby we group things into classes. It is the new home of the universal, which has been chased out of the real. But in giving language a role in this view propounds a purely designative theory of what this role amounts to. It generates a thoroughly designative theory of meaning.

It does so, first, in rejecting the expressive theory of the cosmos, in refusing to see the things which surround us as embodiment of the Ideas; and secondly, in seeing words as acquiring meaning only in being used as names for things. Words mean because they designate something. So we cease to see everything which exists as a sign. The only signs are those which are recognized as such, and they are signs because they signify something.

This theory of language came into its own in the seventeenth-century scientific revolution, which we associate with such names as Descartes, Bacon and Hobbes. This revolution involved a polemical rejection of the vision of the world as meaningful order, and its replacement by a conception of the world as objective process, in the sense of 'objective' described above. The thoroughly designative theory of meaning was one of its main pillars.

The philosophies of the seventeenth century remade our conceptions of man, thought and knowledge to fit the new dispensation. The very notion of what thought is changes. Once we no longer think of discourse-thought as part of the furniture of the real, then we focus on our subjective thinking as a process in its own right.

It is the process by which we are aware of things. How can this be? Once discourse has lost its ontic status, it is not so much the discursive dimension in thought which seems to account for this, but rather its representative dimension. Once we focus on thought as a process going on only in our minds, and we ask how can we know about things in thought, the obvious answer seems to be that thought in some way mirrors or represents things.

And so we get the new conception of thought as made up of ideas, of little units of representation, rather like inner ghostly snapshots. This is the famous 'way of ideas', inaugurated by Descartes and taken up by his successors both rationalist and empiricist, and which dominates psychology and epistemology for the next two centuries. As the writers of the Port Royal *Logique* put it: 'nous ne pouvons avoir aucune connoissance de ce qui est hors de nous que par l'entremise des idées qui sont en nous'.[1] And they conclude from this that these ideas themselves must be the focus of our study. Thought as a kind of inner incorporeal medium becomes of central interest.

But it is through our ideas that we know what is outside. How do we do this? No longer by grasping the form of the real, for there are none such. Rather knowing things outside means grasping how things are put together. And this means that we put them together in ideas as they are in reality.

So the method of thought becomes the famous resolutive-compositive one. We break things in our ideas down into their component elements, and then we put them together in idea as they are in reality. That is what understanding is, for Galileo, Descartes, Hobbes. As Hobbes puts it in *De Cive* (11.14):

> for everything is best understood by its constitutive causes. For as in a watch, or some such small engine, the matter, figure and motion of the wheels cannot be well known, except it be taken insunder and viewed in its parts; so as to make a more curious search into the rights of states and duties of subjects, it is necessary, I say, not to take them insunder, but yet that they be so considered as if they were dissolved . . .

This means, of course, that our thought too must be broken down into its component bits. These bits are the ideas of seventeenth- and eighteenth-century epistemology.

So what is thinking? It is assembling ideas, properly the assembling of clear and distinct ideas, and according to the way components of the world are assembled. Thinking is a mental discourse, to use Hobbes' term; where this is no longer the articulating and making evident of the ancients, but a kind of inner disassembly and reassembly.

But if thinking is mental discourse, what is the role of language? Sometimes it seems, in reading the writings of seventeenth- and eighteenth-century thinkers, that its role is as much negative as positive, that words can mislead us and take our attention away from the ideas. Language is seen by them as the great seducer, tempting us to be satisfied with mere words, instead of focusing on the ideas they designate.

But no one held the view that we should try to do without language altogether. This was evidently impossible. For any relatively complex or long drawn-out thought we plainly need words; all thinkers concur in this. And indeed, this is not only intuitively evident, it is implicit in their nominalistic starting point. It is through words that we marshal our ideas, that we group them in one way rather than another. Words allow us to deal with things in generalities, and not one by one.

And this is the role which this age assigns to language. It is through words that we marshal our ideas, not painstakingly, one by one, in which case we would not get very far in constructing an understanding of the world, and would lose through forgetfulness as fast as we gained through insight; rather we marshal them in groups and classes. This is Hobbes' doctrine when he likens reasoning to reckoning; where we get our global result by casting up a number of partial sums, and not simply by counting one by one. Condillac in the next century has basically the same idea when he says that language gives us 'empire sur notre imagination'.

From this role of language we can see why words are so dangerous. If we use them to marshal ideas, they must be transparent. We must be able to see clearly what the word designates. Otherwise where we think we are assembling our ideas to match the real, we will in fact be building castles of illusion, or composing absurdities. Our instruments will have taken over, and instead of controlling we shall be controlled.

Language for the theory of these centuries is an instrument of *control* in the assemblage of ideas which is thought or mental discourse. It is an instrument of control in gaining knowledge of the world as objective process. And so it must itself be perfectly transparent; it cannot itself be the locus of mystery, that is, of anything which might be irreducible to objectivity. The meaning of words can only consist in the ideas (or things) they designate. The setting up of a designative connection is what gives a word meaning. We set these up in definitions, and that is why thinkers of this period constantly, almost obsessionally, stress the importance of recurring to definitions, of checking always to see that our words are well-defined, that we use them consistently.

The alternative is to lose control, to slip into a kind of slavery; where it is no longer I who make my lexicon, by definitional fiat, but rather it takes shape independently and in doing this shapes my thought. It is an alienation of my freedom as well as the great source of illusion; and that is why the men of this age combated the cosmos of meaningful order with such determination.

As Locke puts it, 'every man has so inviolable a liberty to make words stand for what ideas he pleases;.[2] Even the great Augustus has no power over my lexicon.

III

The seventeenth-century revolution which in a way did so much to establish our modern modes of thought gave us a thoroughly, polemically, designative theory of meaning. This was challenged in the late eighteenth century by a climate of thought and feeling which is loosely called Romanticism. This term is certainly loose, because it is stretched to include many people, Goethe for instance, who did not define themselves as Romantics and who were not Romantics in any exact sense. But it is a handy label, and I want to go on using it here.

One of the founding texts of this expressivist reaction is Herder's *On the Origin of Language* (1772). (Herder himself was not properly speaking a Romantic; but one of the originators of the *Sturm und Drang*.) In an important passage of his work, Herder turns to consider one of the typical origin stories of eighteenth-century designative theory, that of Condillac in his *Essai sur l'origine des connaissances humaines*.[3] It is a fable of two children in the desert, who come to invent language.

We assume certain cries and gestures as natural expressions of feeling. Condillac argues that each, seeing the other, say, cry out in distress, would come to see the cry as a sign of something (e.g., what causes distress), and would come to use it to refer. The children would thus have their first word. Their lexicon would then increase slowly, item by item.

Herder rebels against this whole conception. For, as he says, it presupposes just what we want to explain. It takes the relation of signifying for granted, as something the children already grasp, or that can unproblematically occur to them ('ils parvinrent insensiblement à faire, avec réflexion, ce qu'ils n'avoient fait que par instinct' [para 3]). Condillac, says Herder, presupposes 'das ganze Ding Sprache schon vor der ersten Seite seines Buches erfunden'. His explanation amounts to saying, 'es enstanden Worte, weil Worte da waren, ehe sie da waren'.[4]

The problem is that Condillac presupposes that his children already understand what it is for a word to stand for something, what it is therefore to talk about something with a word. But *that* is just the mysterious thing. Anyone can be taught the meaning of a word, or even guess at it, or even invent one, once they have language. But what is this capacity which we have and animals do not to endow sounds with meaning, to grasp them as referring to, as used to talk about things?

Let us look at this. I have the word 'triangle' in my lexicon. This means that I can recognize things as triangles, identify them, pick them out as such. I can say, for example, 'This is a triangle.' But what does this capacity amount to? Let us see by comparing it with an analogous animal capacity. I might train an animal (a rat), to react differentially, say, to go through a door which had a triangle painted on it, as against one which had a circle. So my rat would be in a sense recognizing a triangle.

But there is a crucial difference: the rat in a sense recognizes the triangle, because he reacts to it. But the human language-user recognizes that this is a triangle, he recognizes that 'triangle' is the right word to use here; that this is the right description. This capacity to recognize that X is the right description is essentially invoked in our capacity to use language. Of course, we are not usually reflecting as we talk that the words we use are the appropriate ones; but the implicit claim in speaking language is that they are appropriate; and we can all understand the challenge that someone might make at any point: 'Is X the right word?', or 'Do you really mean X?' And we would all be able to give some kind of reply.

So only beings who can describe things as triangles can be said to recognize them as triangles, at least in the strong sense. They do not just react to triangles, but recognize them as such. Beings who can do this are conscious of the things they experience in a fuller way. They are more reflectively aware, we might say.

And this is Herder's point. To learn a word, to grasp that 'triangle' stands for triangles, is to be capable of this reflective awareness. That is what needs to be explained. To account for language by saying that we learn that the word 'a' stands for a's, the word 'b' for b's, is to explain nothing. How do we learn what 'standing for' involves, what it is to describe things, briefly, to acquire the reflective awareness of the language user?

Herder uses the term 'reflection' (*Besonnenheit*) for this awareness. And his point against Condillac is that this kind of reflection is inseparable from language. It cannot precede our learning our first word, which is what Condillac implicitly assumes. This is because only someone capable of using language to describe is capable of picking things out as — or recognizing things as —, in the strong sense.

But this means that language is not just a set of words which designate things; it is the vehicle of this kind of reflective awareness. This reflection is a capacity we only realize in speech. Speaking is not only the expression of this capacity, but also its realization.

But then the expressive dimension of language becomes fundamental again. In order for given words to mean something, to designate their respective objects, we have to be able to speak, that is, give expression to this reflective awareness, because it is only through this expression, through speech, that this reflective awareness comes about. A being who cannot speak cannot have it. We only have it, in contrast to animals, in that we talk about things. Expression realizes, and is therefore fundamental.

This is once again an expressive theory. But this time it is an expressive theory of language, rather than an expressive theory of the cosmos. On the traditional view, creation expresses the ideas of God; but these exist before/outside creation. The new expressive theory of human language that we find in Herder is, by contrast, constitutive; that is, reflective consciousness only comes to exist in its expression. The expressive dimension is fundamental to language, because it is only in expression that language comes to be.

The theorists of the Romantic period were, of course, very influenced by the earlier expressivism of the cosmos, as we might call it. We could say that in a sense they transposed what belongs to God on this older theory on to man. For man like God embodies his ideas and makes them manifest. But unlike God, man needs his expression in order to make his ideas manifest to himself. Which is another way of saying that his ideas do not properly exist before their expression in language or some other of the range of media men deploy. That is what is meant by saying that language, or expression in general, is constitutive of thought.

In this connection, it is no accident that the Romantic period sees a revolution in our conception of art. The traditional view understood art in terms of mimesis. Art imitates the real. It may select, imitate only the best, or what conforms to the ideas, but basically what it attempts to do is hold the mirror up to nature. The Romantics gave us a quite different conception, by which, in one formulation, the artist strives to imitate not nature, but the author of nature. Art is now seen not as imitation, but as creative expression. The work of art does not refer beyond itself to what it imitates; rather it manifests something; it is itself the locus in which the meaning becomes manifest. It should be a symbol, rather than an allegory, to recur to the distinction which the men of that generation often invoked.

As Herder put it: 'the artist is become a creator God'.[5] The artist creates in his work, as it were, a miniature universe, a whole which has its goal in itself, and does not refer beyond to anything else. Novalis makes the comparison with the divine creation in these terms: 'artistic creation is thus as much an end in itself as the divine creation of the universe, and one is as original and as grounded on itself as the other: because the two are one, and God reveals himself in the poet as he gives himself corporeal form in the visible universe'.

But to return to the theory of language, we see that language is no longer an assemblage of words, but the capacity to speak (express/realize) the reflective awareness implicit in using words to say something. Learning to use any single word presupposes this general capacity as background. But to have the general capacity is to possess a language. So that it seems that we need the whole of language as the background for the introduction of any of its parts, that is, individual words.

This may seem to pose insuperable obstacles for any account of the acquisition of language; and indeed, Herder in spite of the title of his work (*Ueber den Ursprung der Sprache*) ducks the issue altogether. But it does point to a feature of language which seems undeniable, its holism. One might say that language as a whole is presupposed in any one of its parts.

Herder again is the one who formulated this insight. It is ultimately implicit in the point above, that to use a word to describe is to identify something as —. When I say 'This is a triangle', I recognize it as a triangle. But to be able to recognize something as a triangle is to be able to recognize other things as non-triangles. For the notion 'triangle' to have a sense for me, there must be something(s) which with it contrasts; I must have some notion of other kinds of figures, that is, be able to recognize other kinds of figure for the kinds they are. 'Triangle' has to contrast in my lexicon with other figure terms. Indeed, a word only has the meaning it does in our lexicon because of what terms it contrasts with. What would 'red' mean if we had no other colour terms? How would our colour terms change if some of our present ones dropped out?

But in addition, to recognize something as a triangle is to focus on this property; it is to pick it out by its shape, and not by its size, colour, what it is made of, its smell, aesthetic properties, and so on. Here again some kind of contrast is necessary, a contrast of property dimensions. For to say of something 'This is a triangle' is to apply this word as the *right* word, the appropriate descriptive term. But someone could not be applying a word as the right word and have no sense whatever of what made it the right word, did not even grasp for instance that something was a triangle in virtue of its shape, and not its size or colour.

So it appears that a word like 'triangle' could not figure in our lexicon alone. It has to be surrounded by a skein of other terms, some which contrast with it, and some which situate it, as it were, give its property dimension, not to speak of the wider matrix of language in which the various activities are situated in which our talk of triangles figures: measurement, geometry, design-creation and so on.

The word only makes sense in this skein, in what Humboldt (who followed and developed Herder's thoughts on language) called the web (*Gewebe*) of language. In touching one part of language (a word), the whole is present.[6]

This expressive doctrine thus presents us with a very different picture of language from the empiricist one. Language is not an assemblage of separable instruments, which lie as it were transparently to hand, and which can be used to marshal ideas, this use being something we can fully control and oversee. Rather it is something in the nature of a web, and to complicate the image, is present as a whole in any one of its parts. To speak is to touch a bit of the web, and this is to make the whole resonate. Because the words we use now only have sense through their place in the whole web, we can never in principle have a clear oversight of the implications of what we say at any moment. Our language is always more than we can encompass; it is in a sense inexhaustible. The aspirations to be in no degree at all a prisoner of language, so dear to Hobbes and Locke, is in principle unrealizable.

But at the same time, we need to connect this with another feature of language on this scheme which Humboldt also brought to the fore. What is crucial to language is what is realized in speech, the expression/realization of reflection. Language is not, once again, a set of instruments: words which have been attached to meanings; what is essential to it is the activity in which by speaking words we pick things out as — (among other things, as we shall see). The capacity which language represents is realized in speech.

As Humboldt puts it, we have to think of language as speech, and this as activity, not realized work; as *energgeia*, not *ergon*.

But if the language capacity comes to be in speech, then it is open to being continuously recreated in speech, continually extended, altered, reshaped. And this is what is constantly happening. Men are constantly shaping language, straining the limits of expression, minting new terms, displacing old ones, giving language a changed gamut of meanings.

But this activity has to be seen against the background of the earlier point about language as a whole. The new coinages are never quite autonomous, quite uncontrolled by the rest of language. They can only be introduced and make sense because they already have a place within the web, which must at any moment be taken as given over by far the greater part of its extent. Human speakers resemble the sailors in Neurath's image of the philosopher, who have to remake their ship in the open sea, and cannot build it from the base in a dry-dock.

What then does language come to be on this view? A pattern of activity, by which we express/realize a certain way of being in the world, that of reflective awareness, but a pattern which can only be deployed against a background which we can never fully dominate; and yet a background that we are never fully dominated by, because we are constantly reshaping it. Reshaping it without dominating it, or being able to oversee it, means that we never fully know what we are doing to it; we develop language without knowing fully what we are making it into.

From another angle: the background web is only there in that we speak. But because we cannot oversee it, let alone shape it all, our activity in speaking is never entirely under our conscious control. Conscious speech is like the tip of an iceberg. Much of what is going on in shaping our activity is not in our purview. Our deployment of language reposes on much that is preconscious and unconscious.

So the expressive view yields us a much broader and deeper conception of language. It is an utterly different phenomenon than the assemblage of designative terms which empiricism gave us. But the implicit extensions go further. The designative theory sees language as a set of designators, words we use to talk about things. There is an implicit restriction of the activities of language. Language primarily serves to describe the world (although designative terms can also be given extended uses for questioning and giving commands).

The expressive theory opens a new dimension. If language serves to express/realize a new kind of awareness; then it may not only make possible a new awareness of things, an ability to describe them; but also new ways of feeling, of responding to things. If in expressing our thoughts about things, we can come to have new thoughts; then in expressing our feelings, we can come to have transformed feelings.

This quite transforms the eighteenth-century view of the expressive function of language. Condillac and others conjectured that at the origin of language was the expressive cry, the expression of anger, fear, or some emotion; this later could acquire designative meaning and serve as a word. But the notion here was that expression was of already existing feelings, which were unaltered in being expressed.

The revolutionary idea of expressivism was that the development of new modes of expression enables us to have new feelings, more powerful or more refined, and certainly more self-aware. In being able to express our feelings, we give them a reflective dimension which transforms them. The language user can feel not only anger but indignation, not only love but admiration.

Seen from this angle, language cannot be confined to the activity of talking about things. We transform our emotions into human ones not primarily in talking about them, but in expressing them. Language also serves to express/realize ways of feeling without talking about them. We often give expression to our feelings in talking about something else. (For example, indignation is expressed in condemnation of the unjust actions, admiration in praise of the remarkable traits.)

From this perspective, we cannot draw a boundary around the language of prose in the narrow sense, and divide it off from those other symbolic-expressive creations of man: poetry, music, art, dance, etc. If we think of language as essentially used to say something *about* something, then prose is indeed in a category of its own. But once one takes language as being expressive in this way, that is, where the expression constitutes what it expresses, then talking *about* is just one of the provinces constituted by language; the constitution of human emotion is another, and in this some uses of prose are akin to some uses of poetry, music and art.

In the Romantic period, there was a tendency to see this constituting of the human emotions as the most important function of language in a broad sense. Language realizes man's humanity. Man completes himself in expression. It was natural in such a context to exalt art above other forms of expression, above the development of merely descriptive language; or at least to give it equal weight and dignity. It was then that art began to replace religion for many as the centrally important dimension of human life – which it remains for many today.

But the expressive view not only transformed and extended the conception of the uses of language. It also transformed the conception of the subject of language. If language must be primarily seen as an activity – it is what is constantly created and recreated in speech – then it becomes relevant to note that the primary locus of speech is in conversation. Men speak together, to each other. Language is fashioned and grows not principally in monologue, but in dialogue, or better, in the life of the speech community.

Hence Herder's notion that the primary locus of a language was the *Volk* which carried it. Humboldt takes up the same insight. Language is shaped by speech, and so can only grow up in a speech community. The language I speak, the web which I can never fully dominate or oversee, can never be just *my* language, it is always largely *our* language.

This opens up another field of the constitutive functions of language. Speech also serves to express/constitute different relations in which we may stand to each other: intimate, formal, official, causal, joking, serious, and so on. From this point of view, we can see that it is not just the speech community which shapes and creates language, but language which constitutes and sustains the speech community.

IV

If we attempt to gather all this together, we can see that the expressive conception gives a view of language as a range of activities in which we express/realize a certain way of being in the world. And this way of being has many facets. It is not just the reflective awareness by which we recognise things as —, and describe our surroundings; but also that by which we come to have the properly human emotions, and constitute our human relations, including those of the language community within which language grows. The range of activity is not confined to language in the narrow sense, but rather encompasses the whole gamut of symbolic expressive capacities in which language, narrowly construed, is seen to take its place. This activity, even as regards the production of normal prose about the world, is one which we can never bring under conscious control or oversight in its entirety; even less we can aspire to such oversight of the whole range.

If we now look back over the route we have been travelling, we see how language has become central to our understanding of man. For if we hold on to the intuition that man is the rational animal, the animal possessing logos or discourse-thought, at least in that we concur that this has something to do with what distinguishes us from other animals, then the effect of the expressive doctrine is to make us see the locus of our humanity in the power of expression by which we constitute language in the broadest sense, that is, the range of symbolic forms. For it is these which make thought possible. It is this range of expressions which constitute what we know as logos.

The whole development, through the seventeenth-century designative theory and the Romantic expressive view, has brought language more and more to the centre stage of our understanding of man; first as an instrument of the typically human capacity of thinking, and then as the indispensable medium without which our typically human capacities, emotions, relations would not be.

If we follow the expressive view, then we have to come to understand this medium, and the extraordinary range of activities which constitute it, if we are ever to hope to understand ourselves. What I want to suggest is that we have all in fact become followers of the expressive view; not that we accept the detail of the various Romantic theories, but in that we have all been profoundly marked by this way of understanding thought and language, which has had a major impact on our civilization. I would venture to claim that even those who would want to reject expressive theories as metaphysical rubbish and obfuscatory mystification are nevertheless deeply affected by this outlook.

I want to make at least a feeble attempt briefly to defend this outrageous claim. My point now is that the profound influence of the expressive view in modern culture is what underlies our fascination for language, our making it such a central question of twentieth-century thought and study.

This would also explain why language is more enigmatic to us than to previous ages – admittedly another highly controversial claim. For on the expressive view, language is no longer merely the external clothing of thought, nor a simple instrument which ought in principle to be fully in our control and oversight. It is more like a medium in which we are plunged, and which we cannot fully plumb. The difficulty is compounded in that it is not just the medium in virtue of which we are capable of the human emotion and of standing in specifically human relations to each other. And flowing from this the capacity we want to understand is not just that by which we produce prose about things which surround us, but also those by which we make poetry, music, art, dance, and so on, even in the end those by which we have such thing as a personal style.

This means that the phenomenon of language becomes much broader as well as deeper when we move from a designative to an expressive perspective. We are tempted to ask what this range of capacities have in common. And even if we have been taught by Wittgenstein to resist this temptation, the question cannot but arise of how they hold together as a 'package'. For this they seem to do. It is not an accident that the only speaking animal is also the one who dances, makes music, paints, and so on. Finding the centre of gravity of this range is a much more difficult and baffling question than tracing how words designate, that is, until we come to see that the latter question leads us back to the former.

But this is what the expressive understanding of language puts on our agenda; that we find this centre of gravity, or, in other terms, come to some insight about this extraordinary capacity we have for expression.

Or we can get to the heart of the same issues in another way, if we ask what is the characteristic excellence of expression. On the designative view, this was clear. Language was an instrument. It was at its best when it best served its purpose, when the terms designated clearly distinct ideas, and we maintained their definition clearly before us in our reasoning. On this understanding language was an all-purpose tool of thought. But for the expressivist, it is an activity which constitutes a specific way of being in the world, which Herder referred to as 'reflection', but which it is hard to find a word for just because we are so baffled to define what I called its centre of gravity.

Another way of asking what this centre of gravity is is to ask when this way of being is at its best, its fullest, in other words, what constitutes its excellence. When are our expressive powers most fully realized? We can no longer assume that just attaining maximum clarity about the things we describe and explain constitutes perfection.

But to know what it is to realize our expressive powers to the fullest must be to know something about the characteristic perfection of man, on the premises of the expressive understanding; and so this question must come on our agenda.

Again, the question of what expression is can arise in another way, We try to understand how expression can *arise*, how a new medium of thought or understanding can come to be through expression. And since we cannot study the genesis of language in human life, our question takes the form of asking when we come close now to forging new modes of expression; what happens when we extend our capacity of expression? How does this come about?

For a variety of reasons, many contemporaries have thought it plausible that it is in artistic creation that we come closest to understanding this, to understand the mystery of original expression; and this is one of the reasons why art is so central to our self-understanding.

But the baffling nature of language extends to more than the nature of expression. It also touches the question, who expresses? We saw above that language for the Romantics could not be seen as the creation of the individual. And indeed, it is hard to fault them on this. We are all inducted into language by an existing language community. We learn to talk not only in that the words are given to us by our parents and others, but also in that they talk to us, and hence give us the status of interlocutors. This is what is involved in the centrally important fact that we are given a name. In being given a name we are made into beings that one addresses, and we are inducted into the community whose speaking continually remakes the language. As interlocutors, we learn to say 'I' of ourselves, one of the key stages in our becoming language users.

Language originally comes to us from others, from a community. But how much does it remain an activity essentially bound to a community? Once I learn language I can just continue to use it, even extend it, quite monologically, talking and writing only for myself? Once again, the designative view tends to make us see this as perfectly possible. My lexicon is under *my* control. And common sense tends to side here at first sight with the designative view. Surely, I very often do talk to myself, I can even invent private names for people, and why not also private terms for objects which surround me.?

Of course, I can invent private terms. But the question is whether my speech does not always remain that of an interlocutor in a speech community in an essential way. We might ask whether my conception of what it makes sense to say, of how things may be perspicuously described, of how things can be illuminatingly classified, of how my feelings can be adequately expressed, whether all these are not profoundly shaped by a potential terrain of intersubjective agreement and full communication. I may break away now from my interlocutors, and adopt quite another mode of expression, but is it not always in view of a fuller, more profound and authentic communication, which provides the criterion for what I now recognize as an adequate expression?

So the question remains open as to whether the subject of speech is not always in some sense, and on some level, a speech community.

Another related question concerns the place of the subject in expression. It is in a sense the question, What is expressed? or, What comes to expression? Of course, our developing language, in so far as it is descriptive language, responds to the shape of things around us. But we have seen that there is another dimension to language, that by which its development shapes our emotions and relations. Expression shapes our human lives. The question is, what is it that, in coming to expression, so shapes our lives as humans?

For the expressivists of the late eighteenth century and the Romantic period, the answer was quite unproblematical. Expression was self-expression. What comes to full expression are my desires, my aspirations, my moral sentiments. What comes to light in the full development of expressive power is precisely that what was striving for expression all along was the self. This may not have been so in the earlier stages of human history, when men were prone to see themselves simply as immersed in a larger cosmos and not also as centres of autonomous will and desire. But as it comes to greater self-clarity expression comes to be recognized as self-expression.

But the basic expressivist insights might also suggest another account. What comes about through the development of language in the broadest sense is the coming to be of expressive power, the power to make things manifest. It is not unambiguously clear that this ought to be considered as a self-expression/realization. What is made manifest is not exclusively, not even mainly, the self, but a world. Why think here primarily in terms of self-expression?

Now the expressivists of the Romantic period did not really need to pose this question, because in a sense they could accept both answers at once. They could do so, because of the notion, common in the Romantic period, of God as a kind of cosmic subject, of which we finite subjects are in a sense emanations. This view, which hovers on the brink of pantheism, allows us to see what we make manifest in our language both as our own and as God's, since God lives in us. We expresss both ourselves, and a larger reality of which we are a part.

With the receding of this too indulgent pantheism (as it must appear to us), we are left with the choice. Is the expression which makes us human essentially a self-expression, in that we are mainly responding to our way of feeling/experiencing the world, and bringing this to expression? Or are we responding to the reality in which we are set, in which we are included of course, but which is not reducible to our experience of it?

The common sense of our society takes perhaps too easily the position of the Romantics, without even the excuse for their pantheistic justification. It assumes that in our paradigm-expressive activities, for instance, in artistic creation, we are expressing ourselves, our feelings and reactions. But this answer is also challenged. Some contemporaries would argue that our most expressive creations, hence those where we are closest to deploying our expressive power at the fullest, are not self-expressions; that they rather have the power to move us because they manifest our expressive power itself and its relation to our world. In this kind of expression, we are responding to the way things are, rather than just exteriorizing our feelings.

Heidegger springs to mind in this connection. Something like this view may lie behind this passage, quoted from *Dichterisch wohnet der Mensch*:

> Man behaves as if he were the creator and master of language, whereas on the contrary, it is language which is and remains his sovereign . . . For in the proper sense of these terms, it is language which speaks. Man speaks insofar as he replies to language by listening to what it says to him. Language makes us a sign and it is

> language which first and last conducts us in this way towards the being of a thing.[7]

On this view what we strive to bring to expression is not primarily the self. Expressivism here becomes radically anti-subjectivist. And of course, this issue raises from another angle the one mentioned above, about the characteristic excellence of expression, and hence of man.

These questions are all difficult and deep. I mean by that latter term not only that they touch fundamental questions about ourselves, but that they are baffling and very difficult to formulate, let alone find a clear strategy to investigate. But they are among the questions which the expressive view puts on our agenda. My hypothesis is that we are fascinated and baffled by language in part because we are heirs to this outlook.

But I must face the objection which must have been urging itself forward all this time: surely I cannot be claiming that we all accept the main doctrines of the expressive view of language, that there are no more designativists, or even more implausibly, that there are no more proponents of objectifying science? Of course, I agree, that would be absurd. The stock of objectifying science is as high as ever. The virtually inarticulate belief that only an objective account is a truly satisfactory one has invaded the sciences of man, has shaped the procedures of widely practised academic disciplines, like psychology, sociology, political science, much of linguistics. Moreover one of the underlying motives of an objective account that we saw with the seventeenth-century designative theory, that it seems to promise control over the domain under study, is as forcefully operative today as then; indeed, more so.

But in spite of this, I want to maintain my claim that the expressivist reasons for bafflement are to some extent shared by all of us. I should like to offer two grounds for this.

The first is that much of the Romantic view of language has come to be generally accepted by both metaphysical camps, objectivists and their opponents. We now see language capacity as residing in the possession of an interconnected lexicon, only one part of which is used at any time. We see that the individual term is defined in relation to the others. Ferdinand de Saussure made this point at the beginning of the century, and it is now common property.

At the same time we recognize the central importance of speech activity for language. Language as a code (Saussure's *langue*) can be seen as a kind of precipitate of speech (Saussure's *parole*). Speech activity itself is complex: the declarative sentence is not just the result of concatenating words with their attached meanings. It involves doing different things, picking out an object of reference, and saying something about this object. These different functions and their combination in the declarative utterance determine to a significant degree the kind of language we have. But on top of this we also recognize that speech activity goes well beyond the declarative utterance, and includes questions, orders, prayers, etc.

We are also ready to recognize that this activity involves mechanisms of which we are not fully aware and which we do not fully control. We do not find strange a thesis like Chomsky's, that our grasp of grammaticality involves the application of transformations of which we are not consciously aware, relating a depth structure to a surface structure. We accept without too much demur that there may well be a 'depth structure' to our language activity.

And we are perhaps even ready to agree that the language which is evolved through this speech activity is the language of a community and not just of an individual, in other words, that the crucial speech activities are those of the community. We may not be entirely sure what this means, but we have a sense that in some meaning it contains an important truth.

Of course, this does not mean that everyone has become an expressivist. We are not in any sense forced to abandon the metaphysical stance in favour of objective accounts. But what we now have to do is apply them in a new way. We see language as a whole, as an activity with – potentially at least – a depth structure. The task is now to give an objective account of this depth structure and its operation, which underlies the activity of language we observe. This is now the agenda.

In this the science of language is simply one example of a global shift in the objectivist sciences of man since the eighteenth century. The shift is away from a set of theories in terms of 'surface' or observable realities, principally the contents of the mind available to introspection, in favour of theories in terms of 'deep' or unobservable mechanisms or structures. The shift is one aspect of the virtually total disappearance of the seventeenth- and eighteenth-century 'way of ideas', the attempt to understand the mind in terms of its introspectable contents, the science that came to be called 'ideology' at the moment when it had passed its peak.

This was grounded in the view, common to Descartes and his empiricist critics, that the contents of the mind were in principle open to transparent inspection by the subject himself. Thinking was, as we saw, 'mental discourse', which ought to be entirely self-possessed and self-transparent. This view seems very implausible today, where the importance of unconscious structures and processes in thought seems very plausible, indeed, close to undeniable.

But the scientific goals and norms of the seventeenth and eighteenth centuries easily survived the demise of the 'way of ideas'. In place of the 'surface' psychologies of the past, we now have explanation by-passing consciousness; in some cases by ignoring the psychological altogether, and explaining behaviour in terms of stimulus and response; or else in terms of a depth theory which is physiological; in others by what remains a 'psychological' theory but one drawing heavily on mechanisms unavailable to consciousness, such as Freudian psychoanalysis, or computer-modelled theories of our intelligent performances. In place of 'surface' sociologies, based on the adjustment of conscious interests, or the existence or absence of individual habits of mind, we have theories of social structure, in which individuals are caught up in a dynamic which they do not and perhaps cannot understand; where the explanation is at the level of the social whole, and of properties of this whole which are not evident to the participants. These follow the laws or obey the constraints of historical materialism or structural-functionalism.

Now in many of these cases, for example, Freud, Marx, structural-functionalism, the depth structures elaborated obviously owe a lot to earlier Romantic theorizing. But the fact remains that the intent of these theories is to give an objectivistic explanation.

And in this, of course, they are following a lead set by the 'hard' sciences of nature, which also have had recourse more and more to unobservable depth structures, even including some of which violate our ordinary macroscopic understanding of things.

If we were to try to explain this shift which has gradually taken place over the last two centuries, away from the way of ideas, then undoubtedly the example of the hard sciences, always the paradigms of objectivistic science, is an important factor. But it cannot be the only one. Something would have to be said about the change in our condition. Perhaps it is that in modern mass societies we feel less of a sense that the factors which are decisive for our behaviour are under our purview – that what society claims of us is something we give knowingly even if not willingly – than did the educated classes of the earlier epoch. I think something like this is true, but even so, a great deal remains to be explained. Why do we understand ourselves so readily in depth-psychological terms? Something very important about the whole development of modern society is waiting here to be uncovered.

But in any case, the science of language has followed this pattern. We are no longer satisfied with surface accounts of the application of words to ideas. We want an account in terms of depth structure. But many want the same scientific goals to be paramount.

But although the metaphysical goals survive unscathed into the new sciences of depth structure, the fact that so much has been taken on board from the Romantic conception makes it inevitable that something like the same questions arise as those expressivism puts on the agenda. For instance, there is a continuing issue about how to understand the notion of depth structure, as the philosophical debates around Chomsky's work attest. Is depth structure to be understood as the operation of an unconscious capacity, for instance, do we know how to make transformations, even though we are unaware of doing so? This seems to many unbearably paradoxical. Or should we see depth structures in terms of underlying operations, analogous to those in machines? But then what is their relation to the intelligent and conscious uses of language? From either direction, some mystery surrounds the status of the language capacity as a whole which plainly underlies our ability to say specific things on specific occasions. The baffling questions the expressive view gives rise to will not disappear just because we stick to our objectivist metaphysics. Some seem to arise inescapably with the intuition that language involves some global underlying capacity, and not just a set of particulate dispositions to utter certain words in certain circumstances.

This threatens to create something of a dilemma for objectivistic thought, and leads to the characteristic gamut of modern would-be scientific theories. At one extreme are those who are highly sensitive to the metaphysical dangers of allowing depth explanations. They would like ideally to develop a behaviourist theory, in which the utterance of certain words is made a function of environmental stimulation. Skinner is the most spectacular protagonist of this view.

But the weakness of this strategy is that the explanatory power of such a theory is very poor, and it even comes close to absurdity at times. And so we gain greatly in plausibility by moving along the spectrum, to what we might call 'neo-designative' theories of meaning, like that, for example, of Donald Davidson. This theory can be called 'neo-designative' because it attempts to give an account of meaning in terms of the truth conditions of sentences. These truth conditions are observable states of affairs in the world; hence once again we have the basic *démarche* of a theory which tries to explain the meaning of language in terms of the relation of linguistic elements to extra-linguistic reality. Only here, the modern theory has profited from our understanding of language as a structured reality; so that the elements so related are not words, but declarative sentences.

These theories – another example might be explanations of the functioning of language on the model of information-processing mechanisms – are more plausible than behaviourism, but they still give no recognition to the expressive dimension. But it is possible to move further along the spectrum, to give some recognition to this, while trying to explain it in objectivistic terms.

Two examples spring to mind, which however are not concerned with theories of language in the narrow sense, but with – in different ways – symbolic expression. These are the views of Marx and Freud.

Freud recognizes symbolic expression, in our symptoms as well as in what he calls symbols. But these are explained in terms of desires, which are not themselves desires for symbolic expression, nor do they involve such expression in their proper fulfilment. On the contrary, the symbolic proliferation results from their blocking or inhibition. The symptom gives my object of desire in symbolic form, because I cannot (will not allow myself to) go after it in reality. Moreover these desires should ultimately be explicable physiologically; hence Freud's electrical and hydraulic languages.

With Marx, we also have a recognition of symbolic expression in ideological consciousness: religion, for instance, gives us a distorted expression of the human social condition of its age. With the liberation of classless society, and the victory of scientific over ideological consciousness, such symbolic forms of awareness are swept aside. And from the standpoint of scientific consciousness, the ieological symbolism is fully explicable, again in terms which have nothing to do with a motivation directed to symbolic expression. This rather is seen as a distortion of the reality, and hence of the underlying motives, which come to clear self-recognition in scientific consciousness.

This account may be somewhat unfair to Marxism, as it may also be to Freud, in giving an unduly reductive cast to their explanations. But whether we have here portrayed true or vulgar Marxism and Freudianism, the theories obviously have their weaknesses, in that they have trouble dealing with the place of expression, of symbolism in normal, undistorted or non-pathological life. When they try to say something in the domain of aesthetics, for instance, Marxism and Freudianism must develop more refined interpretations on pain of sounding philistine and implausibly reductive.

We have examples of such developed – and semiologically sensitive – Marxism and Freudianism in contemporary French structuralism (e.g., in different ways, Lacan, Barthes, Althusser). But this structuralism has taken a step further along the spectrum. It allows expression a central place in human life. It understands that man is the language animal, in that language is more than a tool for man, but somehow constitutes a way of being which is specifically human. We have to understand the growth of language as bound up with the development of a form of life which it makes possible. So that the question can arise of the characteristic excellence of language, of when expression is at its best.

As a matter of fact, modern structuralism owes quite a bit to the reflections of expressivist philosophers. For instance, Lévi-Strauss read Merleau-Ponty with interest. Lacan has been very influenced by Hegel and Heidegger (his Hegel being mediated through Kojève, who picked Heideggerian themes out of Hegel).

But the intent remains 'scientific', that is objectivist. In Lévi-Strauss' case, for instance, drawing from the work of Marcel Mauss, the basic idea – at least of his early theory – seems to be that language arises in a drive to classify, which in turn must be understood as ultimately aimed at social/moral order. We order our lives through classifications, of things forbidden and allowed, enjoined or neutral. The classificatory scheme, of our totems, of segments of the universe, is ordered to a classification of partners and actions, which alone makes possible social integration.

This theory sees the expressive function as central; sees it as necessary indeed to the very existence of human society. But it lays claim too to objectivity, presumably in that its account of language is functional and reductive. For the function which explains language is not the manifestation of anything, but the maintenance of a social order. (In this it shows the Durkheimian roots of so much French social thought.) Once more language is to be explained in terms of something else.

But as we come to this end of the spectrum, the questions which the expressive view brings forward become harder and harder to avoid. With contemporary structuralism, great mysteries surround the status of the underlying structures, for example, their relation to the uses of language in everyday life, and their relations to the individual subject. These are comparable to the questions that arise from the expressive view; indeed, in some cases the questions are the same.

I ran through the gamut in order to illustrate the dilemma of modern objectivist theories of language. They can avoid the intrusion of the baffling questions concerning the nature of expression only by espousing narrower and more primitive theories which are either implausible, or which fail to explain an important range of the phenomena of language, or both. Or they can win plausibility and explanatory range, but at the cost of opening themselves to these questions.

This is the first ground I would put forward for my claim that we are all affected to some degree by the expressivist reasons for bafflement about language. It concerns the predicament of scientific theorizing about language. My second ground can be put much more tersely. Regardless of scientific considerations, modern students of language remain children of our age, and immersed in its culture. And this has been so massively affected by the Romantic-expressivist rebellion, that no one can remain untouched by it. This effect is particularly visible in our understanding of art, its nature and its place in human life. One of the most obtrusive effects is the concern of much contemporary art with the process of its own creation, with the properties of its own medium, with the experimental creation of new media. Expression itself becomes its theme; how it is possible, just what it consists in, and what point it can give to human life. The artist becomes his own subject, and/or the process of creation his theme.

It is very difficult to live in this civilization and not have the problem of expression obtrude on us, with all its enigmatic force. And that is the reason, I want to maintain, why we are all so concerned and fascinated with language, so that even the most tough-minded and empiricist philosophies, like logical empiricism, are 'linguistic' in cast.

V

I hope that this historical odyssey has cast light on our contemporary fascination with language. I hope that it has also shown why we find it baffling, and has done something to explain the paradox that, with all the advance of science, this central human function seems more mysterious to us than to our eighteenth-century predecessors.

In fact, seen from this historical perspective, the development towards our present understanding of language as both central and enigmatic seems irreversible. We cannot recapture the earlier perspectives from which language could appear more marginal or less problematic. The view of the universe as an order of signs is lost for ever, at least in its original form, after the coming of modern science and the modern notion of freedom; and the view of language as a set of designative signs, fully in our control and purview, is lost forever with the seventeenth-century view of the punctual subject, perfectly transparent to himself, whose soul contained nothing that he could not observe. From where we stand, we are constantly being forced to the conception of man as a language animal, one who is constituted by language.

But I do not hope for agreement on this. Because in our bafflement, we naturally split into two camps. This reflects the pull on us of the contradictory metaphysical demands: for the clarity and control offered by an objective account of ourselves and our world, on the one hand, and towards a recognition of the intrinsic, irreducible nature of expression, on the other. There are very few of us who do not feel the force of both these demands. And perhaps just for this reason we divide with polemical fervour into opposing parties, expressors and designators.

The battle between expressors and designators is one front in the global war between the heirs of the Englightenment and the Romantics; such as we see in the struggle between technocracy and the sense of history or community, instrumental reason versus the intrinsic value of certain forms of life, the domination of nature versus the need for the reconciliation with nature. This general war rages over the battle fronts of language as well. Heidegger is one of the prophets of the stance of 'letting things be', one of the great critics of modern technological consciousness; the neo-designators defend a notion of reason as instrumental reason. All this is no accident. It shows only how much rides on this issue.

The issue concerns the nature of man, or what it is to be human. And since so much of this turns on what it is to think, to reason, to create; and since all of these point us towards language, we can expect that the study of language will become even more a central concern of our intellectual life. It is in a sense the crucial locus of the theoretical battle we are having with ourselves.

As a civilization, we live with a compromise. In our scientific understanding, we tend to be men of the Enlightenment, and we accept the predominance of Enlightenment – one might say, utilitarian – values in setting the parameters of public policy. Growth, productivity, welfare are of fundamental importance. But it is recognized that, without prejudice to the perhaps ultimately available scientific explanation which will be reductive, people experience things in expressive terms: something is 'more of me'; or I feel fulfilled by this, not by that; or that prospect really 'speaks to me'. Along with this tolerance of experience goes a parallel in the public domain. The main limits of public policy are set by the requirements of production within the constraints of distribution, and these are meant to be established by scientific means, and in a utilitarian spirit. But private experience must be given its expressive fulfilment. There is a 'Romantik' of private life, which is meant to fit into a smoothly running consumer society.

However effective this compromise may be politically, it is a rotten one intellectually; it combines the crassest scientism (objectivism) with the most subjectivist forms of expressivism. But I suppose I say it is rotten mainly because I think that both of these are wrong; and that they leave out the really fruitful line of inquiry, a contemporary expressivism which tries to go beyond subjectivism in discovering and articulating what is expressed.

But even leaving aside my commitments, it is certain that in the absence of a strong expressivist critique, scientism remains smugly satisfied with its half-baked explanations, and the subjectivist conception of experience veers towards formless sentimentalism. The issue of language goes by default; which means the issue of what it is to be human goes too.

NOTES

1 Antoine Arnaud and Pierre Nicole, *La Logique ou l'art de penser* (Paris, 1970), p. 63.
2 Essay, III. ii. 8.
3 Part II, sect. I, ch. I.
4 *Treatise on the Origin of Language*, in J. G. Herder, *Sprachphilosophie* (Hamburg, 1960), pp. 12, 13.
5 Quoted in T. Todorov, *Théories du symbole* (Paris, 1977), p. 185.
6 Another very persuasive argument is the famous one in Wittgenstein's *Philosophical Investigations*, i.258ff., dealing with sensation E. If you try to give the name 'E' to an inner sensation, and avoid saying anything else about it, not even that it is a sensation, then you find yourself just wanting to make an inarticuate noise. For in saying nothing else, you deprive 'E' of the status of a word. You cannot know what you are saying. Cf. also his arguments against private ostensive definition; *Investigations*, i.29.
7 *Dichterisch wohmet der Mensch*, in Martin Heidegger, *Voträge und Aufsätze*, part II (Pfullingen, n.d.), p. 64.

5

'From the Native's Point of View': On the Nature of Anthropological Understanding

CLIFFORD GEERTZ

I

Several years ago a minor scandal erupted in anthropology: one of its ancestral figures told the truth in a public place. As befits an ancestor, he did it posthumously, and through his widow's decision rather than his own, with the result that a number of the sort of right-thinking types who are with us always immediately rose to cry that she, an in-marrier anyway, had betrayed clan secrets, profaned an idol, and let down the side. What will the children think, to say nothing of the layman? But the disturbance was not much lessened by the ceremonial wringing of the hands; the damn thing was, after all, already printed. In much the same fashion as James Watson's *The Double Helix* exposed the way in which biophysics in fact gets done, Bronislaw Malinowski's *A Diary in the Strict Sense of the Term* rendered established accounts of how anthropologists work fairly well implausible. The myth of the chameleon fieldworker, perfectly self-tuned to his exotic surroundings, a walking miracle of empathy, tact, patience, and cosmopolitanism, was demolished by the man who had perhaps done most to create it.

The squabble that arose around the publication of the *Diary* concentrated, naturally, on inessentials and missed, as was only to be expected, the point. Most of the shock seemed to have arisen from the mere discovery that Malinowski was not, to put it delicately, an unmitigated nice guy. He had rude things to say about the natives he was living with, and rude words to say in it. He spent a great deal of his time wishing he was elsewhere. And he projected an image of a man about as little

Reprinted by permission of the author from Clifford Geertz, 'From the Native's Point of View: On the Nature of Anthropological Understanding', *Bulletin of the Academy of Arts and Sciences*, vol. 28 (1974), no. 1, pp. 26–45. This article re-appeared in Clifford Geertz, *Local Knowledge* (New York: Basic Books 1982).

complaisant as the world has seen. (He also projected an image of a man consecrated to a strange vocation to the point of self-immolation, but that was less noted.) The discussion was made to come down to Malinowski's moral character or lack of it, and the genuinely profound question his book raised was ignored; namely, if it is not, as we had been taught to believe, through some sort of extraordinarily sensibility, an almost preternatural capacity to think, feel, and perceive like a native (a word, I should hurry to say, I use here 'in the strict sense of the term'), how is anthropological knowledge of the way natives, think, feel, and perceive possible? The issue the *Diary* presents, with a force perhaps only a working ethnographer can fully appreciate, is not moral. (The moral idealization of fieldworkers is a mere sentimentality in the first place, when it is not self-congratulating or a guild pretense.) The issue is epistemological. If we are going to cling – as, in my opinion, we must – to the injuction to see things from the native's point of view, where are we when we can no longer claim some unique form of psychological closeness, a sort of transcultural identification, with our subjects? What happens to *verstehen* when *einfühlen* disappears?

As a matter of fact, this general problem has been exercising methodological discussion in anthropology for the last ten or fifteen years; Malinowski's voice from the grave merely dramatizes it as a human dilemma over and above a professional one. The formulations have been various: 'inside' versus 'outside', or 'first person' versus 'third person' descriptions; 'phenomenological' versus 'objectivist', or 'cognitive' versus 'behavioural' theories; or, perhaps most commonly 'emic' versus 'etic' analyses, this last deriving from the distinction in linguistics between phonemics and phonetics, phonemics classifying sounds according to their internal function in language, phonetics classifying them according to their acoustic properties as such. But perhaps the simplest and most directly appreciable way to put the matter is in terms of a distinction formulated, for his own purposes, by the psychoanalyst Heinz Kohut, between what he calls 'experience-near' and 'experience-distant' concepts.

An experience-near concept is, roughly, one that someone – a patient, a subject, in our case an informant – might himself naturally and effortlessly use to define what he or his fellows see, feel, think, imagine, and so on, and which he would readily understand when similarly applied by others. An experience-distant concept is one that specialists of one sort or another – an analyst, an experimenter, an ethnographer, even a priest or an ideologist – employ to forward their scientific, philosophical or practical aims. 'Love' is an experience-near concept, 'object cathexis' is an experience-distant one. 'Social stratification' and perhaps for most peoples in the world even 'religion' (and certainly 'religious system') are experience-distant; 'caste' and 'nirvana' are experience-near, at least for Hindus and Buddhists.

Clearly, the matter is one of degree, not polar opposition – 'fear' is experience-nearer than 'phobia', and 'phobia' experience-nearer than 'ego dyssyntonic'. And the difference is not, at least so far as anthropology is concerned (the matter is otherwise in poetry and physics), a normative one, in the sense that one sort of concept is to be preferred as such over the other. Confinement to experience-near concepts leaves an ethnographer awash in immediacies, as well as entangled in vernacular. Confinement to experience-distant ones leaves him stranded in abstractions and smothered in jargon. The real question, and the one Malinowski raised by demonstrating that, in the case of 'natives', you don't have to be one to know one, is what roles the two sorts of concepts play in anthropological analysis. Or, more exactly, how, in each case, ought one to deploy them so as to produce an interpretation of the way a people lives which is neither imprisoned within their mental horizons, an ethnography of witchcraft as written by a witch, nor systematically deaf to the distinctive tonalities of their existence, an ethnography of witchcraft as written by a geometer.

Putting the matter this way – in terms of how anthropological analysis is to be conducted and its results framed, rather than what psychic constitution anthropoligists need to have – reduces the mystery of what 'seeing things from the native's point of view' means. But it does not make it any easier, nor does it lessen the demand for perceptiveness on the part of the fieldworker. To grasp concepts that, for another people, are experience-near, and to do so well enough to place them in illuminating connection with experience-distant concepts theorists have fashioned to capture the general features of social life, is clearly a task at least as delicate, if a bit less magical, as putting oneself into someone else's skin. The trick is not to get yourself into some inner correspondence of spirit with your informants. Preferring, like the rest of us, to call their souls their own, they are not going to be altogether keen about such an effort anyhow. The trick is to figure out what the devil they think they are up to.

In one sense, of course, no one knows this better than they do themselves; hence the passion to swim in the stream of their experience, and the illusion afterwards that one somehow has. But in another sense, that simple truism is simply not true. People use experience-near concepts spontaneously, unselfconsciously, as it were colloquially; they do not, except fleetingly and on occasion, recognize that there are any 'concepts' involved at all. That is what experience-near means – that ideas and the realities they inform are naturally and indissolubly bound up together. What else could you call a hippopotamus? Of course the gods are powerful, why else would we fear them? The ethnographer does not, and, in my opinion, largely cannot, perceive what his informants perceive. What he perceives, and that uncertainly enough, is what they perceive 'with' – or 'by means of', or 'through' . . . or whatever the word should be. In the country of the blind, who are not as unobservant as they look, the one-eyed is not king, he is spectator.

Now, to make all this a bit more concrete, I want to turn for a moment to my own work, which, whatever its other faults, has at least the virtue of being mine – in discussions of this sort a distinct advantage. In all three of the societies I have studied intensively, Javanese, Balinese, and Moroccan, I have been concerned, among other things, with attempting to determine how the people who live there define themselves as persons, what goes into the idea they have (but, as I say, only half-realize they have) of what a self, Javanese, Balinese, or Moroccan style, is. And in each case, I have tried to get at this most intimate of notions not by imagining myself someone else, a rice peasant or a tribal sheikh, and then seeing what I thought, but by searching out and analyzing the symbolic forms – words, images, institutions, behaviours – in terms of which, in each place, people actually represented themselves to themselves and to one another.

The concept of person is, in fact, an excellent vehicle by means of which to examine this whole question of how to go about poking into another people's turn of mind. In the first place, some sort of concept of this kind, one feels reasonably safe in saying, exists in recognizable form among all social groups. The notions of what persons are may be, from our point of view, sometimes more than a little odd. They may be conceived to dart about nervously at night shaped like fireflies. Essential elements of their psyches, like hatred, may be thought to be lodged in granular black bodies within their livers, discoverable upon autopsy. They may share their fates with *doppelgänger* beasts, so that when the beast sickens or dies they sicken or die too. But at least some conception of what a human individual is, as opposed to a rock, an animal, a rainstorm, or a god, is, so far as I can see, universal. Yet, at the same time, as these offhand examples suggest, the actual conceptions involved vary from one group to the next, and often quite sharply. The Western conception of the person as a bounded, unique, more or less integrated motivational and cognitive universe, a dynamic center of awareness, emotion, judgment, and action organized into a distinctive whole and set contrastively both against other such wholes and against its social and natural background, is, however incorrigible it may seem to us, a rather peculiar idea with the context of the world's cultures. Rather than attempting to place the experience of others within the framework of such a conception, which is what the extolled 'empathy' in fact usually comes down to, understanding them demands setting that conception aside and seeing their experiences within the framework of their own idea of what selfhood is. And for Java, Bali, and Morocco, at least, that idea differs markedly not only from our own but, no less dramatically and no less instructively, from one another.

II

In Java, where I worked in the fifties, I studied a small, shabby inland county-seat sort of place; two shadeless streets of whitewashed wooden shops and offices, and even less substantial bamboo shacks crammed in helter-skelter behind them, the whole surrounded by a great half-circle of densely packed rice-bowl villages. Land was short, jobs were scarce, politics was unstable, health was poor, prices were rising, and life was altogether far from promising, a kind of agitated stagnancy in which, as I once put it, thinking of the curious mixture of borrowed fragments of modernity and exhausted relics of tradition that characterized the place, the future seemed about as remote as the past. Yet in the midst of this depressing scene there was an absolutely astonishing intellectual vitality, a philosophical passion really, and a popular one besides, to track riddles of existence right down to the ground. Destitute peasants would discuss questions of freedom of the will, illiterate tradesmen discoursed on the properties of God, common laborers had theories about the relation between reason and passion, the nature of time, or the reliability of the senses. And, perhaps most importantly, the problem of the self – its nature, function, and mode of operation – was pursued with the sort of reflective intensity one could find among ourselves in only the most recherché settings indeed.

The central ideas in terms of which this reflection proceeded, and which thus defined its boundaries and the Javanese sense of what a person is, were arranged into two sets of contrasts, at base religious, one between 'inside' and 'outside', and one between 'refined' and 'vulgar'. These glosses are, of course, crude and imprecise; determining exactly what the terms involved signified, sorting out their shades of meaning, was what all the discussion was about. But together they formed a distinctive conception of the self which, far from being merely theoretical, was the one in terms of which Javanese in fact perceived one another and, of course, themselves.

The 'inside'/'outside' words, *batin* and *lair* (terms borrowed, as a matter of fact, from the Sufi tradition of Muslim mysticism, but locally reworked) refer on the one hand to the felt realm of human experience and on the other to the observed realm of human behaviour. These have, one hastens to say, nothing to do with 'soul' and 'body' in our sense, for which there are in fact quite other words with quite other implications. *Batin*, the 'inside' word, does not refer to a separate seat of encapsulated spirituality detached or detachable from the body, or indeed to a bounded unit at all, but to the emotional life of human beings taken generally. It consists of the fuzzy, shifting flow of subjective feeling perceived directly in all its phenomenological immediacy but considered to be, at its roots at least, identical across all individuals, whose individuality it thus effaces. And similarly, *lair*, the 'outside' word, has nothing to do with the body as an object, even an experienced object. Rather, it refers to that part of human life which, in our culture, strict behaviourists limit themselves to studying – external actions, movements, postures, speech – again conceived as in its essence invariant from one individual to the next. These two sets of phenomena – inward feeling and outward actions – are then regarded not as functions of one another but as independent realms of being to put in proper order independently.

It is in connection with this 'proper ordering' that the contrast between *alus*, the word meaning 'pure', 'refined', 'polished', 'exquisite', 'ethereal', 'subtle', 'civilized', 'smooth', and *kasar*, the word meaning 'impolite', 'rough', 'uncivilized', 'coarse', 'insensitive', 'vulgar', comes into play. The goal is to be *alus* in both the separated realms of the self. In the inner realm this is to be achieved through religious discipline, much but not all of it mystical. In the outer realm, it is to be achieved through etiquette, the rules of which here are not only extraordinarily elaborate but have something of the force of law. Through mediation the civilized man thins out his emotional life to a kind of constant hum; through etiquette, he both shields that life from external disruptions and regularizes his outer behavior in such a way that it appears to others as predictable, undisturbing, elegant, and rather vacant set of choreographed motions and settled forms of speech.

There is much more to all this, because it connects up to both an ontology and an aesthetic. But so far as our problem is concerned, the result is a bifurcate conception of the self, half ungestured feeling and half unfelt gesture. An inner world of stilled emotion and an outer world of shaped behavior confront one another as sharply distinguished realms unto themselves, any particular person being but the momentary locus, so to speak, of that confrontation, a passing expression of their permanent existence, their permanent separation, and their permanent need to be kept in their own order. Only when you have seen, as I have, a young man whose wife – a woman he had in fact raised from childhood and who had been the center of his life – has suddenly and inexplicably died, greeting everyone with a set smile and formal apologies for his wife's absence and trying, by mystical techniques, to flatten out, as he himself put it, the hills and valleys of his emotion into an even, level plain ('That is what you have to do', he said to me, 'be smooth inside and out') can you come, in the face of our own notions of the intrinsic honesty of deep feeling and the moral importance of personal sincerity, to take the possibility of such a conception of selfhood seriously and appreciate, however, inaccessible it is to you, its own sort of force.

III

Bali, where I worked in another small provincial town, though one rather less drifting and dispirited, and, later, in an upland village of highly skilled musical instruments makers, is of course in many ways similar to Java, with which it shared a common culture to the fifteenth century. But at a deeper level, having continued Hindu while Java was, nominally at least, Islamized, it is quite different. The intricate, obsessive ritual life – Hindu, Buddhist, and Polynesian in about equal proportions – whose development was more or less cut off in Java, leaving its Indic spirit to turn reflective and phenomenological, even quietistic, in the way I have just described, flourished in Bali to reach levels of scale and flamboyance that have startled the world and made the Balinese a much more dramaturgical people with a self to match. What is philosophy in Java is theater in Bali.

As a result, there is in Bali a persistent and systematic attempt to stylize all aspects of personal expression to the point where anything idiosyncratic, anything characteristic of the individual merely because he is who he is physically, psychologically, or biographically, is muted in favor of his assigned place in the continuing and, so it is thought, never-changing pageant that is Balinese life. It is dramatis personae, not actors, that endure; indeed, it is dramatis personae, not actors, that in the proper sense really exist. Physically men come and go, mere incidents in a happenstance history, of no genuine importance even to themselves. But the masks they wear, the stage they occupy, the parts they play, and most important, the spectacle they mount remain, and comprise not the façade but the substance of things, not least the self. Shakespeare's old-trouper view of the vanity of action in the face of morality – all the world's a stage and we but poor players, content to strut our hour, and so on – makes no sense here. There is no make-believe; of course players perish, but the play does not, and it is the latter, the performed rather than the performer, that really matters.

Again, all this is realized not in terms of some general mood the anthropologist in his spiritual versatility somehow captures, but through a set of readily observable symbolic forms: an elaborate repertoire of designations and titles. The Balinese have at least a half-dozen major sorts of labels, ascriptive, fixed, and absolute, which one person can apply to another (or, of course to himself) to place him among his fellows. There are birth-order markers, kinship terms, caste titles, sex indicators, tekononyms, and so on and so forth, each of which consists not of a mere collection of useful tags but a distinct and bounded, internally very complex, terminological system. When one applies one of these designations or titles (or, as is more common, several at once) to someone, one therefore defines him as a determinate point in a fixed pattern, as the temporary occupant of a particular, quite untemporary, cultural locus. To identify someone, yourself or somebody else, in Bali is thus to locate him within the familiar cast of characters – 'king', 'grandmother', 'third-born', 'Brahman' – all of which the social drama is, like some stock company roadshow piece – *Charley's Aunt* or *Springtime for Henry* – inevitably composed.

The drama is of course not farce, and especially not transvestite farce, though there are such elements in it. It is an enactment of hierarchy, a theater of status. But that, though critical, is unpursuable here. The immediate point is that, in both their structure and their mode of operation, the terminological systems conduce to a view of the human person as an appropriate representative of a generic type, not a unique creature with a private fate. To see how they do this, how they tend to obscure the mere materialities – biological, psychological, historical – of individual existence in favor of standardized status qualities would involve an extended analysis. But perhaps a single example, the simplest further simplified, will suffice to suggest the pattern.

All Balinese receive what might be called birth-order names. There are four of these, 'first-born', 'second-born', 'third-born', 'fourth-born', after which they recycle, so that the fifth-born child is called again 'first-born, the sixth 'second-born', and so on. Further, these names are bestowed independently of the fates of the children. Dead children, even stillborn ones, count, so that in fact, in this still high-birthrate high-mortality society, the names do not really tell you anything very reliable about the birth-order relations of concrete individuals. Within a set of living siblings, someone called 'first-born' may actually be first, fifth, or ninth-born, or, if someone is missing, almost anything in between, and someone called 'second born' may in fact be older. The birth-order naming system does not identify inviduals as individuals, nor is it intended to; what it does is to suggest that, for all procreating couples, births form a circular succession of 'firsts', 'seconds', 'thirds', and 'fourths', an endless four-stage replication of an imperishable form. Physically men appear and disappear as the ephemerae they are, but socially the acting figures remain eternally the same as new 'firsts', 'seconds', and so on emerge from the timeless world of the gods to replace those who, dying, dissolve once more into it. All the designation and title systems, so I would argue, function in the same way: they represent the most time-saturated aspects of the human condition as but ingredients in an eternal, footlight present.

Nor is this sense the Balinese have of always being on stage a vague and ineffable one either. It is, in fact, exactly summed up in what is surely one of their experience-nearest concepts: *lek*. *Lek* has been variously translated or mistranslated ('shame' is the most common attempt); but what it really means is close to what we call stage fright. Stage fright consists, of course, in the fear that, for want of skill or self-control, or perhaps by mere accident, an aesthetic illusion will not be maintained, that the actor will show through his part. Aesthetic distance collapses, the audience (and the actor) lose sight of Hamlet and gain it, uncomfortably for all concerned, of bumbling John Smith painfully miscast as the Prince of Denmark. In Bali, the case is the same: what is feared is that the public performance to which one's cultural location commits one will be botched and that the personality – as we would call it but the Balinese, of course, not believing in such a thing, would not – of the individual will break through to dissolve his standardized public identity. When this occurs, as it sometimes does, the immediacy of the moment is felt with excruciating intensity and men become suddenly and unwillingly creatural, locked in mutual embarrassment, as though they had happened upon each other's nakedness. It is the fear of *faux pas*, rendered only that much more probable by the extraordinary ritualization of daily life, that keeps social intercourse on its deliberately narrowed rails and protects the dramatistical sense of self against the disruptive threat implicit in the immediacy and spontaneity even the most passionate ceremoniousness cannot fully eradicate from face-to-face encounters.

IV

Morocco, Middle Eastern and dry rather than East Asian and wet, extrovert, fluid, activist, masculine, informal to a fault, a Wild West sort of place without the bar-rooms and the cattle drives, is another kettle of selves altogether. My work there, which began in the mid-sixties, has been centered around a moderately large town or small city in the foothills of the Middle Atlas, about twenty miles south of Fez. It's an old place, probably founded in the tenth century, conceivably even earlier. It has the walls, the gates, the narrow minarets rising to prayer-call platforms of a classical Muslim town, and, from a distance anyway, it is a rather pretty place, an irregular oval of blinding white set in the deep-sea-green of an olive grove oasis, the mountains, bronze and stony here, slanting up immediately behind it. Close up, it is less prepossessing, though more exciting: a labyrinth of passages and alleyways, three quarters of them blind, pressed in by wall-like buildings and curbside shops and filled with a simply astounding variety of very emphatic human beings. Arabs, Berbers, and Jews; tailors, herdsmen, and soldiers; people out of offices, people out of markets, people out of tribes; rich, super-rich, poor, super-poor; locals, immigrants, mimic Frenchmen, unbending medievalists, and somewhere according to the official government census for 1960, an unemployed Jewish airplane pilot – the town houses one of the finest collections of rugged individuals I, at least, have ever come up against. Next to Sefrou (the name of the place), Manhattan seems almost monotonous.

Yet no society consists of anonymous eccentrics bouncing off one another like billiard balls, and Moroccans, too, have symbolic means by which to sort people out from one another and form an idea of what it is to be a person. The main such means – not the only one, but I think the most important and the one I want to talk about particularly here – is a peculiar linguistic form called in Arabic the *nisba*. The word derives from the triliteral root, *n-s-b*, for 'ascription', 'attribution', 'imputation', 'relationship', 'affinity', 'correlation', 'connection', 'kinship'. *Nsīb* means 'in-law'; *nsab* means 'to attribute or impute to'; *munāsaba* means 'a relation', 'an analogy', 'a correspondence'; *mansūb* means 'belonging to', 'pertaining to'; and so on to at least a dozen derivatives, from *nassāb* ('genealogist') to *nīsbīya* ('[physical] relativity').

Nisba itself, then, refers to a combination morphological, grammatical, and semantic process that consists in transforming a noun into what we would call a relative adjective but what for Arabs is just another sort of noun by adding *ī* (f., *īya*): *Ṣefrū*/Sefrou – *Ṣefrūwī*/native son of Sefrou; *Sūs*/region of southwestern Morocco – *Sūsī*/man coming from that region; *Beni Yazğa*/a tribe near Sefrou – *Yazğī*/a member of that tribe; *Yahūd*/the Jews as a people, Jewry – *Yahūdī*/a Jew; *ʿAdlun*/ surname of a prominent Sefrou family – *ʿAdlūnī*/a member of that family. Nor is the procedure confined to this more or less straightforward 'ethnicizing' use, but is employed in a wide range of domains to attribute relational properties to persons. For example, occupation (*ḥrār*/silk – *ḥrārī*/silk merchant); religious sect (*Darqāwā*/a mystical brotherhood – *Darqāwī*/an adept of that brotherhood or spiritual status), (*ʿAli*/The Prophet's son-in-law – *ʿAlawī*/descendant of the Prophet's son-in-law, and thus of the Prophet).

Now, as once formed, nisbas tend to be incorporated into personal names – Umar Al-Buhadiwi/Umar of the Buhadu Tribe'; Muhammed Al-Sussi/Muhammed from the Sus Region – this sort of adjectival attributive classification is quite publicly stamped on to an individual's identity. I was unable to find a single case where an individual was generally known, or known about, but his or her nisba was not. Indeed, Sefrouis are far more likely to be ignorant of how well-off a man is, how long he has been around, what his personal character is, or where exactly he lives, than they are of what his nisba is – Sussi or Sefroui, Buhadiwi or Adluni, Harari or Darqawi. (Of women to whom he is not related that is very likely to be all that he knows – or, more exactly, is permitted to know.) The selves that bump and jostle each other in the alleys of Sefrou gain their definition from associative relations they are imputed to have with the society that surrounds them. They are contextualized persons.

But the situation is even more radical than this; nisbas render men relative to their contexts, but as contexts themselves are relative, so too are nisbas, and the whole thing rises, so to speak, to the second power: relativism squared. Thus, at one level, everyone in Sefrou has the same nisba, or at least the potential of it – namely, Sefroui. However, within Sefrou such a nisba, precisely because it does not discriminate, will never be heard as part of an individual designation. It is only outside of Sefrou that the relationship to that particular context becomes identifying. Inside it, he is an Adluni, Alawi, Meghrawi, Ngadi, or whatever. And similarly within these categories: there are, for example, twelve different nisbas (Shakibis, Zuinis, and so forth) by means of which, among themselves, Sefrou Alawis distinguish one another.

The whole matter is far from regular: what level or sort of nisba is used and seems relevant and appropriate (to the users, that is) depends heavily on the situation. A man I knew who lived in Sefrou and worked in Fez but came out from the Beni Yazgha tribe settled nearby – and from the Hima lineage of the Taghut subfraction of the Wulad Ben Ydir fraction within it – was known as a Sefroui to his work fellows in Fez, a Yazghi to all of us non-Yazghis in Sefrou, an Ydiri to other Beni Yazghas around, except for those who were themselves of the Wulad Ben Ydir fraction, who called him a Taghuti. As for the few other Taghutis, they called him a Himiwi. That is as far as things went here, but not as far as they can go, in either direction. Should, by chance, our friend journey to Egypt, he would become a Maghrebi, the nisba formed from the Arabic word for North Africa. The social contextualization of persons is pervasive and, in its curiously unmethodical way, systematic. Men do not float as bounded psychic entities, detached from their backgrounds and singularly named. As individualistic, even wilful, as the Moroccans in fact are, their identity is an attribute they borrow from their setting.

Now as with the Javanese inside/outside, smooth/rough phenomenological sort of reality dividing, and the absolutizing Balinese title systems, the nisba way of looking at persons – as though they were outlines waiting to be filled in – is not an isolated custom, but part of a total pattern of social life. This pattern is, like the others, difficult to characterize succinctly, but surely one of its outstanding features is a promiscuous tumbling in public settings of varieties of men kept carefully segregated in private ones – all-out cosmopolitanism in the streets, strict communalism (of which the famous secluded woman is only the most striking index) in the home. This is, indeed, the so-called mosaic system of social organization so often held to be characteristic of the Middle East generally: differently shaped and coloured chips jammed in irregularly together to generate an intricate overall design within which their individual distinctiveness remains none the less intact. Nothing if not diverse, Moroccan society does not cope with its diversity by sealing it into castes, isolating it into tribes, dividing it into ethnic groups, or covering it over with some common-denominator concept of nationality, though, fitfully, all have now and then been tried. It copes with it by distinguishing, with elaborate precision, the contexts – marriage, worship, and to an extent diet, law, and education – within which men are separated by their dissimilitudes, and those – work, friendship, politics, trade – where, however warily and however conditionally, they are connected by them.

To such a social pattern, a concept of selfhood which marks public identity contextually and relativistically, but yet does so in terms – tribal, territorial, linguistic, religious, familial – that grow out of the more private and settled arenas of life and have a deep and permanent resonance there, would seem particularly appropriate. Indeed, the social pattern would seem virtually to create this concept of selfhood, for it produces a situation where people interact with one another in terms of categories whose meaning is almost purely positional, location in the general mosaic, leaving the substantive content of the categories, what they mean subjectively as experienced forms of life, aside as something properly concealed in apartments, temples and tents. Nisba discriminations can be more specific or less, indicate location within the mosaic roughly or finely, and they can be adapted to almost any changes in circumstance. But they cannot carry with them more than the most sketchy, outline implications concerning what men so named as a rule are like. Calling a man a Sefroui is like calling him a San Franciscan: it classifies him, but it does not type him; it places him without portraying him.

It is the nisba system's capacity to do this – to create a framework within which persons can be identified in terms of supposedly immanent characteristics (speech, blood, faith, provenance, and the rest) – and yet to minimize the impact of those characteristics in determining the practical relations among such persons in markets, shops, bureaus, fields, cafés, baths and roadways that makes it so central to the Moroccan idea of the self. Nisba-type categorization leads, paradoxically, to a hyper-individualism in public relationships, because by providing only a vacant sketch, and that shifting, of who the actors are – Yazghis, Adlunis, Buhadiwis, or whatever – it leaves the rest, that is, almost everything, to be filled in by the process of interaction itself. What makes the mosaic work is the confidence that one can be as totally pragmatic, adaptive, opportunistic and generally ad hoc in ones relations with others – a fox among foxes, a crocodile among crocodiles – as one wants without any risk of losing one's sense of who one is. Selfhood is never in danger because, outside the immediacies of procreation and prayer, only its coordinates are asserted.

V

Now, without trying to tie up the dozens of loose ends I have not only left dangling in these rather breathless accounts of the senses of selfhood of nearly ninety million people but have doubtless frazzled even more, let us return to the question of what all this can tell us, or could if it were done adequately, about 'the native's point of view' in Java, Bali and Morocco. Are we, in describing symbol uses, describing perceptions, sentiments, outlooks, experience? And in what sense? What do we claim when we claim that we understand the semiotic means by which, in this case, persons are defined to one another? That we know words or that we know minds?

In answering this question, it is necessary, I think, first to notice the characteristic intellectual movement, the inward conceptual rhythm, in each of these analyses, and indeed in all similar analyses, including those of Malinowski – namely, a continuous dialectical tacking between the most local of local detail and the most global of global structure in such a way as to bring them into simultaneous view. In seeking to uncover the Javanese, Balinese or Moroccan sense of self, one oscillates restlessly between the sort of exotic minutiae (lexical antithesis, categorical schemes, morphophonemic transformations) that make even the best ethnographies a trial to read and the sort of sweeping characterizations ('quietism', 'dramatism', 'contextualism') that make all but the most pedestrian of them somewhat implausible. Hopping back and forth between the whole conceived through the parts that actualize it and the parts conceived through the whole that motivates them, we seek to turn them, by a sort of intellectual perpetual motion, into explications of one another.

All this is, of course, but the now familiar trajectory of what Dilthey called the hermeneutic circle, and my argument here is merely that it is as central to ethnographic interpretation, and thus to the penetration of other people's modes of thought, as it is to literary, historical, philological, psychoanalytic, or biblical interpretation, or for that matter to the informal annotation of everyday experience we call common sense. In order to follow a baseball game one must understand that a bat, a hit, an inning, a left fielder, a squeeze play, a hanging curve, and a tightened infield are, and what the game in which these 'things' are elements is all about. When an *explication de texte* critic like Leo Spitzer attempts to interpret Keats's 'Ode on a Grecian Urn', he does so by repetitively asking himself the alternating question 'What is the whole poem about?' and 'What exactly has Keats seen (or chosen to show us) depicted on the urn he is describing?', emerging at the end of an advanced spiral of general observations and specific remarks with a reading of the poem as an assertion of the triumph of the aesthetic mode of perception over the historical. In the same way, when a meaning-and-symbols ethnographer like myself attempts to find out what some pack of natives conceive a person to be, he moves back and forth between asking himself, 'What is the general form of their life?' and 'What exactly are the vehicles in which that form is embodied?', emerging in the end of a similar sort of spiral with the notion that they see the self as a composite, a persona, or a point in a pattern. You can no more know what *lek* is if you do not know what Balinese dramatism is than you can know what a catcher's mitt is if you do not know what baseball is. And you can no more know what mosaic social organization is if you do not know what a nisba is than you can know what Keat's Platonism is if you are unable to grasp, to use Spitzer's own formulation, the 'intellectual thread of thought' captured in such fragment phrases as 'Attic shape', 'silent form', 'bride of quietness', 'cold pastoral', 'silence and slow time', 'peaceful citadel', or 'ditties of no tone'.

In short, accounts of other peoples' subjectivities can be built up without recourse to pretentions to more-than-normal capacities for ego effacement and fellow feeling. Normal capacities in these respects are, of course, essential, as is their cultivation, if we expect people to tolerate our intrusions into their lives at all and accept us as persons worth talking to. I am certainly not arguing for insensitivity here, and I hope I have not demonstrated it. But whatever accurate or half-accurate sense one gets of what one's informants are, as the phrase goes, really like does not come from the experience of that acceptance as such, which is part of one's own biography, not of theirs. It comes from the ability to construe their modes of expression, what I would call their symbol systems, which such an acceptance allows one to work toward developing. Understanding the form and pressure of, to use the dangerous word one more time, natives' inner lives is more like grasping a proverb, catching an allusion, seeing a joke – or, as I have suggested, reading a poem – than it is like achieving communion.

6
Appearance and Reality in Politics

WILLIAM E. CONNOLLY

PENETRATING APPEARANCES

Certain social and political theorists, most notably Plato, Hegel, Marx and Freud, distinguish a society's real structure from the appearance it presents to its participants. Bound up with this distinction are those between theory and ideology, thought and action, the actual and the possible, and consciousness and self-consciousness. The goal of theory, when these distinctions are prominent, is to pierce through appearance to the real structure, to allow (at least some) participants to see things as they really are, and either to reconcile the newly self-conscious agents to necessity or to encourage them to bring the society into closer harmony with their real interests.

The discrepancy between appearance and reality can assume a variety of forms. That which is particular may present itself as a universal, as when the calculating ethic appears universal to its bearers while it is really dramatically accentuated in their particular order. Or a causal relation can be inverted in consciousness, as when God appears to be the author of man while man is really the author of God. Or a partial truth can be mistakenly construed as the whole story, as when the appearance of free exchange in the market between labor and capital is really circumscribed by the need for labor to sell itself to those who control the means of production. Or the future vision which helps to unify society may actually be unrealizable, as when a populace identifies with the project of creating a society of affluence for the benefit of future generations while the future beneficiaries will not be able to sustain allegiance to the result once accomplished. And each of these forms can be reversed, as when a universal presents itself as a particular, and so on.

Not only the discrepancy, but also the connection, between appearances and realities can vary. Thus the belief that God will continue to

Reprinted by permission of Cambridge University Press from William E. Connolly, *Appearance and Reality in Politics* (New York: Cambridge University Press, 1982), pp. 63–89, 202–5;

nourish the soil will not by itself provide the soil with nourishment if God refuses. But the belief that the future pursued in common now will prove satisfying to future generations helps to nourish present practices geared to that purpose, even if the future beneficiaries eventually will repudiate the actual achievement. A political theory must pay attention to both the discrepancies and the connections between appearances and realities.

Consider a simplified example of the sort of relationship to be examined here. A person thinks he is persuaded to participate in a strike by arguments another gives in good faith. But the agent giving the arguments consciously withholds some considerations which, were they known to our striker, would tip the balance in the other direction. The first person manipulates the second. This face-to-face relation of manipulation is in some respects a microcosm of the relations we will examine, but it deviates from them in other respects. It is similar, first, in that the appearance of persuasion to the first party is essential to the actual relationship of manipulation. The appearance is not a mere ephiphenomenon which, if peeled away, will expose the underlying reality unchanged; it helps to constitute the reality it misrepresents. Secondly, a change in the appearance of the relationship will in some degree reconstitute the reality. If the recipient recognizes what has been going on, he may sever the friendship; or continue in it but seek to forestall manipulation in the future; or demand such changes unsuccessfully and find himself subjected now to coercion; or pretend he is still deceived to avoid open coercion. But a change in the appearance will in some way alter the real relation; moreover the stage will be set for efforts to revise it more fully. Thirdly, there may be some reluctance on the part of the recipient to recognize the real relation because he stands in a dependent status to the manipulator. The belief that he is persuaded supports the image he wishes to project to self and others as one who acts freely, while recognition of the reality would require him either to struggle against heavy odds to secure autonomy or to acknowledge his dependent status. The real relationship was not just invisible to him; he was an active participant in making it so.

But the simple model also omits dimensions of the macroscopic relationships to be examined. First, it is not necessary that some agents be in the know while others are not. Secondly, in the larger setting the appearances take the form of a complex web of concepts and beliefs in which each element receives some support from many others. It is more difficult to reach secure ground from which these tangled webs can be unravelled. This condition, in conjunction with the tendency of the identity of the participants to be bound up with the appearances they help to construct and defend, greatly complicates the task of tracing the relations between appearance and reality. Thirdly, because the institutional order is loosely structured so that a successful reform in one instituton would have to be associated with a corollary series of reforms in others, a shift in the appearance the order presents may alter its performance without necessarily allowing the reconstruction or solidification now desired. This condition, in conjunction with the quest for identity on the part of participants, fosters ambivalence and ambiguity in the political self-interpretations of some constituencies.

Certain theoretical traditions are impaired in their ability to comprehend the relations between appearance and reality in politics. Their epistemic prejudices support the misinterpretation of such an order (should such an order exist). Thus the pure theory of interpretation, which identifies social reality with the interpretation of participants and presumes that the standards of rationality acknowledged within an order are fully appropriate to it, cannot comprehend a deep disjuncture between appearance and reality. Theorists working within this framework can expose modest discrepancies between implicit dimensions within a self-interpretation and its explicit articulation, but such discrepancies, important in their own right, do not suffice to comprehend the sort of relationships we are examining.[1]

Structural theorists, while sometimes oriented to the discrepancy between appearance and reality, none the less underplay possible complexities in the relationship. If the subjectivity and intersubjectivity of participants are treated merely as effects to be explained, and if the participants are treated as unable in principle to attain reflexive awareness of the theory which explains those effects, the theory which emerges may gloss over ambiguities and possibilities immanent within the order.

While doubtless preparing particular pitfalls for myself I will try to avoid the two identified by adopting the following strategy. We begin with an initial presentation of the political self-interpretation of a particular constituency. A series of hypothetical revisions is then introduced into the initial interpretation, each of which purports to comprehend dimensions of the order missed in the first account. The preliminary interpretation can be identified as the ideology of sacrifice and the hypothetical revisions as, respectively, the liberal, utopian, and structural moments. The ideology of sacrifice provides its bearers with a sense of dignity, though that dignity is preserved by misrepresenting important features of social life and is vulnerable potentially to invalidation by the action of other groups. Each of the hypothetical moments to follow captures a dimension missed in the initial interpretation, but none can sustain modes of conduct consistent with the wish of the participants to see themselves as free and dignified. The identity the participants seek to maintain is tied to a set of beliefs they struggle to secure: the belief that one voluntarily accepts the roles one plays; that these roles serve worthy private and public purposes; that one lives in a political order which is relatively transparent to its citizens and capable of promoting the collective ends they accept; and that the sacrifices persistently required in the order are necessary to the most worthy purposes of private and public life. The struggle to sustain these beliefs in turn generates implications for the political priorities, alliances, and conflicts established by the believers.

Lodged within the connection, first, between the effort to maintain a sense of dignity and the beliefs about the larger order needed to support that sense, and secondly, between beliefs about the order and their implications for political practice, is space for a potential disjuncture between the real structure of the order and the appearance it presents to a range of participants. This is the space we shall explore.

The intent of the total interpretation is to identify the pressures which generate the self-construction of the ideology of sacrifice, those aspects of social and political life screened out by that interpretation, and the consequences which would emerge were the invisible elements to become more visible to participants. The account is explanatory, not in revealing law-like relations among discrete elements, but in showing how structural limits *encourage* or *provoke* participants to adopt specific orientations to political conduct. The terms 'encourage' and 'provoke' identify precisely the loose and open quality of these relationships – terms like 'cause' and 'produce' are too imprecise. The porous texture and equivocal character of unreflective self-interpretations, and reflexive capacities of those who act on such interpretations, and the play or flexibility within the structural dimension of social life, together imply that a more formal account would gloss over uncertainties and ambiguities located within the object of inquiry.

The dialectic to be constructed is to be viewed as a thought experiment. The preliminary portrait of the ideology of sacrifice is exaggerated; subordinate elements within it are suppressed. Each of the subordinate strains is then exaggerated in its turn so that, by identifying the political orientation implicit within each strain, we can ascertain why it remains underdeveloped in fact within the established order. This progressive introduction of counterfactuals eventually brings out more clearly how a dense and ambiguous background of undeveloped perspectives is condensed into an operative set of political practices. It provides a way to penetrate appearances without reducing them to epiphenomena or treating them as exhaustively constitutive of political reality.

After the entire interpretation has been offered we will return to the meta-theoretical level, probing the difficulties in ascertaining the extent to which such an account is valid or invalid.

HIDDEN INJURIES AND STRUCTURAL CONSTRAINTS

Consider a group of white, married, male blue-collar workers in the United States today. Each is a principal breadwinner in a family with young children and each has a reasonable degree of job security. The breadwinner does not see himself as working simply to maximize his family's short range consumption opportunities. He voluntarily sacrifices now so that his children can escape the circumstances in which he finds himself.[2] He chooses to accept the work routines, authoritarian controls and overtime he dislikes in order to improve the mobility of his children. His claim to the respect of his wife and children grows out of this willingness to sacrifice, and the respect they give him lends dignity to his life activity.

This orientation to work and family helps to condition the worker's interpretive reaction to welfare recipients, intellectuals, student dissidents, feminists, deviants, and criminals. For the conduct and rhetoric of each of these types threatens to invalidate the ideology of sacrifice.

If the welfare recipient claims that unemployment is created by structural causes rather than by the personal defects of the recipient, the worker's very possession of a job may appear to be more a matter of luck than of self-discipline and desert. If the recipient calls for higher levels of support the worker's own sacrifice may begin to look foolish. If radicals claim that common crimes are implicitly acts of rebellion against an order that breeds criminals, they inadvertently condemn the worker for bowing passively to that order. Or: they mock his exercise of self-restraint by relieving the criminal of responsibility for stealing under existing social conditions. If feminists claim that women are imprisoned in the home, the worker's sacrifice is reinterpreted as a restraint on her freedom and dignity. If radicals treat equality of opportunity as a fraud they unwittingly undermine the worker's hopes for his children's future and render his sacrifice fruitless. If university students debunk the privileged way of life they are about to enter they ridicule the purpose which informs the worker's life activity. And even if the worker succeeds in projecting his children into higher circles they may then become, he fears, the kind of people who look down on people like him.

The worker is caught in a bind. To repudiate the ideology of sacrifice is to lose the claim to respect available under present circumstances, but to affirm it is to set the worker against the very constituencies with whom he must be allied if significant changes in this undignified life-situation are to be generated. The ideology of sacrifice generates political orientations that help to perpetuate the worker's plight while the plight generates pressures to perpetuate the ideology. Yet this bind itself cannot be acknowledged without undermining the identity available to the worker. The worker is thus under a double pressure, first, to accept the ideology and, secondly, to resist the suggestion that its role in securing his identity outstrips its truth value. If this ideology is to be secured he must claim that those who challenge it in various ways are either irresponsible or indulge themselves in utopian dreams.

It is important to see that the beliefs in the foreground of the ideology of sacrifice support a set of background beliefs concerning the necessity and desirability of the institutional structure within which it is forged. We have seen how the principle of equal opportunity, and thus the institution of labor mobility, is supported by this interpretation. It sustains a similar understanding of instrumental work. For if it were held that work could be organized in other ways the sacrifice would take on a new appearance. Its proponents would see themselves less as responsible agents making the most of the necessities of modern life and more as white Uncle Toms performing unnecessary and undignified tasks in a servile way. Distressing questions about the risks and responsibilities in organizing a political challenge to these forms would emerge. Moreover, instrumental work and the associated institutions of bureaucratic rationality, production for private profit, and sharply graded incentive systems, are justified in the name of economic growth. The ideology of sacrifice is most at home with itself if it does not question the viability of the end justifying these means. It supports thereby the priorities of the established order and the legitimacy of its dominant institutions.

Our portrayal has already moved beyond the self-interpretation of the participants towards an account of why they might strive to retain it in the face of contrary evidence. To fix that preliminary account we can say that while the reaction to criminals, feminists, environmentalists, and radicals does pick out discrepancies between the conduct of the target groups and that of the workers, it also magnifies these differences, distorts the motives of the target groups, and suppresses inner doubts on the part of the workers about the point of their sacrifice and the truth of the ideology sustaining it. The test of the claim that the self-interpretation involves a powerful element of self-deception is launched, first, by ascertaining if the workers' interpretation of the motives and situation of the target groups is inflated, secondly, if evidence available to correct this inflation is ignored, and thirdly, if the attribution of this defensive ideology of sacrifice to the workers helps to render intelligible conduct and conflicts which would otherwise remain vaguely mysterious.

Suppose the range of workers acknowledges that this external account is approximately correct. They acknowledge that their previous beliefs about the accused and themselves formed a spiral of partial self-deceptions needed to secure a sense of dignity under adverse conditions.

We must expect this new interpretation eventually to support revisions in the personal identities and political commitments of those accepting it. They will externalize a range of doubts that had been internalized. They may begin to probe previously suppressed questions about the legitimacy of a system which, as they now see it, requires them to seek dignity in such undignified ways. Perhaps they will begin to locate themselves within the same class as many of those formerly accused of freeloading, to see the accused and themselves as members of a subordinate class which reaps the fewest rewards, receives insufficient space to carve out a dignified life, and is called upon to bear the largest sacrifices when the larger economy is under pressure.

The reinterpretation will reconstitute political alliances and cleavages; it will politicize grievances previously relegated to a non- or semi-political status such as the right to a job, class inequality, and the social preconditions of self-respect. The diminished sense of individual agency accompanying the demise of the ideology of sacrifice will be offset, at least initially and to some degree, by the enhanced sense of the working class as a potential agent of collective change. It ushers in the liberal moment.

This sense of collective agency and dignity is itself quite vulnerable to invalidation. For the changes sought cannot be superimposed on top of the established institutions. The institutions must be reconstituted as well. The right to a job cannot be guaranteed for everyone without setting an inflationary spiral into motion, reducing income levels and job security from another direction. Controlling inflation while retaining full employment, in turn, would require significant changes in the social infrastructure of consumption, accentuating collective goods (e.g., public transport, parks and recreational facilities, community housing, public health care) and reducing dependence on individual consumption (e.g., cars and single unit houses). The desired reduction in inequality could not be pushed very far without undercutting the flow of private investment into the system of production for private profit, and if that obstacle were surmounted its realization would require even more significant shifts from individualized to collective forms of consumption. Each of these changes in turn would require significant shifts in the role of the state, the status of private profit, the structure of work organization and incentives, and the mobilization of the economy around the expectation of constant economic growth.[3]

It is one thing to call for reforms within an established order and another to conclude that those reforms must be situated within a massive set of institutional changes. If the participants continue to believe that the established institutions, because they are essential to industrial society as such, are invulnerable to significant change, the initial sense of collective agency will dissipate. They may lapse into the old ideology. More likely, they will resign themselves to an inescapable fate while resenting even more deeply those dissident constituencies who unwittingly condemn them for their resignation.

The new, embryonic self-interpretation is inherently unstable. Its retention requires a deeper probing of doubts suppressed within the old view. The initial step is to reinterpret the established institutions, to see them not as a given set of 'natural' forms required to promote the necessary goals of economic growth aqnd affluence, but as a set of potentially alterable human constructions requiring conduct and promoting ends which no longer automatically attract the allegiance of people implicated within them. The focus now is on the nature of these institutions and on the relation between the roles they impose and the changing aspirations of the role-takers.[4]

If a populace believes that the good life, the good life it can build in common, is one of affluence; if it believes that affluence will both satisfy in itself and create the freedom its recipients need to experience fulfilling relations and activities, the beliefs will legitimize those institutions promoting such desirable results. If the ends appear to be the natural ends of human life, the institutions essential to them will assume a nature-like appearance too. Complaints about the strains created by instrumental work, production for private profit, labor mobility, income stratification, accentuation of private over collective consumption, state subsidies for economic growth, the rapid obsolescence of old skills and old workers, environmental destruction, the dangerous dependence on crucial resources located in foreign countries, and the limits to intellectual development posed by technical education – these complaints will be muted and self-mocking in tone. For it would be irrational to favor the end and to oppose the means. Better to be ironic about the occasional inconsistency between one's appreciation of the good life pursued and lack of appreciation of the pursuit itself.

But it is because these practices are experienced and justified primarily as instruments to ends outside themselves that they are susceptible eventually to inner erosion. Such institutions can be drained of normative significance if

1 The ends pursued, once attained by a large minority, seem empty to the privileged beneficiaries.
2 Many members of the subordinate population increasingly suspect that they and their progeny will sacrifice only so that others can enjoy the good life.

3 The very attainment of the previously postulated ends now seem to destroy prized aspects of social life which the pursuers tacitly had assumed would remain intact.

Large numbers of people today, it can be argued, have moved toward one or more of these orientations. These are some of the very constituencies whose rhetoric and conduct placed the initial ideology of sacrifice under so much pressure.

For the institutions justified earlier by the future affluence and leisure they would generate are now largely intact. The future is now. The enthusiasm to build a life of affluence and free time for future generations can no longer be so readily mobilized once the gap between the original projection of vague aspirations and the concrete experience of the actual achievements is revealed historically.[5] The old purposes sustaining allegiance to the old role requirements cannot so easily sustain the innocent allegiance of a new generation of role-bearers. They must continue to work, politic, consume, rear children, invest, and bargain within these forms. But their allegiance to them weakens, their motivation to excel within them declines, and their performance deteriorates.

The expression of disillusionment varies across categories of age, class, occupational sector, region, race, and gender; its tonalities shift with variations in the level of international tensions and with the crests and troughs of the business cycle. But it does find expression. Its first clear manifestation was the youth movement of the 1960s, a movement in which those destined to fill privileged roles expressed disaffection from the role requirements, the larger purposes they served, and the sacrifices imposed by the whole complex on the subordinate population. Most other manifestations are, for reasons to be explained, indirect.

These manifestations include the problem of worker motivation in several sectors of the work force, the rise of the environmental movement, repudiation by many women of traditional household roles, the retreat by many into fundamentalist religion, the rise of hedonist movements, and – once the economic crunch set in – the competitive scramble amongst highly educated youth over the remaining slots in the few professions with intrinsically fulfilling work.[6]

This new interpretation of prevailing institutions and objectives crystallizes disaffection from the civilization of productivity while affirming the possibility of reconstituting the old institutions to serve new purposes. If it can also cast new light on old orientations, if it can retrospectively account for the ambivalence and exaggeration lodged inside the ideology of sacrifice, it can hope to become the new self-interpretation of those once gripped by that ideology. We shall test its power to account for the deep hostility toward the welfare state in a later chapter. Our concentration now will be on its ability to detect and explain the ambivalence within the old orientation, as it finds expression in charges hurled at a range of critics and victims of the system.

The accusations formerly advanced against radicals, welfare recipients, feminists and minority activists did contain a moment of truth, for the conditions of existence of these constituencies do vary in some ways from those of the worker, and they often press their claims without attending closely to the worker's circumstances. But the intensity with which the accusations were levelled and the exaggerations they contained can now be comprehended overtly by those adopting the revised interpretation of the civilization of productivity. For these dimensions reveal a vulnerability within the accusers themselves. The tendency of the accusers, first, to exaggerate the differences between their own behaviour and that of the accused, and, secondly, to deny the real grievances felt by these constituencies, protected a disorienting discrepancy within themselves between the beliefs and aspirations appropriate to their life situation and their declining allegiance to those orientations. The self whose indulgence was resented was in part the self of the other who appeared to escape the disciplines accepted by responsible people. But it was also that part of oneself which remained subjected to those disciplines and yet vaguely opposed to them. This ambivalence towards the roles with which one is intimately involved is difficult to acknowledge. To do so is to acknowledge a certain disaffection from the self one has become. And when one seems surrounded by those who believe that the imperatives of the civilization support the ends proper to humanity itself the overt expression of discontent with them must appear to be irresponsible or self-indulgent. One opens oneself to harsh charges to which there is no ready reply. Moreover, to express these discontents openly while continuing to carry out the same role assignments is to admit that one does not exercise self-discipline in pursuit of freely chosen ends. It is to call one's freedom into question.

To retain, thereby, the appearance of one whose outer conduct reflects inner convictions one is encouraged to adopt a hostile stance to those whose conduct seems to express repudiation of those convictions. The denial of the grievances of Blacks and welfare recipients is part of the process by which those in marginally more secure circumstances subvert questions about their own dignity, integrity and freedom. The state treats those others too permissively, one insists; and the insistence controls that part of oneself which one must not treat too permissively.

The situation portrayed here is fraught with irrationality. But the irrationality is not characterized adequately by saying that the participants resist necessary means to desirable ends or that policies recognizably in the interests of the collectivity are not in the interests of any individual. Contemporary social scientists have imposed more weight upon these formulae than they can bear. The tendency to force recognized irrationalities in the order into the frame of these timeless formulae is understandable. For they provide the most powerful categories through which those who lack a theory of intersubjectivity can come to grips with the symptoms of declining allegiance to the civilization of productivity. But the hegemony of these categories must be resisted. They legitimize ruthless policies designed to coerce those who appear to lack sufficient self-discipline to adjust private interests to collective imperatives or to accept necessary means to desired ends.

The central contentions advanced so far can be summarized by reference to three dimensions of irrationality within the civilization of productivity which are reducible to neither of these standard formulae.

First, a set of established social ends is progressively experienced by participants as empty or defeated by the institutional means now seen to be necessary to their attainment, while the institutional means to them are increasingly felt to be inescapable. The contradictory tendency here embodies a temporal or historical dimension whereby abstractly specified ends targeted for achievement in a distant future later decline in their ability to secure allegiance as their actual content is experienced concretely. And, as part of the same historical trajectory, the institutions which sustain those purposes are progressively solidified. The concrete experience necessary to crystallize disaffection and the appearance of institutional intractibility, move in tandem.[7]

Secondly, the experienced inescapability of the institutional means to these ends conflicts with the wish of the workers to identify themselves as agents freely shaping their own lives. This potential contradiction can be alleviated, at least in appearance, by suppressing the inner disaffection from the ends themselves, by denying the progressive force of the evidence against them. In appearing now to affirm these ends one appears to adopt voluntarily the roles necessary to their attainment. This resolution stands at the level of appearance – which is not to say it is a mere idea disconnected from practice – to the extent that the overt affirmation is belied by other aspects of conduct in work, school, family and politics. These inchoate expressions of disaffection stand as symptoms to the extent they are not incorporated into a coherent self-interpretation.

Thirdly, to identify with the institutions which impose these disciplines and appear so intractible it is helpful to view them either as nature-like in form or as rational means to universal ends. For it is never a constraint on our freedom as a politically organized populace to fail to change the unchangeable or to refrain from reconstituting that which is already rational. But this nature-like interpretation of, say, instrumental work and production for private profit preserves the sense of collective agency by misreading the constitution of the institutions. It denies the extent to which they are historical human constructions shaped in part by previous power constellations and priorities gripping many participants. This misreading bears long term political consequences. For, as we shall see in a later chapter, it sets up the welfare state to be the screen upon which the deeper disaffection from the civilization of productivity is projected; it increases the load imposed upon the welfare state in maintaining the civilization of productivity; and it depletes the supply of civic virtue available to the state in carrying out its expanded tasks of social coordination.

The irrationality at each of these levels supports those at others. The set together does not reside so much in the character of the participants or in the structure of the institutional complex abstracted from its participants. It resides, rather, in the disjunction between the question for identity and an institutional complex, partially constituted by the concepts, beliefs and aspirations of its role-bearers, impaired in its ability to secure reflective allegiance to the purposes it must serve.

Pretend now that the newly revised interpretation becomes the self-interpretation of the youngest contingent of workers. They accept it partly because it makes sense of blind spots and discrepancies in the old orientation and partly because it seems to orient them politically where the previous interpretation did not. Previously they were forced to conclude that, though the ideology of sacrifice was self-defeating, no other acceptable identity was available to them in the established order. Now they agree that the established institutional priorities cannot retain their reflective allegiance and that the institutions themselves are susceptible to change. The new forms envisaged are not merely to be instruments to ends outside themselves, but the instrumentalities must be infused to some extent with activities and relationships that are intrinsically fulfilling. It is not, they now say eagerly, that the sphere of necessity – organizing production, working, learning, rearing children, and politics – can be eliminated; but once the ends of productivity, private affluence and leisure are displaced from their overriding position, these practices themselves can be reshaped to create more room for fulfilling social relationships, collective consumption and public deliberation over common areas of concern.

If the problem at this stage is seen to be one of public consciousness, then the point of politics is to change that consciousness. Encounter groups, experiments in community life designed to demonstrate the viability of new social forms, public demonstrations, and a politics of theater are likely to bloom. The point is to expose ideas and norms implicit in the old roles, to shock the audience into recognition of its own complicity in the way of life that breeds discontent, and to articulate new ideas and norms to be insinuated inside new institutional arrangements. This is the utopian moment. It is, if you will, Charles Reich brought inside the factory gates.

The utopian moment contains a political insight. For to articulate implicit disaffection and to expose unrecognized complicity in a corrupt order is to increase the responsibility of those so implicated to change those institutions. My responsibility to contribute to the elimination of some undesirable outcome increases (other things being equal) as my *knowledge* increases of the implicit and reversible tendency of my previous conduct to support it. And this is the knowledge the new politics is designed to disseminate.

But the utopian moment is susceptible to shattering dissillusionment. Technocratic elites, tied to the established order, will greet the new strategies with incomprehension and hostility. If the technocrats believe that the opposite of instrumental rationality in the pursuit of established ends is irrationality, if they therefore conclude that theatrical gestures impede the serious business of production and politics, then they must on principle refuse to 'reason' or 'bargain' with those who repudiate reason itself. Those who break the rules of the game must be broken. And this response, if widespread, sours the utopian initiative. Treated as irrational, it tends increasingly to live up to the charge. And it loses its ability to expose deeper irrationalities in the established order.

Underlying the inability to establish enclaves in the established order, and implicit in the repressive response, is a deeper reality. The institutions attacked, now that they are firmly established, have acquired a life of their own: the possibilities for change are now structurally constrained. Though the reinterpretation did improve selectively upon the view it displaced, though social institutions are constituted in part by the concepts, beliefs, and aspirations of the participants, changes in those beliefs and commitments cannot suffice to reconstitute an institutional complex. The interdependence and intermeshing of each institution with others creates an institutional structure strongly resistant to serious reconstitution. The growing discrepancy between the role requirements and the new aspirations can impede profoundly the performance of the old order, but this (by now) conscious disaffection does not automatically produce a political strategy sufficient to adapt that order to newly emerging objectives. The previous understanding of these institutions as an unchangeable part of nature, or as required by the criteria of reason as such, expressed in mystified form a truth overlooked in the reinterpretation.

Social relations are not *simply* communicative relations amongst (disembodied) agents. Two types of constraint operate on such relationships. First, social relations among human beings – who themselves embody natural needs for food and shelter and remain susceptible to the sorts of pains and injuries afflicting non-rational animals – require complex transactions between persons and nature if social life is to continue. No society can persist long if interruptions in such transactions do not soon propel new transactions into existence or allow the (perhaps modified) reinstatement of the old. An established heritage of skills, machinery, and organization mobilized in support of these transactions cannot easily be scrapped. Secondly, the institutions implicated in those transactions can become so intertwined that a significant change in one eventually requires corollary changes in others if necessary transactions with nature are to continue. How tightly such contemporary forms are interlocked now is a matter legitimately open to controversy. But powerful constraints do flow out of this complex of institutional dependencies and interconnections.

Suppose that a new political coalition, mobilized to reorient the economy of growth, successfully elects candidates to the major governmental posts. Its representatives, facing a minority opposition in Congress, none the less have an initial majority strong enough to enact policies designed to propel the welfare state, situated in a privately incorporated economy of growth, into a socialist polity oriented to new aspirations. The elected officials must face in two directions at once. They must strive to enact programs congruent with their mandate while maintaining a level of economic performance sufficient to meet the needs of the populace.

To carry out its agenda the welfare state must generate sufficient tax revenues. The flow of tax revenues depends on the investment and production decisions of private owners. And those decisions in turn are influenced by the extent to which the welfare state supports the conditions of growth. The *dependency* of the welfare state on the economy it would reconstitute, combined with its increasingly *dominant role* in maintaining economic performance, presses it toward policies perpetuating the political economy of growth.

Suppose state officials, in alliance with organized workers, legally sanction a series of reforms in productive arrangements; they broaden work routines, extend participation in corporate decisions, and try to enhance the social utility of corporate products. If the reforms are instituted in an economy where private profit creation continues to be the basic motor of the system, a dilemma may emerge. Either the worker–consumer participants will have to adapt their policy agendas to the imperatives of private profit creation or the firms involved will falter nationally and internationally. If the participants adjust to these imperatives the reforms will be more apparent than real; if they do not the firms will soon face crises.

The answer would seem to be to nationalize the pertinent units first and then to institute the reforms. But the very national and international intertwining of these institutions gives corporate owners powerful leverage to defeat such attempts. They might transfer essential funds to foreign investments in anticipation of such moves, weakening the performance of the economy and arousing the fears of dependent employees. They might deploy the advantages available to any privileged minority in the policy-making process to delay or veto proposed changes. They might finance, say, disruptive strikes by truckers who feel threatened by these changes, interrupting thereby the nation's flow of goods and services. The possibilities here are quite large because of the complex interdependencies among the established modes of work, investment, distribution, consumption, state revenue creation, state efficacy in implementing policies, the military, the legitimacy of state policies, state accountability, the absence of accountability amongst economic units, and the international scope of capitalist enterprise.

As the performance of the system was impeded by these reactions, the state's response to it would itself be structurally constrained. It might be compelled to impose new disciplines and sacrifices on those least essential to corporate growth and least able to resist the impositions – on marginal workers in the market sector, the unemployed, welfare recipients, low level public employees, school children, the elderly, the sick, prisoners, the mentally retarded. It might have to sanction the extension of Taylorist modes of work and control into higher occupational levels in order to maintain productive efficiency and to discipline a work force losing the self-discipline it once exercised – even though the authoritarian, routinized mode of work is itself the source of much of the disaffection from the civilization of productivity.[8] It might have to tolerate high levels of inflation to cope with the imperatives facing it, even though inflationary spirals, with their corrosive effects on established income differentials, generate a large constellation of discontented constituencies each claiming to suffer unjustly by comparison to at least one other group previously behind it in the income hierarchy.

If the constraints were extremely tight – that issue remains open – the institutional result could eventually approach the shape of an historical dilemma. The future, once built, loses its normative grip on those implicated in it; but since its structure is largely established, powerful constraints to its reconstitution persist. Moreover, because the state is under pressure to promote growth, productive efficiency, and private consumption within the established order it is extremely difficult for a viable political movement to articulate the underlying disaffection in ways which could orient state action. The disaffection itself seems unreal to those gripped by it because it is not articulated as a set of concrete grievances within the established order. And it is not articulated partly because leaders competing for state office cannot identify existing state resources capable of responding to these issues.

It might not appear too difficult to get those who have already acknowledged disaffection from the civilization of work to move toward this newly revised interpretation. For they must expect any credible interpretation to explain why an advanced capitalist system perpetuates itself even amidst periods of instability and the periodic revolt of youthful constituencies. Moreover, looking to their own previous denial of disaffection, they might see inside it an implicit awareness that the established order is quite intractable. The ideology of sacrifice treated the established institutional matrix as nature-like, as the unchangeable background of politics: it thus recognized, if darkly, its structural resistance to significant change.

But if political interpretation involves both a question for truth and a search for a secure identity, the newly revised interpretation faces a treacherous path. As it stands now, its strategic implications are underdetermined because its structural dimension is underspecified. Perhaps there are openings in this order not yet detected in the interpretation; or perhaps the constraints eventually will emerge as contradictions which must be resolved; or perhaps the preconditions for the evolution of a new order more congruent with the newly emerging aspirations are undermined by the very efforts of the state to maintain economic performances. We can say, minimally, that the utopian moment is over for those who accept an interpretation in which structural interdependencies and constraints play an important role. We can also anticipate a reactive movement to stem the dialectic of disaffection, one which will struggle aggressively to suppress clear manifestations of discontent while repressing their more diffused expression in the wider populace. Those who would oppose such a regressive movement must strive to redefine public issues so that middle class liberals and radicals do not continue to press constituencies oriented to the ideology of sacrifice into a defensively aggressive posture.

This critical interpretation, when all its parts are assembled, treats prevailing appearances as forms in need of transcendence. But another reading might converge with this one at many points while insisting that participants must none the less become reconciled to the limits of the prevailing order. If those limits are treated as unbreakable necessities, that which is irrational within one account becomes rational in the next. Attention to this rejoinder, implicit today within new, defensive versions of liberalism, will help to bring out further dimensions in the interpretation advanced here.

The rejoinder goes something like this. There is a vacancy in the interpretation. The account is parasitic upon an idealized view of the previous history of capitalist development which is both unacknowledged and incorrect. This order – and others as well – has always been marked by struggle, selective oppression, resistance, cycles and calamity. But the critical interpretation implicitly treats the past as a smooth surface which is only now subject to rupture. When we reconstruct appropriately our understanding of the past we will not be so critical of limits apparent in the present. For such limits, though not exactly the same ones, face every society.

There is a certain irony in this rejoinder, at least as it is offered in the context of American intellectual life. For it has taken two decades of radical reinterpretation to break the consensus reading of American history which previously prevailed within liberalism. Inside the irony is a misconception of the sort of account advanced here. The thesis is not that the growth of American capitalism has proceeded smoothly until certain flaws in its priorities became more visible to a range of participants. Rather, expressions of hope and solace previously available to defeated and forgotten constituencies are less available. And the control of these constituencies is both more necessary to the maintenance of the order and more difficult than it was. These shifts insinuate themselves into our political life during periods of quiescence and unrest, infecting the performance of the dominant institutions and depleting the supply of civic resources we can draw upon in trying to shore them up.

But the major thesis of the new liberals refers not to the past but to the untouchable limits in the present. Earlier, optimistic versions, holding that the welfare state could maintain affluence and liberty while significantly reducing inequality and insecurity, are now giving way to this tougher doctrine; and this ideological shift serves to acknowledge some of the themes advanced here. The themes are then given a different reading. We must work within the admittedly narrow confines of this order because it is utopian to try to stretch the limits themselves. We must get tougher with those who impair or disrupt the system of productivity, doing so to preserve important virtues only it can preserve. Such an orientation recasts the relations between appearances and realities sketched here by relocating the lines which separate the rational from the irrational.

I do not believe that a definitive response can be made to this sort of rejoinder. But considerations can be advanced which support opening theoretical explorations and political movements it would close off.

Theodore Adorno's reply to a similar thesis advanced under different circumstances provides the right launching pad:

> Criticism of tendencies in modern society is automatically countered, before it is fully uttered, by the argument that things have always been like this. The accuser is further informed that . . . the grounds for his indignation are common knowledge, trivial, so that no one can be expected to waste his interest in them . . . Connivance makes use of the trick of attributing to its opponent a reactionary and untenable theory of decline – for is not horror indeed perennial? – in order by the alleged error in his thinking to discredit his concrete insight into the negative, and to blacken him who remonstrates against darkness as an obfuscator.[9]

Perfect, as far as it goes. It goes far enough to expose the potential for obfuscation accompanying efforts to treat evils within a particular order as universals, not far enough to establish the presumption in favor of treating them as particulars potentially susceptible to significant reconstitution. The case for retaining an open and exploratory orientation to future possibilities will be considered later in this study. For now it suffices to note that the interpretation advanced here incorporates a contestable position on that issue.

THE REALITY OF APPEARANCES

All of this might seem too laden with counterfactuals and counter-counterfactuals to be eliminating or realistic. Perhaps the consciousness of participants does enter into political relations, but *could* the participants become self-conscious in the ways suggested? I believe the question should be reversed. Given the capacity people in modern society have to think critically about the roles they play, the purposes they serve, and the assumptions underlying those activities, what sorts of impediments limit critical reflection into them? And how are the participants constrained from acting upon such reconsidered judgements once articulated? When the question is reformulated the multiplication of counterfactuals emerges as the most promising way, first, to explain why the ideology of sacrifice retains a powerful hold over large sections of the working class even though the identity it provides is so thin and vulnerable, and, secondly, to comprehend the complex obstacles facing any dissident orientation to thought and practice aiming to displace that ideology.

The ideology of sacrifice persists, despite the ambivalence within it, because a decade of tentative explorations by adventurous youth bumped into the various reactions and constraints we have identified. No secure enclaves could be found which allowed the participants to establish new bearings while launching families, working, preparing children for the future available in this society, and maintaining ties to an older generation whose own sense of achievement had been threatened by the exploratory forays. Some of these ties and responsibilities can be broken in pursuit of a better way of life, but it is extremely difficult to deny all of them over a long period of time if the political progress sought is consistently obstructed.

To specify the constraints facing such exploratory movements is thus to explain why disaffection from the civilization of productivity in fact finds only a limited and indirect political expression. Once the defining institutions of that civilization are wheeled into place even dissident political movements are pressed to define objectives congruent with the established order. But such a structural bias means that no organized movement *articulates* inchoate disaffection, crystallizing it into a coherent set of grievances and aspirations. The disaffection itself thereby remains vague and undefined. It tends to be denied by those experiencing it because it seems so unreal, so disconnected from the demands and possibilities of everyday life; and it seems so unreal because it lacks an institutional framework within which it can be translated into concrete proposals. When defenders of the established order then define the behavioural expression of these vague anxieties as the misbehaviour of a new generation of hedonists and irrationalists, those who would otherwise explore such orientations in themselves tend instead to deny, to submerge, the doubts.[10] They may indeed attack dissidents who continue to project such irrational fantasies on to the public realm, and the attack may help to control such unspeakable tendencies in their own conduct and attitudes.

Epistemic pressures (the lack of articulation and specificity) and social pressures (the inability to secure identity over a lifetime outside of the established institutional forms) coalesce to block the explicit expression of disaffection while the very historical development of the institutions works to undercut allegiance to the ends they serve.

An interpretive account begins with the self-understanding of the participants, but it must eventually explore implicit beliefs, unexpressed doubts, vaguely articulated hopes, and repressed anxieties which help to account for their conduct. Moreover, these discrepancies must be explained, and one promising route (though it does not exhaust the possibilities) is to explore institutional interdependencies which encourage some understandings and aspirations, while rendering others inconsistent with the wish of the participants to see themselves as responsible agents freely choosing to play the roles available to them.

An interpretation wishing both to respect appearances and to reveal what they conceal can be disciplined, but it should not pretend to be politically neutral. For that which is implicit or repressed is not exactly like the explicit or the expressed minus the single difference that it is hidden or unstated. Implicit beliefs, hopes, and fears are vague and undisciplined. They are not public enough to be subjected to scrutiny, criticism and refinement from a variety of angles over a sustained period of time by a number of different people. Thus to clarify them is to give them a distinct shape and accent previously absent; to convince those to whom they are attributed to accept the new formulation is partly to draw out what was there already and partly to change it and its role in their lives. In the sphere of political reflection discovery and creation are not neatly separable. And since ideas, beliefs, and aspirations enter into political relations, that means that political reflection, once it is heard and heeded, or heard and repudiated, never leaves things as they were.[11]

The interpretive conversion of the implicit into the explicit, the identification of internal discrepancies, and the characterization of inchoate disaffection and aspirations, though anchored in the lives of the participants, will bear necessarily the imprint of one's own anthropology. The interpretation offered here, for instance, projects a multi-layered or faceted view of persons and social relations. It requires distinctions between explicit and implicit beliefs and between conscious and unconscious purposes; it affirms the possibility of deception, distortion, ambivalence, and projection in relations with others and oneself; it insists that some degree of self-consciousness, autonomous action, and moral integrity are possible human achievements; it recognises an attenuated, historicized conception of natural human ends whereby some institutionalized ends cannot sustain the allegiance of a populace unless they are mystified or specified in futuristic terms. And if any of these ingredients had to be rejected on logical or experiential grounds, the interpretation within which they are housed would require revision.

One never confronts social reality in an unmediated way, then, for the appearence it assumes in the theory reflects to some extent the anthropology accepted by the theorist; and the anthropologically mediated interpretation, to the extent that it enters into the future thought and action of those whose conduct is subjected to interpretation, introduces new projects, alliances, and cleavages into political life. How can such a standpoint be disciplined by reason and evidence?

One can, first, compare the anthropology advanced to the one (or ones) accepted by the populace one is studying. This provides preliminary bearings. But the explicit convictions of the populace seldom exhaust their actual orientations; and, as we have seen, to bring out subordinate dimensions and presuppositions of such interpretations is to introduce additional elements in need of critical scrutiny. Moreover, even if the fit were tight, that would not guarantee the truth of both accounts. We have argued previously, for instance, that a populace can be moved at one time by vaguely specified aspirations without realizing that their later specification and realization will tend to undermine commitment to them. Such a test, then, is not only necessary, but necessarily contaminated by some of the very factors in need of critical scrutiny.

Secondly, one can show how a particular anthropology renders intelligible a range of ideologies and political conflicts which appear mysterious or merely unexplained from other standpoints. Such an account might draw upon an anthropology with some ingredients not presently acknowledged or recognized by the participants. Thirdly, and closely connected, one can show how certain assumptions help us to *identify* modes of behavior previously ignored and thus unexplained within other anthropologies. The peresistent claim of Freudian theory to serious attention, for instance, flows from its impressive performance in these two areas, and the performance lends credibility to 'wild' assumptions within it that would otherwise be shrugged off.

Fourthly, one can compare, as anthropologists themselves do, the possibilities and limits identified as universals in a particular anthropology to actual forms of life *appearing* to be at odds with these expectations in some respects. Here too, though, appearances may still deceive; and the deception, once covered, may allow retention of elements initially jeopardized.

Fifthly, one can, as Peter Strawson and Jürgen Habermas have both done recently, explore presuppositions rooted in one's own reactive attitudes and speech acts to ascertain whether they square with assumptions explicitly incorporated into one's anthropology.[12] As part of this enterprise one can ask whether the assumptions made about others in explaining their conduct are consistent with those made in appraising it morally, and whether assumptions I make about myself as the author of an argument square with those I make about myself as a member of society whose conduct is susceptible to explanation.

Sixthly, one can explore the logic or illogic of notions central to an anthropology (notions such as rationality, self-deception, unconscious purposes, and autonomous action) to see whether each is internally coherent and whether all can be housed within the same framework.

None of these test-levels provides an ultimate court of appeal in the sense that conclusions reached there automatically override contradictory conclusions reached at other levels. With respect to our sixth level, for instance, a large number of philosophers previously argued that ideas such as self-deception and unconscious purposes were impermissible in scientific inquiry because they did not cohere with neutral requirements of scientific theory. But the apparent explanatory power of theories employing these notions justified resistance to this conclusion. And more recently revisionists have argued that the *rules of analysis* accepted in shuffling such notions outside the rubric of science (e.g., the analytic–synthetic dichotomy, a strict falsification principle) and the *restrictive analogies* within which these criticism were developed (e.g., self-deception as analogous to one person deceiving another, construing personal identity in terms of a 'simple' rather than a 'complex' model) distorted the findings emerging from the analysis of such notions.[13] Such rules and analogies themselves can be placed under pressure (seventh) when a theory not fitting these norms reveals strength in other respects.

But perhaps it can be argued that *for us today* some of these tests are more fundamental than others. For given our current powers of conceptualization and self-understanding, a set of implicit assumptions about ourselves built into the identity we seek to sustain could only be denied by lapsing into a series of pragmatic contradictions. If that were so, any explanatory theory of politics which explicitly or implicitly denies the validity of these assumptions must today be repudiated.

The reactive relations we enter into – as in my resentment when I conclude that another has slighted me intentionally and unjustifiably, or my indignation when I rebuke another who fails to abide by shared standards in his relation with a third person – presuppose my own belief in our common capacity to live up to shared norms, to pursue goals arrived at deliberately, and to be held responsible for failure to live up to such standards. And the existential questions we periodically pose ('What shall I do? How shall I live my life?') presuppose a capacity for self-conscious criticism and for the reactive reconstitution of previous habits of conduct. Aware of ourselves as agents not exhausted by the multiple roles we play, we are aware of ourselves as agents able to subject those norms to reflective criticism and revision. We define ourselves today, to some degree, by contrast to earlier peoples less conscious of the historical variety amongst ways of life and thus more thoroughly inclined to view their individual and collective life as expressions of fate given by God or Nature. The contrast helps to crystallize our sense of ourselves as responsible agents, capable of acting freely, and worthy, under the appropriate conditions, of being held responsible for what we do and what we become.

It is immensely difficult, perhaps now impossible, to give up the presuppositions built into the reactive relations and habits of self-conscious criticism we display in daily conduct. The attempt to do so would be blocked repeatedly by our tendency to affirm in conduct what we deny in abstract theory. The identity which supports the political self-interpretation we have explored critically is not itself to be repudiated. These are appearances which we must treat as realities.

Such a contention rests upon a reconstituted form of the transcendental argument, deviating from its classical predecessor in two respects: it does not insist that only one reading of the human capacities for reason, responsibility, and self-consciousness must be accepted by all contemporary theorists, but it does set limits within which alternative readings of these capacities and norms can be articulated now. And it does not claim that no future advance in our theories about nature and society could force a revision in these limits, but it does claim that our own reading today cannot remain internally coherent unless it falls within them.

Stuart Hampshire summarizes a qualified form of such a modified transcendental argument:

> Within language as we know it, a limit is set to the possibility of varying the ways in which we think about our actions, by our nature as perceiving and thinking beings who are intentional agents moving among other things. One must start from the truisms that set these limits . . . We cannot claim an absolute and conditional finality for these truisms since the deduction of them is always a deduction within language as we know it. But the deduction only shows that we are not in a position to describe any alternative forms of communication between intentional agents which do not exmplify these truisms.[14]

Two implications flow from these contentions.

First, the self-identity attributed in this essay to the authors of the ideology of sacrifice is indeed a defensible, laudable vision of self-supportable by reasoned argument. It is not this identification of oneself as a person worthy of being held responsible for one's actions and character that should be displaced (though its *social* preconditions and dimensions should be incorporated more fully into the self-consciousness of its bearers), but the established role imperatives which require many to construct the ideology of sacrifice to preserve a fragile, blunted form of that identity within the established order. The tendency of technocratic theorists to repudiate this underlying identity whenever its expression conflicts with prevailing role requirements is susceptible to criticism from this perspective. The technocratic theorist might argue that state officials, trying to manage a complex economy, should be released from the obligation to legitimize their policies to a wider populace or, more directly, to that conception of role-bearers appropriate to scientific explanation and social control is incompatible with the self-conceptions of the role-bearers themselves. Such an account, once its import is elaborated, must appear to us today to be quite implausible and to be thoroughly contemptuous of those whose conduct is to be explained. For the theorist, in constructing and defending the explanation, must claim to exercise the very capacities he strips from the human objects of inquiry. The self-identity of the one is affirmed while that of the other is repudiated; and no ground is provided for differentiating the one from the other.

Secondly, the best way to discipline those anthropological speculations which must somehow be incorporated into any social theory is to run coherence tests across the multiple test levels we have identified. Such a process will identify discrepancies to be resolved if the theory is to retain its acceptability, and it will render some anthropologies more plausible than others. But, because each identified discrepancy can be resolved in a number of ways, because some ingredients in every anthropology refer to hypothetical limits and possibilities that have not yet been established historically, and because the introduction of a revised anthropology into the self-interpretation of participants might generate recognition of new limits or possibilities not clearly anticipated in current speculation, we must not expect any single, tightly formulated, anthropology to be so thoroughly grounded in experience and logic that every other candidate is eliminated from the running. Some orientations will appear more plausible than the others and reasons can be specified in support of such a judgement.[15] But it is not to be anticipated that the number of legitimate candidates will reduce to one.

Political interpretation is not merely politically engaged, then, it is engaged in a special way. One's moral ideals and fears enter into theory through the very specification of its anthropological dimension. The theory conveys a recommendation, undetermined by available evidence, to crystallize our self-understanding in a particular way in the hope, vain as it usually is, that this articulation will help to solidify the reality portrayed or to obstruct the outcome feared or to promote the achievement pursued. That is certainly a feature of the interpretation advanced here, as it is of those ranged against it. The warning conveyed by this particular interpretation found its most condensed expression in an earlier era: 'In our times we can neither endure our faults not the means of correcting them.'[16]

NOTES

1 The recent debates over Peter Winch's arguments in *The Idea of a Social Science* (London: Routledge and Kegan Paul, 1958) explore these issues. Winch himself did not consistently support the relativist position attributed to him, but the critiques do point out weaknesses in such a relativism. See the collection by Brian Wilson (ed.), *Rationality* (Oxford: Oxford University

Press, 1970) as well as several chapters in Alasdair MacIntyre, *Against the Self Images of the Age* (New York: Schocken Books, 1971).

2 The interpretation at this level is indebted directly to the study of Richard Sennett and Jonathan Cobb, *The Hidden Injuries of Class* (New York: Random House, 1973). Sennett and Cobb themselves reject theories of false consciousness, arguing that the ideology of the worker is a self-creation and not imposed on him from above. I will concur with the view that it is a self-creation and dissent from the conclusion that this makes false consciousness an impossibility. The Sennet–Cobb study has been widely criticized because the method they employ is closer to a *dialogue* with the respondent than a *survey* of their attutides. Such methodological critiques are unfounded. Taken seriously, they would make it impossible to inquire into the depth interpretations of any segment of the population. Of course these methods run the risk of introducing biases into the findings. But the proper approach here is not to perfect and thus sterilize the interview instrument but to devise a series of indirect tests. Does the ideology of sacrifice emerging out of these dialogues help to render intelligible modes of conduct which seemed mysterious before this background interpretation was present? If so, we have impressive evidence that the interpretation uncovered through dialogue actually enters into the self-interpretation of the respondents. To criticize these methodological critiques of the Sennett–Cobb study is to repudiate not the quest for evidence but rather its narrow confinement to the instrument of survey analysis.

3 It is not my intention to show why these changes are implied by a successful program to reduce inequality and provide job security for everyone. Michael Best and I have offered such arguments in *The Politicized Economy* (Lexington, Mass.: D. C. Heath, 1976). More immediately to the point, the new version of Liberalism to be examined later in this study now concedes that such objectives are not attainable within the prevailing institutional structure.

4 My argument at this point is indebted to the analyses by Jürgen Habermas in *Legitimation Crisis*, trans. Thomas McCarthy (Boston: Beacon Press, 1973) and Charles Taylor, 'Interpretation and the Sciences of Man', *The Review of Metaphysics* (Spring, 1971), pp. 4–51.

5 Charles Taylor puts the point in this way: 'The notion of a horizon to be attained by future greater production verges on the absurd in contemporary America. Suddenly the horizon which was essential to the sense of meaningful purpose has collapsed, which would mean that like so many other enlightenment dreams, the free productive, bargaining society can only sustain man as a goal, not as a reality' ('Interpretation and the Sciences of Man', p. 43).

6 This escalation of pressure for positions in law, medicine and college teaching occurred even when high-paying jobs were more available in business, accounting and public bureaucracies.

7 This analysis does not make reference to the earlier wrenching of people from the land to fill the cities and the factories. My argument does not presuppose that people once ran eagerly from the country to the city. But

once in the city for a few generations the abstract goals for the civilization productivity begin to take hold. The differences between the United States and European countries in this respect would play a central role in any theory designed to compare and contrast their modes of development, and, particularly, the comparative rates of scepticism and resistance to that development.

8 The pressure for an expansion of Taylorism and the extensive inroads already made in this direction are examined effectively in Harry Braverman, *Labor and Monopoly Capital* (New York: Monthly Review Press, 1974).

9 Theodore Adorno, *Minima Moralia*, trans. E. F. N. Jephcott (London: New Left Books, 1974), p. 233.

10 Daniel Bell, in *The Cultural Contradictions of Capitalism* (New York: Basic Books, 1977), interprets the revolt of the 1960s as a new hedonism generated by the success of capitalism itself. He misses, I contend, the deeper disaffection inside that revolt, misconstruing the difficulties in formulating it and giving it concrete political expression within the established order as a manifestation of irrationalism on the part of the disaffected.

11 This finding remains intact even when it is acknowledged that the low quality, availability, or pertinence of any particular account may make its general influence negligible. One is tempted to say that the general likelihood of political indoctrination increases proportionately with the tendency amongst political intellectuals to obscure this intrinsic feature of political reflection and discourse. Very general, epistemological orientations set a framework for practical political judgement which is not neutral. For an excellent, short defence of this thesis, see Brian Fay, *Social Theory and Political Practice* (London: George Allen and Unwin, 1975).

12 See Peter Strawson, 'Freedom and Resentment' in his *Studies in the Philosophy of Thought and Action* (New York: Oxford University Press, 1968), pp. 71–96. Habermas, *Legitimation Crisis*, pt III. The import of Strawson's effort for political theory is discussed in William E. Connolly, *The Terms of Political Discourse* (Lexington, Mass.: D. C. Heath, 1974), chs 2 and 6.

13 Numerous examples of such shifts in the controlling rules and analogies are to be found in Jonathan Glover (ed.), *The Philosophy of Mind* (Oxford: Oxford University Press, 1976). The collected essays deal with pertinent issues such as the criteria of psychoanalytic interpretation (B. A. Farrell), self-deception (Patrick Gardiner), roles and self-consciousness (Gerald Cohen), the expression of feelings (Stuart Hampshire) and personal identity (Derek Parfit).

14 Stuart Hampshire, *Thought and Action* (New York: The Viking Press, 1959), p. 67. A philosophy of mind and a social theory are properly viewed as mutually enabling and restraining modes of thought. If a social theory projects a complex anthropology in which unconsciousness, pre-conscious, conscious, and self-conscious levels of thought and action are recognized, its claims are increasingly subject to revision and adjustment by the conceptual distinction required to *distinguish* between these levels and the

connections required to support the assumption that, to some degree, ideas can move from one level to another. I believe that an interpretive theorist can do no better than to start with Hampshire's study. My own thinking on these questions, in particular on the role of a modified version of the transcendental argument, has been clarified through discussions with Alan Montefiore and Charles Taylor.

15 Though this specification of anthropological limits was not the central focus of this essay, perhaps I should note that I do not hold that the self can become fully transparent to the agent or that we can anticipate a society in which all the dimensions of life are transparent to the participants. Such a recognition, if it is correct, must be built into any formulation of a socialist ideal of political life, modifying some of the hopes conveyed by Marxist readings of socialist politics. This conclusion is not an abridgement of the view advanced in this essay, but grows out of the philosophy of mind providing it with its conceptual foundations. Here again, Stuart Hampshire is illuminating: 'More of human conduct than we had thought, and aspects of it that we had not expected, may be outside the possible control of practical reason; less of human conduct than we had thought may flow from an unalterable natural endowment' (*Thought and Action*, p. 254).

16 The Roman historian Livy, quoted by Hegel in *The Philosophy of History*, trans. J. Sibree (New York: Dover Publications, 1956), p. 277.

7
The Hermeneutic Claim to Universality

JÜRGEN HABERMAS

I

Hermeneutics refers to an 'ability' we acquire to the extent to which we learn to 'master' a natural language: the art of understanding linguistically communicable meaning and to render it comprehensible in cases of distorted communication. The understanding of meaning is directed at the semantic content of speech as well as the meaning-content of written forms or even of non-linguistic symbolic systems, in so far as their meaning-content can, in principle, be expressed in words. It is no accident that we speak of the art of understanding and of making-oneself-understood, since the ability to interpret meaning, which every language-user possesses, can be stylized and developed into an artistic skill. This art is symmetric with the art of convincing and persuading in situations where decisions have to be reached on practical questions. Rhetoric, too, is based on an ability which is part of the communicative competence of every language user and which can be stylized into a special skill. Rhetoric and hermeneutics have both emerged as teachable arts which methodically discipline and cultivate a natural ability.

This is not so in the case of a philosophical hermeneutic:[1] it is not a practical skill guided by rules but a critique, for its reflexive engagement brings to consciousness experiences of our language which we gain in the course of exercising our communicative competence, that is, by moving within language. It is because rhetoric and hermeneutics serve the instruction and disciplined development of communicative competence that hermeneutic reflection can draw on this sphere of experience. But the reflection upon skilled understanding and making-oneself-

Reprinted by permission of Routledge and Kegan Paul plc from Jürgen Habermas, 'The Hermeneutic Claim to Universality', in *Contemporary Hermeneutics: Hermeneutics and Method, Philosophy and Critique*, Josef Bleicher (ed.) (London: Routledge and Kegan Paul, 1980), pp. 181–211.

understood on the one hand (1), and upon convincing and persuading on the other (2), does not serve the establishing of a teachable art, but the philosophical consideration of the structures of everyday communication.

(1) The art of understanding and making-oneself-understood provides a philosophical hermeneutic with its characteristic insight that the means of natural language are, in principle, sufficient for elucidating the sense of any symbolic complex, however, unfamiliar and inaccessible it may initially appear. We are able to translate from any language into any language. We are able to make sense of objectivations of the most remote epoch and the most distant civilization by relating them to the familiar, i.e. pre-understood, context of our own world. At the same time, the actual distance to other traditions is part of the horizon of every natural language. In addition, the already understood context of one's own world can at any time be exposed as being questionable; it is, potentially, incomprehensible. Hermeneutic experience is circumscribed by the conjunction of these two moments: the intersubjectivity of everyday communication is principally as unlimited as it is restricted; it is unlimited becuse it can be extended *ad libitum*; it is restricted because it can never be completely achieved. This applies to contemporary communication both within a socio-culturally homogeneous language community and across the distance between different classes, civilizations and epochs.

Hermeneutic experience brings to consciousness the position of a speaking subject *vis-à-vis* his language. He can draw upon the self-referentiality of natural languages for paraphrasing any changes metacommunicatively.

It is, of course, possible to construct hierarchies of formal languages on the basis of everyday language as the 'last metalanguage' which would relate to one another as object – to meta, to metametalanguage, etc. The formal construction of such language systems excludes the possibility that for individual sentences the rules of application be determined ad hoc, commented on or changed; and the type-rule prohibits metacommunication about sentences of a language on the level of this object language. Both these things are, however, possible in everyday language. The system of natural language is not closed, but it allows the rules of application for any utterance to be determined ad hoc, commented on or changed; and metacommunication has to employ the language which itself is made the object: every natural language has its own metalanguage. This is the basis for that reflexivity which, in the face of the type-rule, makes it possible for the semantic content of linguistic utterances to contain, in addition to the manifest message, an indirect message as to its application. Such is, for example, the case in a metaphoric use of language. Thanks to the reflexive structure of natural languages, the native speaker is provided with a unique metacommunicative manoeuvring space.

The reverse side of this freedom of movement is a close bond with linguistic tradition. Natural languages are informal; for this reason, speaking subjects cannot confront their language as a closed system. Linguistic competence remains, as it were, behind their backs: they can make sure of a meaning-complex explicitly only to the extent to which they also remain tied to a dogmatically traditioned and implicitly pregiven context. Hermeneutical understanding cannot approach a subject-matter free of any prejudice; it is, rather, unavoidably prepossessed by the context within which the understanding subject has initially acquired his interpretive schemes. This pre-understanding can be thematized and it has to prove itself in relation to the subject-matter in the course of every analysis undertaken with hermeneutic awareness. But even the modification of these unavoidable pre-conceptions does not break through the objectivity of language *vis-à-vis* the speaking subject: in the course of improving his knowledge he merely develops a new pre-understanding which then guides him as he takes the next hermeneutical step. This is what Gadamer means when he states that the 'awareness of effective-history is unavoidably more being than consciousness'.[2]

(2) The art of convincing and persuading, in turn, provides a philosophical hermeneutic with the characteristic insight that it is possible not only to exchange information through the medium of everyday language, but also that, through it, action-orienting attitudes are formed and changed. Rhetoric is traditionally regarded as the art of bringing about a consensus on questions which cannot be settled through compelling reasoning. This is why the classical age reserved the realm of the merely 'probable' for rhetoric, in contrast to the realm in which the truth of statements is discussed theoretically. We are consequently here dealing with practical questions which can be traced to decisions about the acceptance or rejection of standards, of criteria for evaluation and norms of action. These decisions, if arrived at in a rational process, are made neither in a theoretically compelling nor in a merely arbitrary way: they have, in effect, been motivated by convincing speech. The peculiar ambivalence between conviction and persuasion, which attaches to any consensus arrived at through rhetorical means, not only evidences the element of force which to this day has not been removed from the determination of socio-political objectives – however much of it is based on discussion. More importantly, this equivocality is also an indication of the fact that practical questions can only be resolved dialogically and for this reason remain within the context of everyday language.

Rationally motivated decisions can be arrived at only on the basis of a consensus that is brought about by convincing speech; and that means depending on the both cognitively and expressively appropriate means of everyday language.

We can also learn from our experience of rhetoric about the relationship between a speaking subject and his language. A speaker can make use of the creativity of natural language to respond spontaneously to changing situations and to define new situations in principally unpredictable statements. A formal prerequisite for this is a language-structure which makes possible the generation and understanding of an infinite number of sentences by following general rules and by drawing on a finite number of elements. This productivity extends, however, not only to the immediate generation of sentences in general, but also to the long-term process of the formation of interpretive schemes which are formulated in everyday language and which both enable and pre-judge the making of experiences. A good speech which leads to a consensus about decisions on practical questions merely indicates the point where we consciously intervene in this natural–innate process and attempt to alter accepted interpretive schemes with the aim of learning (and teaching) to see what we pre-understood through tradition in a different way and to evaluate it anew. This type of insight is innovatory through the choice of the appropriate word. Thanks to the creativity of natural language the native speaker gains a unique power over the practical consciousness of the members of a community. The career of sophistry reminds us that it can be used for mind-fogging agitation as well as for enlightening people.

There is, however, another side to this power: the specific lack of power of the speaking subject *vis-à-vis* habitualized language-games; they cannot be modified unless one participates in them. This in turn can be successful only to the extent that the rules which determine a language-game have been internalized. To enter into a linguistic tradition necessitates, at least latently, the efforts of a process of socialization: the 'grammar' of language-games has to become part of the personality structure. The sway of a good speech over practical consciousness rests with the fact that a natural language cannot be adequately comprehended as a sytem of rules for the generation of systematically ordered and semantically meaningful symbolic contests; an immanent necessity ties it, in addition, to the context of action and bodily expressions. Rhetoric experience teaches us, in this way, the interconnection of language and praxis. Everyday communication would not only be incomplete but impossible outside the, grammatically ruled, connection with normatively guided interaction and accompanying, intermittent expressions of experiences. The insight that language and action mutually interpret each other is, of course, developed in Wittgenstein's concept of a language-game which is, at the same time, a life-form. The grammar of language-games, in the sense of a complete life-praxis, regulates not only the combining of symbols but, at the same time, the interpretation of linguistic symbols by actions and expressions.[3]

These remarks should serve as a reminder that a philosophical hermeneutic develops those insights into the structure of natural languages which can be gained from the reflexive use of communicative competence: *reflexivity and objectivity are fundamental traits of language, as are creativity and the integration of language into life-praxis*. Such reflexive knowledge, which is comprised by the 'hermeneutic consciousness', is obviously different from a skill in understanding and speech. A philosophical hermeneutic differs equally from linguistics.

Linguistics is not concerned with communicative competence, that is the ability of native speakers to participate in everyday communication through understanding and speaking; it restricts itself to linguistic competence in the narrower sense. This expression was introduced by Chomsky[4] to characterize the ability of an ideal speaker who has a command of the abstract system of rules of natural language. The concept of a language system in the sense of *langue* leaves out of account the pragmatic dimension in which *langue* is transformed into *parole*. It is precisely experiences a speaker makes in this dimension that a philosophical hermeneutic is concerned with. Furthermore, linguistics aims at a reconstruction of the system of rules that allows the generation of all the grammatically correct and semantically meaningful elements of a natural language, whereas a philosophical hermeneutics reflects upon the basic experiences of communicatively competent speakers whose linguistic competence is tacitly presupposed. This distinction between rational reconstruction and self-reflection I would like to introduce by just giving one intuitive example.

Through *self-reflection* a subject becomes aware of the unconscious pre-suppositions of completed acts. Hermeneutic consciousness is thus the outcome of a process of self-reflection in which a speaking subject recognized his specific freedom from, and dependence on, language. This leads to the dissolution of a semblance, both of a subjectivist and an objectivist kind, which captivates naive consciousness. Self-reflection throws light on experiences a subject makes while exercising his communicative competence, but it cannot explain this competence. The rational *reconstruction* of a system of linguistic rules, in contrast, is undertaken with the aim of explaining linguistic competence. It makes explicit those rules which a native speaker has an implicit command of; but it does not as such make the subject conscious of suppositions he is not aware of. The speaker's subjectivity, constituting the horizon within which reflexive experience can be gained, remains excluded in principle.

One could say that a successful linguistic reconstruction makes us conscious of the apparatus of language that is functioning without us being aware of it. This would, however, be an inauthentic use of language, since the consciousness of the speaker is not changed by this linguistic knowledge. What, then, is the relevance of hermeneutic consciousness if a philosophical hermeneutic is as little concerned with the art of understanding and of speech as it is with linguistics, i.e. if its usefulness is equally limited in relation to the pre-scientific exercise of communicative competence as it is for the scientific study of language?

It is nevertheless possible to cite four aspects in which a philosophical hermeneutic is relevant to the sciences and the interpretation of their results. (1) Hermeneutic consciousness destroys the objectivist self-understanding of the traditonal *Geisteswissenschaften*. It follows from the hermeneutic situatedness of the interpreting scientist that objectivity in understanding cannot be secured by an abstraction from preconceived ideas, but only by reflecting upon the context of effective-history which connects perceiving subjects and their object.[5] (2) Hermeneutic consciousness furthermore reminds the social sciences of problems which arise from the symbolic pre-structuring of their object. If the access to data is no longer mediated through controlled observation but through communication in everyday language, then theoretical concepts can no longer be operationalized within the framework of the pre-scientifically developed language-game of physical measuring. The probelms that arise on the level of measuring recur on the level of theory-construction: the choice of a categorical framework and of basic theoretical predicates has to correspond to a tentative preconception of the object.[6] (3) Hermeneutic consciousness also affects the scientistic self-understanding of the natural sciences but not, of course, their methodology. The insight that natural language represents the 'last' metalanguage for all theories expressed in formal language elucidates the empistemological locus of everyday language within scientific activity. The legitimation of decisions which direct the choice of research strategies, the construction of theories and the methods for testing them, and which thereby determine the 'progress of science', is dependent on discussions within the community of scientists. These discussions, which are conducted on the level of meta-theory, are nevertheless tied up in principle to the context of natural language and to the explicative forms of everyday communication. A philosophical hermeneutic can show the reason why it is possible to arrive at a rationally motivated but not at a peremptory consensus on this theoretic level. (4) Hermeneutic consciousness is, finally, called upon in one area of interpretation more than in any other and one which is of great social interest: the translation of important scientific information into the language of the social life-world. 'What would we know of modern physics which so visibly alters our existence from physics alone? Its portrayal, which aims beyond the circle of experts, is dependent on a rhetorical element for its impact. . . . All science that hopes to be of practical use is dependent on rhetoric.'[7]

The objective need to rationally relate technically utilizable knowledge to the practical knowledge of the life-world is explained by the function which scinetific–technological progress has acquired for the maintenance of the system of developed industrial societies. It is my opinion that a philosophical hermeneutics tries to satisfy this need with its claim to universality. Hermeneutic consciousness can open the path towards 'integrating again the experience of science into our own general and human life-experience'[8] only when it is possible to consider 'the universality of human linguisticality as an element that is itself unlimited and that supports everything, not just linguistically transmitted cultural objects',[9] Gadamer refers to Plato's saying that he who considers objects in the mirror of speech arrives at their whole and uncurtailed truth – 'in the mirror of language everything that exists is reflected'.[10]

This specific historical theme, which itself led to the efforts of a philosophical hermeneutic, does not, however, correspond to Plato's statement. It is obviously the case that modern science can legitimately claim to arrive at true statements about 'things' by proceeding monologically instead of considering the mirror of human speech: that is, by formulating theories which are monologically constructed and which are supported by controlled observation. It is because hypothetic–deductive systems of propositions of science do not form an element of everyday speech that the information derived from them is removed from the life-world which is articulated in natural language. Of course, the transference of technically utilizable knowledge into the context of the life-world requires that monologically generated knowledge be made intelligible within the dimension of speech, i.e. within the dialogue of everyday language; and this transference does, of course, represent a hermeneutic problem – but it is a problem that is new to hermeneutics itself. Hermeneutic consciousness does, after all, emerge from a reflection upon our own movement *within* natural language, whereas the interpretation of science on behalf of the life-world has to achieve a mediation *between* natural language *and* monological language systems. This process of translation transcends the limitations of a rhetorical–hermeneutical art which has only been dealing with cultural products that were handed down and which are constituted by everyday language. Going beyond hermeneutic consciousness, that has established itself in the course of the reflexive exercise of this art, it would be the task of a philosophical hermeneutic to clarify the conditions for the possibility to, as it were, step outside the dialogical structure of everyday language and to use language in a monological way for the formal construction of theories and for the organization of purposive rational action.

At this stage I would like to include, parenthetically, some considerations. Jean Piaget's[11] genetic epistemology uncovers the non-linguistic roots of operative thought. It is certainly the case that the latter can only reach maturity through the integration of cognitive schemes, which emerge pre-linguistically within the sphere of instrumental action, with the linguistic systems of rules. But there is sufficient indication that language merely 'sits upon' categories such as space, time, causality and substance, and rules for the formal–logical combination of symbols which possess a *pre*-linguistic basis. With the help of this hypothesis it is possible to understand the monological use of language for the organization of purposive–rational action and for the construction of scientific theories; in these cases, natural language is, in a manner of speaking, removed from the structure of intersubjectivity; without its dialogue-constitutive elements and separated from communication it would be solely under the conditions of operative intelligence. The clarification of this issue is still to be completed; it will, in any case, be of relevance for deciding upon our question. If it is the case that operative intelligence goes back to pre-linguistic, cognitive schemes, and is therefore able to use language in an instrumental way, then the hermeneutic claim to universality would find its limit in the linguistic systems of science and the theories of rational choice. On the basis of this pre-supposition it could be made plausible why monologically constructed systems of language, even though they cannot be interpreted without recourse to natural language, can nevertheless be 'understood' while by-passing the hermeneutic problem; the conditions for understanding would not, at the same time, be the conditions for everyday communication. That would only be the case once the content of rigorously contructed theories were to be translated into the context of the life-world of speech.

I cannot deal with this problem now, but I would like to put the question concerning the validity of the hermeneutic claim to universality in a different way. Can there be an understanding of meaning in relation to symbolic structures formulated in everyday language that is not tied to the hermeneutic pre-supposition of context-dependent processes of understanding, an understanding that in this sense by-passes natural language as the last metalanguage? Since hermeneutical understanding always has to proceed in an ad hoc way and cannot be developed into a scientific method – it can at best be developed into an art – this question is equivalent to the problem of whether there can be a theory appropriate to the structure of natural languages on which a methodical understanding of meaning can be based.

I can envisage two ways which promise success in looking for a solution.

On the one hand we hit upon a non-trivial limit to the sphere of hermeneutical understanding in cases which are dealt with by psychoanalysis – or the critique of ideology where collective phenomena are concerned. Both deal with objectivations in everyday language in which the subject does not recognize the intentions which guided his expressive activity. These manifestations can be regarded as parts of systematically distorted communication. They are comprehensible only to the extent to which the general conditions of the pathology of everyday communication are known. A theory of everyday communication would first of all have to beat a path through to the pathologically blocked meaning-context. If the claim to represent such a theory were justified, then an explanatory understanding would be possible which transcended the limit of the hermeneutical understanding of meaning.

On the other hand, representatives of generative linguistics have for more than a decade been working on a renewed programme of a general theory of natural languages. This theory is meant to provide a rational reconstruction of a regulative system that adequately defines general linguistic competence. If this claim could be fulfilled in such a way that each element of a natural language can definitely be attached to structural descriptions formulated in theoretical language, then the latter could take the place of the hermeneutical understanding of meaning.

I cannot deal with this problem either in the present context. In the following, I shall only consider the question whether a critical science such as psychoanalysis can by-pass the way skilful interpretation is tied to the natural competence of everyday communication with the help of a theoretically based semantic analysis – and thereby refute the hermeneutic claim to universality. These investigations will help us to establish more precisely in what sense it is nevertheless possible to defend the basic hermeneutic tenet that we cannot transcend 'the dialogue which we are', to use Gadamer's romanticist formulation.

II

Hermeneutic consciousness remains incomplete as long as it does not include a reflection upon the limits of hermeneutic understanding. The experience of a hermeneutical limitation refers to specifically incomprehensible expressions. This specific incomprehensibility cannot be overcome by the exercise, however skilful, of one's naturally acquired communicative competence; its stubbornness can be regarded as an indication that it cannot be explained by sole reference to the structure of everyday communication that hermeneutic philosophy has brought to light.

In this case it is not the objectivity of linguistic tradition, the finite horizon of a linguistically articulated understanding of life, the potential incomprehensibility of what is implicitly regarded as self-evident, that stands in the way of the interpretative effort.

In cases where understanding proves difficult owing to great cultural, temporal or social distance it is still possible for us to state in principle what additional information we require in order to fully understand: we know that we have to decipher an alphabet, get to know a vocabulary or rules of application which are specific to their context. Within the limits of tolerance of normal everyday communication it is possible for us to determine what we do not – yet – know when we try to make sense of an incomprehensible complex of meaning. This hermeneutic consciousness proves inadequate in the case of systematically distorted communication: incomprehensibility is here the result of a defective organization of speech itself. Openly pathological speech defects which are apparent, for example, among psychotics, can be disregarded by hermeneutics without impairment of its self-conception. The area of applicability of hermeneutics is congruent with the limits of normal everyday speech, as long as pathological cases are excluded. The self-conception of hermeneutics can only be shaken when it appears that patterns of systematically distorted communication are also in evidence in 'normal', let us call it pathologically unobtrusive, speech. This is the case in the pseudo-communication in which the participants cannot recognize a breakdown in their communication; only an external observer notices that they misunderstand one another. Pseudo-communication generates a system of misunderstandings that cannot be recognized as such under the appearance of a false consensus.

Hermeneutics has taught us that we are always a participant as long as we move within the natural language and that we cannot step outside the role of a reflective partner. There is, therefore, no general criterion available to us which would allow us to determine when we are subject to the false consciousness of a pseudo-normal understanding and consider something as a difficulty that can be resolved by hermeneutical means when, in fact, it requires systematic explanation. The experience of the limit of hermeneutics consists of the recognition of systematically generated misunderstanding as such – without, at first, being able to 'grasp' it.

Freud has drawn on this experience of systematically distorted communication in order to demarcate a sphere of specifically incomprehensible expressions. He always regarded dreams as the 'standard model' for those phenomena which themselves extend innocuous pseudo-communication and parapraxes in everyday life to the pathological manifestions of neuroses, mental illness and psychosomatic complaints. In his writings on the theory of civilization Freud extended the sphere of systematically distorted communication and he used the insights gained in dealing with clinical phenomena as a key for pseudo-normality, i.e. the hidden pathology of societal systems. We shall first of all focus on the sphere of neurotic manifestations that has received the fullest explanation.

There are available three criteria for demarcating neurotically distorted, which here means specifically incomprehensible, forms of expression. On the level of linguistic symbols, distorted communication is apparent in the application of rules which deviate from the publicly accepted rule-system. It is possible for an isolated semantic content of complete fields of meaning, in extreme cases even the syntax, to be affected. Freud examined the content of dreams mainly in relation to condensation, displacement, a-grammaticality and the role of contraries. On the level of the behaviour, a deformed language game is noticeable because of its rigidity and compulsion to repeat. Stereotyped patterns of behaviour recur in situations with the same stimuli which give rise to affective impulses. This inflexibility is an indication that the semantic content of a symbol has lost its specifically linguistic situational independence. When we consider the system of distorted communication as a whole it becomes apparent that there exists a characteristic discrepancy between the levels of communication: the usual congruence between linguistic symbols, actions and accompanying expressions has disintegrated. Neurotic symptoms are merely the most stubborn and manifest evidence of this dissonance. No matter on what level of communication these symptoms appear – in linguistic expression, body-language or compulsive behaviour – it is always the case that a content, which has been excommunicated from its public usage, assumes independence. This content expresses an intention which remains incomprehensible according to the rules of public communication, and is, in this sense, privatized; but it also remains inaccessible to its author. There exists within the self a barrier to communication between the 'I' who is linguistically competent and who participates in intersubjectivity established language-games, and that 'inner exile' (Freud) that is represented by the symbolic system of a private or protogenal language.

Alfred Lorenzer has examined the analytical dialogue between doctor and patient from the point of view of psychoanalysis as a linguistic analysis.[12] He conceives of the depth-hermeneutical decoding of the meaning of specifically incomprehensible objectivations as an understanding of analogous scenes. The aim of analytical interpretation, seen hermeneutically, consists of the clarification of the incomprehensible meaning of symptomatic expressions. As far as neuroses are concerned, these expressions represent part of a deformed language-game within which the patient 'acts': he enacts an incomprehensible scene by contravening, in a conspicuous and steotyped way, existing expectations of behaviour. The analyst tries to render understandable the meaning of a symptomatic scene by relating the latter to analogous scenes in a sitution which contains the key to the coded relationship between the symptomatic scene which the adult patient enacts outside his treatment on the one hand, and to the original scene of his early childhood on the other, in the transfer situation. This is because the analyst is pushed into the role of the conflict-charged primary object. In his role as reflective partner the analyst can interpret the transference as a repetition of scenes of early childhood and can thereby draw up a lexicon of the meanings of these symptomatic expressions which are formulated in a private language. Scenic understanding proceeds, therefore, from the insight that the patient behaves in his symptomatic scenes as he does in certain transference scenes; it aims at a reconstruction of the original scene in which the patient validates in an act of self-reflection.

As Lorenzer has demonstrated by reference to the phobia of Little Hans whom Freud examined, the reconstructed original scene is typically a situation in which a child suffers an intolerable conflict which he then represses. This defence is connected with a process of desymbolization and of symptom-formation. The child excludes the experience of conflictive object-relations from public communication (and thereby renders it inaccessible even to his own Ego); it splits off the part of the representation of the object that is charged with conflict and, in a way, desymbolizes the meaning of the relevant object. The gap that appears in the semantic field is closed by a symptom, in that an unsuspicious symbol takes the place of the symbolic content that has been split off. This symbol is, however, as conspicuous as a symptom since it has gained a private meaning and can no longer be used in accordance with the rules of public language. Scenic understanding establishes an equivalence of meaning between the elements of three patterns: everyday scene, transference scene and original scene; it thereby breaks through the specific incomprehensibility of the symptom and assists in the re-symbolization, i.e. the re-introduction into public communication of a symbolic content that has been split off. The latent meaning underlying the present situation is rendered comprehensible by reference to the unmutilated meaning of the original scene in infancy. Scenic understanding makes possible the 'translation' into public communication of the sense of a pathologically petrified pattern of communication which has so far remained inaccessible, but which determined behaviour.

Scenic understanding is distinguishable from the elementary hermeneutical understanding of meaning by its explanatory potential; it makes accessible the meaning of specifically incomprehensible forms of expression only to the extent to which it is possible to clarify the conditions for the emergence of nonsense in conjunction with the reconstruction of the original scene. The 'what', the meaning-content of sytematically distorted expressions, can only be 'understood' when it is possible to answer, at the same time, the 'why' question, i.e. to 'explain' the emergence of the symptomatic scene by reference to the initial conditions of the sytematic distortion itself.

This understanding can acquire an explanatory function in the narrow sense only if the analysis of meaning does not rely solely on the skilled application of communicative competence but is guided by theoretical assumptions. I name two points of evidence to show that scenic understanding relies on theoretical pre-suppositions which in no way follow automatically from the natural competence of a native speaker.

Scenic understanding is, first of all, tied to a specific hermeneutical form of experimentation. The analytical rule introduced by Frued guarantees a form of communication between doctor and patient which, as it were, fulfils experimental conditions; virtualization of an actual situation and free association on the part of the patient, and goal-inhibited reaction and reflective participation by the analyst, make it possible that a transference occurs which can be used as a foil for the task of 'translation'. Secondly, the analyst's pre-understanding is directed at a small segment of possible meanings: viz. early, conflictive object-relations. The linguistic material that emerges in talks with the patient is classified within a closely circumscribed context of possible double meaning. This context consists of a general interpretation of infant patterns of interaction which is correlated with a theory of personality that exhibits specific phases of development. Both these aspects show that scenic understanding cannot be regarded in the same way as hermeneutical understanding, i.e. as a non-theoretical application of communicative competence which makes theorizing possible in the first place.

The theoretical assumptions tacitly underlying depth-hermeneutical language analysis can be developed in relation to three aspects. The psychoanalyst has a pre-conception of the structure of undistorted everyday communication (1); he traces the systematic distortion of communication back to the confusion of pre-linguistic and linguistic organization of symbols which are separated as two stages in the developmental process (2); he explains the emergence of deformations with the aid of a theory of deviant processes of socialization which extends on to the connection of patterns of infant interaction with the formation of personality (3). I need not here develop these theoretical assumptions in a systematic way; but I would like to illustrate briefly the aspects just mentioned.

1 The first set of theoretical assumptions refers to the structural conditions that have to be met when talking about 'normal' everyday communication.

(a) In non-deformed language-games there exists a congruence of expression on all three levels of communication; those utterances symbolized linguistically, those that are presented in actions, and those embodied in physical expressions do not contradict but complement one another metacommunicatively. Indeed contradictions, which themselves contain a message, are, in this sense, regarded as normal. It is a further aspect of the normal form of everyday communication that a part of extra-verbal meanings, which varies with its socio-cultural context but which remains constant within a language-community, is intentional, i.e. in principle verbalizable.

(b) Normal everyday language follows intersubjectively valid rules: it is public. Communicated meanings are, in principle, identical for all members of a language-community. Verbal utterances are formed in agreement with the valid system of grammatical rules and are applied in a specific context; there also exists a lexicon for all extra-verbal utterances not following grammatical rules which varies within limits between socio-cultural contexts.

(c) In normal speech, the speakers are aware of the categorical difference between subject and object. They differentiate between outer and inner speech and separate private and public existence. The differentiation between reality and appearance is, in addition, dependent on the difference between linguistic symbol, its meaning-content (signification) and the object referred to by the symbol (referent, denotation). Only on this basis is it possible to use linguistic symbols independently of a given situation (decontextualization). The speaking subject becomes capable of distinguishing between reality and appearance to the extent which language acquires for him an existence separate from the denoted objects and the represented state of affairs as well as from private experiences.

(d) It is in normal everyday communication that the intersubjectivity of relations which secures the identity of individuals who mutually recognize one another is formed and maintained. Whereas the analytical use of language allows the identification of states of affairs (i.e. the categorization of objects by means of the identification of the specific, the subsumption of elements under classes, and the inclusion of aggregates), the relexive use of of language secures the relationship of speaking subject to a language-community, which is something that cannot be adequately represented with the mentioned analytical operations. The intersubjectivity of a world, which the subjects can inhabit on the strength of their communication in everyday language alone, is not a generality under which individuals are subsumed in the same way as elements under a class. It is, rather, the case that the relations between I, You (other I) and We (I and the other Is) are established through an analytically paradoxical achievement. The speakers identify themselves with two mutually incompatible dialogic roles and thereby secure the identity of the I as well as that of the group. The one (I) affirms his absolute non-identity *vis-à-vis* the other (You); but at the same time both recognize their own identity by accepting one another as irreplaceable individuals. In this process they are connected by something they share (We), i.e. a group which itself affirms its individuality *vis-à-vis* other groups, so that the same relations are established on the level of intersubjectively united collectives as exist between individuals.[13]

The specific point about linguistic intersubjectivity is that individuated persons can communicate on the basis of it. In the reflexive use of language we formulate what is inalienable and individual in general categories; we do this in such a way that we, as it were, metacommunicatively retract (and confirm with reservation) our direct message in order to express indirectly that part of the I that is non-identical and that cannot be represented by general determinations – even though they are the only means for expressing it.[14] The analytical use of language is embedded within the reflexive use, since the intersubjectivity of everyday communication cannot be maintained without the reciprocal self-representation of speaking subjects. A speaker can distinguish between reality and appearance to the extent to which he has a mastery of those indirect means of communication on the level of metacommunication. It is possible for us to communicate directly about states of affairs, but the subjectivity we encounter in the course of talking to one another appears only as a surface-phenomenon in direct forms of communication. The categorial meaning of indirect forms of communication which give expression to that which is individualized and unsayable is merely ontologized in the concept of an entity that exists in its appearances.

(e) Finally, it is characteristic of normal speech that the sense of substance and causality, space and time differs depending on whether these categories are applied to objects in the world or to the linguistically constituted world of speaking subjects itself. The interpretive scheme 'substance' has a different sense in the identity of objects which can be categorized in an analytically unequivocal way from the one it has for speaking and acting subjects whose Ego-identity cannot be captured in analytically unequivocal operations. The causal interpretive scheme leads to the concept of physical 'cause' if applied to the empirical consequences of events, and also to the concept of 'motive' in the context of intentional action. Space and time are, analogously, schematized differently in respect to the physically measurable properties of objects and events than in respect of the intersubjective experience of contexts of symbolically mediated interaction. In the first case categories are employed as a system of co-ordinates for observations which are checked by the success of instrumental action; in the second case they serve as a frame of reference for subjective experiences of social space and historical time. The parameter of possible experiences in the field of intersubjectivity changes complementarity to the parameter of possible experiences about objectivated objects and events.

2 The second set of assumptions refers to the relationship between two genetically consecutive stages of the human organization of symbols.

(a) The earlier organization of symbols which does not allow the transposition of its contents into grammatically regulated communication can only be investigated through data about the pathology of speech and on the basis of an analysis of the content of dreams. We are here concerned with symbols which direct behaviour and not just with signs since symbols possess an authentic meaning-function; they represent experiences gained in interaction. This layer of paleo-symbols is, however, devoid of all the properties of normal speech.[15] Paleo-symbols are not integrated into a system of grammatical rules. They are unordered elements and do not arise within a system that could be transformed grammatically. It is for this reason that the functioning of pre-linguistic symbols has been compared with that of analogy computers in contrast to digital computers. Freud had already noticed the lack of logical connections in his analyses of dreams. In particular, he points to contraries which have preserved, on the linguistic level, the genetically earlier characteristic of an ensemble of logically irreconcilable, that is contrary, meanings.[16] Pre-linguistic symbols are highly charged affectively and are tied to specific scenes; there is also no separation between linguistic symbol and bodily expression. They are tied to a specific context so closely that symbols cannot vary freely in relation to action.[17] Even though paleo-symbols represent the pre-linguistic basis for the intersubjectivity of co-existence and collective action they do not lend themselves to public communication in the strict sense. This is because the constancy of meaning is low while the proportion of private meanings is, at the same time, high: they cannot yet guarantee an intersubjectively binding identity of meaning. The privatism of the pre-linguistic organization of symbols, which is apparent in all forms of pathological speech, can be traced back to the fact that the distance which is maintained in everday speech between addressor and addressee has not yet been developed, and neither has the distinction between symbolic sign, semantic content and referent. Nor is it as yet possible, by means of paleo-symbols, to differentiate clearly between the level of reality and that of appearance, and between public and private world (adualism).

Pre-linguistic organization of symbols does not, finally, allow only satisfactory categorization of the experienced world of objects. Among the disorders of communication and thought processes apparent in psychotics[18] one can find two extreme forms of malfunctioning; in both cases, the analytical operation of classification is disturbed. There exists, firstly, a structure of fragmentation that does not allow the comprehension of disintegrated individual elements into classes by following general criteria. Secondly, one can find an amorphous structure that does not allow any analysis of aggregates of objects which resemble each other superficially and which are vaguely grouped together. The use of symbols has not become impossible in its entirety. But the inability to form hierarchies of classes and to identify elements of classes indicates in both cases the collapse of the analytical use of language. It is, of course, possible to conclude on the basis of the second variation that an archaic formation of classes is possible by means of pre-linguistic symbols. In any case, we can find so-called primary classes, which are not formed on the abstract basis of the identity of properties, in the early stages of ontogenitic and phylogenetic developments and in cases of speech-pathology. The aggregates in question, in fact, comprehend concrete objects in view of an overarching, subjectively convincing context of motivation irrespective of their identifiable properties. Animistic cosmologies are organized in accordance with such primary classes. Since comprehensive intentional structures cannot be developed without any experience of interaction one can assume that early forms of intersubjectivity are already developed in the pre-linguistic stage of symbol-organization. Paleo-symbols are, apparently, formed in contexts of interaction before they are incorporated into a system of grammatical rules and connected to operative intelligence.

(b) The organization of symbols described above, which is genetically prior to language, is a theoretical construction. It can nowhere be observed. The psychoanalytic decoding of systematically distorted communication pre-supposes such a construction, however, since depth-hermeneutics comprehends confusions of normal speech either as forced regression to earlier stages of communiction or as the intrusion of an earlier form of communication into language. Basing himself on an analyst's experience of neurotic patients, Alfred Lorenzer sees the essence of psychoanalysis, as has been already shown, as the attempt to re-integrate split-off symbolic contents, which led to a privatistic narrowing of public communications, into the general usage of language. Analysis helps to achieve a 'resymbolization' by retracting, and thereby undoing, the process of repression; the latter can, therefore, be regarded as a process of 'desymbolization'. The patient reacts against the analyst's cogent interpretation by the defence mechanism of repression, which is analogous to a taking to flight; this is an operation that takes place through and against language – otherwise it would be impossible to undo the defensive process by hermeneutical means, i.e. through the analysis of language. The fleeing Ego that in situations of conflict is forced to submit to the claims of external reality hides before itself by removing the representatives of the claims of unwelcome drives from the text of its everyday self-understanding. By means of this censorship, the representation of the tabooed object of love is excommunicated from the public use of language and, as it were, pushed back into the genetically earlier stage of paleo-symbols.

The assumption that neurotic behaviour is guided by paleo-symbols and is only subsequently rationalized by linguistic interpretation also provides an explanation for the characteristics of this form of behaviour: for its status as pseudo-communication, stereotyped and compulsive behaviour, emotional attachment, expressive content and inflexible situational tie.

If repression can be regarded as desymbolization then it is possible to provide a language-analytical interpretation for a complementary defensive mechanism that is not directed at the self but at external reality, viz. projection and disavowal. Whereas in the first case the public use of language is mutilated by symptoms that have been formed in place of excommunicated linguistic elements, distortion in the second case is directly attributable to the uncontrolled intrusion of paleo-symbolic derivatives into language. Language analysis does not aim here at the re-transformation of desymbolized contents into linguistically articulate meaning, but at a consciously undertaken excommunication of pre-linguistic elements. In both instances, systematic distortion of everyday communication can be explained by reference to semantic contents which are tied to paleo-symbols and which encyst within language like alien bodies. It is the task of language analysis to dissolve these syndromes, i.e. to isolate both levels of language.

In processes of linguistic creation, however, there occurs a genuine integration; the meaning-potential tied to paleo-symbols is publicly retrieved in the creative use of language and is utilized for the grammatically guided use of symbols.[19] The transference of semantic contents from the pre-linguistic to the linguistic state of aggregation widens the sphere of communicative action at the expense of the unconsciously motivated one. The moment of successful, creative use of language is one of emancipation.

This is not so in the case of jokes. The laughter with which we almost compulsively respond to a joke is witness to the liberative experience of the transition from the stage of paleo-symbols to that of linguistic thought; the funny element consists in the demasking of the ambiguity of the joke which resides in the teller enticing us to regress to the stage of pre-linguistic symbolism, i.e. to confuse identity and resemblance, and at the same time to convict us of the mistake of this regression. The ensuing laughter is one of relief. In our response to a joke, which leads us to retrace, virtually and experimentally, the dangerous passage across the archaic boundary between pre-linguistic and linguistic communication, we become reassured of the control we have achieved over the dangers of a superseded stage of consciousness.

3 Depth-hermeneutics, which clarifies the specific incomprehensibility of distorted communication, can, strictly speaking, no longer be considered in relation to the model of translation, as is the case with ordinary hermeneutical understanding. This is because the controlled 'translation' or pre-linguistic symbolism into language removes obscurities which do not arise within language but through language itself; it is the structure of everyday communication, which provides the basis of translation, which is itself affected. Depth-hermeneutical understanding requires, therefore, a systematic pre-understanding that extends onto language in general, whereas hermeneutical understanding always proceeds from a pre-understanding that is shaped by tradition and which forms and changes itself within linguistic communication. The theoretical assumptions which relate, on the one hand, to two stages in the organization of symbols and, on the other hand, to processes of de- and re-symbolization, to the intrusion of paleo-symbolic elements into language and the conscious excommunication of these interspersals, as well as to the integration of pre-linguistic symbolic contents – these theoretical assumptions can be integrated into a structural model which Freud derived from his experiences gained in the analysis of the mechanism of defence. The constructions of the 'Ego' and the 'Id' interpret the analyst's experience of resistance on the part of the patient.

'Ego' is the portion of the personality that fulfils the task of examining reality and of censuring drives. 'Id' is the name for those parts of the self which have been separated from the Ego and the existence of which becomes accessible in connection with the mechanisms of defence. The 'Id' is indirectly represented by symptoms which fill the gaps in normal discourse that appeared in the course of de-symbolization; It is directly represented by those delusory paleo-symbolic elements which enter language through projection and disavowal. The same clinical experience of 'resistance' which led to the construction of the structures Ego and Id now also shows that defensive processes occur mainly unconsciously. This is why Freud introduced the category of 'Super-ego': an agency of defence unknown to the Ego which is formed through the open-ended identification with the expectations of the primary object. All three categories, Ego, Id and Super-ego, are consequently tied to the specific sense of a systematically distorted communication which analyst and patient enter into with the aim of initiating a dialogical process of enlightenment, and to encourage and guide the patient towards self-reflection. Metapsychology can only be established as meta-hermeneutics.[20]

The structural model implicitly relies upon a model of the deformation of everyday intersubjectivity; the dimensions of Id and Super-ego within the structure of personality clearly correspond to the deformation of that structure of intersubjectivity which is apparent in communication free from domination. The structure model which Freud introduced as the categorial frame of metapsychology can, consequently, be traced back to a theory of the distortion of communicative competence.

Metapsychology consists, in the main, of assumptions about the formation of personality structures which, too, can be explained by reference to the meta-hermeneutical role of psychoanalysis. The understanding of the analyst derives, as we have seen, its explanatory force from the fact that the clarification of systematically inaccessible sense can succeed only to the extent that the origin of this non-sense can itself be explained. The reconstruction of the original scene can do both at the same time; it makes it possible to understand the meaning of deformed language-games and, together with it, to explain the origin of this deformation. This is why scenic understanding pre-supposes a metapsychology in the sense of a theory of the formation of the structure of Ego, Id and Super-ego.

On the sociological level, this finds its correspondence in the theory of the acquisition of the basic qualifications for role-guided behaviour. But both theories are part of a meta-hermeneutic which traces back the psychological development of personality structures and the acquisition of the basic qualifications for role-guided behaviour to the development of communicative competence; this is the socializing introduction into, and practising of, forms of the intersubjectivity of everyday communication. It is now possible to answer our original question: explanatory understanding, in the sense of the depth-hermeneutical decoding of specifically inadequate expressions, does not only necessitate the skilled application of naturally acquired communicative competence, as it is the case with elementary hermeneutical understanding, but also presupposes a theory of communicative competence. The latter covers the forms of the intersubjectivity of language and causes of its deformation. I cannot say that a theory of communicative competence has up until now been attempted in a satisfactory way, never mind been explicitly developed. Freud's metapsychology would have to be freed of its scientistic self-miscomprehension before it could be utilized as a part of a meta-hermeneutic. I would say, however, that each depth-hermeneutical interpretation of systematically distorted communication, irrespective of whether it appears in an analytic encounter or informally, implicitly relies on those demanding theoretical assumptions which can only be developed and justified within the framework of a *theory of communicative competence.*

III

What follows from this hermeneutic claim to universality? Is it not the case that the theoretical language of a meta-hermeneutic is subject to the same reservation as all other theories: that a given non-reconstructed everyday language remains the last meta-language? And would not the application of general interpretations, which are deducible from such theories, to material given in everyday language still require basic hermeneutical understanding which is not replaceable by any generalized measuring procedure? Neither of these questions would any longer have to be answered in accordance with the hermeneutic claim to universality if the knowing subject, who necessarily has to draw on his previously acquired linguistic competence, could assure himself explicitly of this competence in the course of a theoretical reconstruction. We have so far bracketed this problem of a general theory of natural language. But we can already refer to this competence, which the analyst (and the critic of ideologies) has to employ factually in the disclosure of specifically incomprehensible expressions, in advance of all theory construction. Already the *implicit knowledge of the conditions of systematically distorted communiction*, which is pre-supposed in an actual form in the depth-hermeneutical use of communicative competence, *is sufficient for the questioning of the ontological self-understanding of the philosophical hermeneutic* which Gadamer propounds by following Heidegger.

Gadamer turns the context-dependency of the understanding of meaning, which hermeneutic philosophy has brought to consciousness and which requires us always to proceed from a pre-understanding that is supported by tradition as well as to continuously form a new pre-understanding in the course of being corrected, to the ontologically inevitable primacy of linguistic tradition.[21] Gadamer poses the question: 'Is the phenomenon of understanding adequately defined when I state that to understand is to avoid misunderstanding? Is it not, rather, the case that something like a 'supporting consensus' precedes all misunderstanding.[22] We can agree on the answer, which is to be given in the affirmative, but not on how to define this preceding consensus.

If I understand correctly, then Gadamer is of the opinion that the hermeneutical clarification of incomprehensible or misunderstood expressions always has to lead back to a consensus that has already been reliably established through converging tradition. This tradition is objective in relation to us in the sense that we cannot confront it with a principled claim to truth. The pre-judgmental structure of understanding not only prohibits us from questioning that factually established consensus which underlies our misunderstanding and incomprehension, but makes such an undertaking appear senseless. It is a hermeneutical requirement that we refer to a concrete pre-understanding which itself, in the last analysis, goes back to the process of socialization, i.e. the introduction into a shared tradition. None of them is, in principle, beyond criticism; but neither can they be questioned abstractly. This would only be possible if we could examine a consensus that has been achieved through mutual understanding by, as it were, looking into it from the side and subjecting it, behind the backs of the participants, to renewed demands for legitimation. But we can only make demands of this kind in the face of the participants by entering into a dialogue with them. In this case we submit, yet again, to the hermeneutic demand to accept, for the time being, the clarifying consensus which the resumed dialogue might arrive at, as a supporting agreement. It would be senseless to abstractly suspect this agreement, which, admittedly, is contingent, of being false consciousness since we cannot transcend the dialogue which we are. This leads Gadamer to conclude to the ontological priority of linguistic tradition over all possible critique; we can consequently criticize specific traditions only on the basis that we are part of the comprehensive context of the tradition of a language.

On first sight, these considerations seem plausible. They can, however, be shaken by the depth-hermeneutical insight that a consensus achieved by seemingly 'reasonable' means may well be the result of pseudo-communication. Albrecht Wellmer has pointed out that the Enlightenment tradition generalized this insight which is hostile to tradition. However much the Enlightenment was interested in communication, it still demanded that Reason be recognized as the principle of communication, free from force in the face of the real experience of communication distorted by force:

> The Enlightenment knew what a philosophical hermeneutic forgets – that the 'dialogue' which we, according to Gadamer, 'are', is also a context of domination and as such precisely no dialogue. . . . The universal claim of the hermeneutic approach [can only] be maintained if it is realized at the outset that the context of tradition as a locus of possible truth and factual agreement is, at the same time, the locus of factual untruth and continued force.[23]

It would only be legitimate for us to equate the supporting consensus which, according to Gadamer, always precedes any failure at mutual understanding with a given factual agreement, if we could be certain that each consensus arrived at in the medium of linguistic tradition has been achieved without compulsion and distortion. But we learn from depth-hermeneutic experience that the dogmatism of the context of tradition is subject not only to the objectivity of language in general but also to the repressivity of forces which deform the intersubjectivity of agreement as such and which systematically distort everyday communication. It is for this reason that every consensus, as the outcome of an understanding of meaning, is, in principle, suspect of having been enforced through pseudo-communication: in earlier days, people talked about delusion when misunderstanding and self-misunderstanding continued unaffected under the appearance of factual agreement. Insight into the pre-judgmental structure of the understanding of meaning does not cover the identification of actually achieved consensus with a true one. It, rather, leads to the ontologization of language and to the hypostatization of the context of tradition. A critically enlightened hermeneutic that differentiates between insight and delusion incorporates the meta-hermeneutic awareness of the conditions for the possibility of systematically distorted communication. It connects the process of understanding to the principle of rational discourse, according to which truth would only be guaranteed by *that* kind of consensus which was achieved under the idealized conditions of unlimited communication free from domination and could be maintained over time.

K.-O. Apel rightly emphasized that hermeneutical understanding can, at the same time, lead to the critical ascertainment of truth only to the extent to which it follows the regulative principle: to try to establish universal agreement within the framework of an unlimited community of interpreters.[24] Only this principle can make sure that the hermeneutic effort does not cease until we are aware of deceptions within a forcible consensus and of the systematic distortion behind seemingly accidental misunderstanding. If the understanding of meaning is not to remain *a fortiori* indifferent towards the idea of truth then we have to anticipate, together with the concept of a kind of truth which measures itself on an idealized consensus achieved in unlimited communication free from domination, also the structures of solidary co-existence in communication free from force. Truth is that characteristic compulsion towards unforced universal recognition; the latter is itself tied to an ideal speech situation, i.e. a form of life, which makes possible unforced universal agreement. The critical understanding of meaning thus has to take upon itself the formal anticipation of a true life. This has already been expressed by G. H. Mead:[25]

> Universal discourse is the formal ideal of communication. If communication can be carried through and made perfect, then there would exist a kind of democracy . . . in which each individual would carry just the response in himself that he knows he calls out in the community. That is what makes communication in the significant sense the organising process in the community.

The idea of truth, which measures itself on a true consensus, implies the idea of the true life. We could also say: it includes the idea of being-of-age (*Mündigkeit*).[26] It is only the formal anticipation of an idealized dialogue, as the form of life to be realized in the future, which guarantees the ultimate supporting and contra-factual agreement that already unites us; in relation to it we can criticize every factual agreement, should it be a false one, as false consciousness. It is, however, only when we can show that the anticipation of possible truth and a true life is constitutive for every linguistic communication which is not monological that we are in a position not merely to demand but to justify that regulative principle of understanding. Basic meta-hermeneutic experience makes us aware of the fact that critique, as a penetrating form of understanding which does not rebound off delusions, orients itself on the concept of ideal consensus and thereby follows the regulative principle of rational discourse. But to justify the view that we not only do, but indeed have to, engage in that formal anticipation in the course of every penetrating understanding, is not enough merely to refer to experience alone. To attempt a systematic justification we have to develop the implicit knowledge, that always and already guides the depth-hermeneutical analysis of language, into a theory which would enable us to deduce the principle of rational discourse from the logic of everyday language and regard it as the necessary regulative for any actual discourse, however distorted it may be.

Even without anticipating a general theory of natural language, the above considerations would suffice to criticize two conceptions which follow not so much from hermeneutics itself but from what seems to be to be a false ontological self-understanding of it.

1 Gadamer deduced the rehabilitation of prejudice from his hermeneutic insight into the pre-judgmental structure of understanding. He does not see any opposition between authority and reason. The authority of tradition does not assert itself blindly but only through its reflective recognition by those who, while being part of tradition themselves, understand and develop it through application. In response to my criticism,[27] Gadamer clarifies his position once again.[28]

> I grant that authority exercises force in an infinite number of forms of domination. . . . But this view of obedience to authority cannot tell us why these forms all represent ordered states of affairs and not the disorder of the brachial use of force. It seems to me to follow necessarily when I consider recognition as being determined in actual situations of authority. . . . One only needs to study such events as the loss or decay of authority . . . to see what authority is and what sustains it; it is not dogmatic force but dogmatic recognition. But what is dogmatic recognition, however, if it is not that one concedes to authority a superior knowledge.

The dogmatic recognition of tradition, and this means the acceptance of the truth-claims of this tradition, can be equated with knowledge itself only when freedom from force and unrestricted agreement about tradition have already been secured within this tradition. Gadamer's argument pre-supposes that legitimizing recognition and the consensus on which authoirty is founded can arise and develop free from force. The experience of distorted communication contradicts this pre-supposition. Force can, in any case, acquire permanence only through the objective semblance of an unforced pseudo-communicative agreement. Force that is legitimated in such a way we call, with Max Weber, authority. It is for this reason that there has to be that principle proviso of a universal agreement free from domination in order to make the fundamental distinction between dogmatic recognition and true consensus. Reason, in the sense of the principle of rational discourse, represents the rock which factual authorities have so far been more likely to crash against than build upon.

2 If, then, such opposition between authority and reason does in fact exist, as the Enlightenment has always claimed, and if it cannot be

superseded by hermeneutic means, it follows that the attempt to impose fundamental restrictions upon the interpreter's commitment to enlightenment becomes problematic, too. Gadamer has, in addition, derived the re-absorption of the moment of enlightenment into the horizon of currently existing convictions, from his insight into the pre-judgmental structure of understanding. The interpreter's ability to understand the author better than he had understood himself is limited by the accepted and traditionally established certitudes of the socio-cultural life-world of which he is part:[29]

> How does the psychoanalyst's knowledge relate to his position within the social reality to which he belongs? The emancipatory reflection which he initiates in his patients necessitates that he inquires into the more conscious surface interpretations, breaks through masked self-understanding, sees through the repressive function of social taboos. But when he conducts this reflection in situations which are outside the legitimate sphere of an analyst and where he is himself a partner in social interaction, then he is acting out of part. Anyone who sees through his social partners to something hidden to them, i.e. who does not take their role-acting seriously, is a 'spoil-sport' who will be avoided. The emancipatory potential of reflection which the psychoanalyst draws on therefore has to find its limit in the social consciousness within which both the analyst and his patient are in agreement with everyone else. As hermeneutic reflection has shown us, social communality, despite existing tensions and defects, always refers us back to a consensus on the basis of which it exists.

There is, however, reason to assume that the background consensus of established traditions and of language-games may be a forced consensus which resulted from pseudo-communication; this may be so not only in the individual, pathological case of disturbed family systems, but also in societal systems. The range of a hermeneutical understanding that has been extended into critique must, consequently, not be tied to the radius of convictions existing within a tradition. A depth-hermeneutic which adheres to the regulative principle of rational discourse has to seek out remaining natural–historical traces of distorted communication which are still contained even within fundamental agreements and recognized legitimations; and since it can find them there, too, it follows that any privatization of its commitment to enlightenment, and the restriction of the critique of ideology to the role of a treatment as it is institutionalized in the analyst–patient relationship, would be incompatible with its methodic point of departure. The enlightenment, which results from radical understanding, is always political. It is, of course, true that criticism is always tied to the context of tradition which it reflects. Gadamer's hermeneutic reservations are justified against monological self-certainty which merely arrogates to itself the title of critique. There is no validation of depth-hermeneutical interpretation outside of the self-reflection of all participants that is successfully achieved in a dialogue. The hypothetical status of general interpretations leads, indeed, to *a priori* limitations in the selection of ways in which the given immanent commitment of critical understanding to enlightenment can at any time be realized.[30]

In present conditions it may be more urgent to indicate the limits of the false claim to universality made by criticism rather than that of the hermeneutic claim to universality. Where the dispute about the grounds for justification is concerned, however, it is necessary to critically examine the latter claim, too.

NOTES

1 H. G. Gadamer, 'Rhetorik, Hermeneutik und Ideologiekritik', in *Kleine Schriften*, I (Tübingen, 1967), pp. 113–30.
2 Ibid., p. 127.
3 Cf. J. Habermas, *Erkenntnis und Interesse* (Frankfurt, 1968) translated as *Knowledge and Human Interest* (London, 1968), p. 206.
4 N. Chomsky, *Aspects of the Theory of Syntax* (Cambridge, Mass., 1965).
5 Gadamer shows this in the second part of *Truth and Method*.
6 Cf. J. Habermas, 'Zur Logik der Sozialwissenschaften', in *Phil-Rundschau*, Supplement 5 (1967), ch. III.
7 Gadamer, 'Rhetorik, Hermeneutik und Ideologiekritik', p. 117.
8 Gadamer, 'Die Universalität des hermeneutischen Problems' in *Kleine Schriften*, I (Tübingen, 1967), p. 109 (translated as 'The universality of the hermeneutical problem').
9 Gadamer, 'Rhetorik, Hermeneutik und Ideologiekritik', p. 118.
10 Ibid., p. 123.
11 Cf. H. G. Furth's excellent examination, *Piaget and Knowledge* (Englewood Cliffs, NJ, 1969).
12 A. Lorenzer, *Symbol und Verstehen im psychoanalytischen Prozess. Vorarbeiten zu einer Metatheorie der Psychoanalyse* (Frankfurt, 1970).
13 This is also apparent in our relationship with foreign languages. We can, in principle, learn every foreign language since all natural languages can be traced back to a general system of generative rules. But, yet, we acquire a foreign language only to the extent to which we, at least potentially, undergo at a late stage the process of socialization of native speakers – and, thereby, again at least potentially, grow into an individual language community; natural language can be general only as something concrete.

14 For the concept of non-identity, see T. W. Adorno, *Negative Dialektik* (Frankfurt, 1966), translated as *Negative Dialectics* (London, 1973).

15 Cf. S. Arieti, *The Intrapsychic Self* (New York, 1967), especially ch. 7 and ch. 16; also H. Werner and B. Kaplan, *Symbol Formation* (New York, 1967); P. Watzlawick, J. H. Beavin, D. D. Jackson, *Pragmatics of Human Communication* (New York, 1967), especially ch. 6 and ch. 7.

16 Cf. A. Gehlen, *Urmensch und Spätkultur* (Bonn, 1956); A. S. Diamond, *The History and Origin of Language* (London, 1959).

17 Lorenzer (*Symbol and Verstehen*, p. 88) finds the same characteristics in the unconscious representatives which direct neurotic modes of behaviour: the confusion of living expression and symbol, the close co-ordination with a particular mode of behaviour, the scenic content, context-dependency.

18 Cf. S. Arieti, *The Intrapsychic Self*, p. 286; Werner and Kaplan, p. 253, and L. C. Wynne, 'Denkstörung und Familienbeziehung bei Schizophrenen', in *Psyche*, May 1965, p. 82.

19 S. Arieti, *The Intrapsychic Self*, p. 327.

20 Cf. J. Habermas (1968a), p. 290.

21 Cf. C. V. Bormann, 'Die Zwiedeutigkeit der hermeneutischen Erfahrung', in *Philosophische Rundschau*, 16 (1969), p. 92 (also in K. O. Apel et al., *Hermeneutik und Ideologiekritik* (Frankfurt, 1971), pp. 83–119) for Gadamer's meta-critique to my objections to the third part of *Truth and Method*, where he gives an ontological interpretation of the hermeneutic consciousness.

22 Gadamer, 'Die Universalität des hermeneutischen Problems', p. 104.

23 A. Wellmer, *Kritische Gesellschaftstheorie und Positivismus* (Frankfurt, 1969), p. 48, translated as *Critical Theory of Science* (New York, 1974).

24 K.-O. Apel, 'Szientismus oder transzendentale Hermeneutik?' in Bubner, R., Cramer, K., Wiehl, R. (eds), *Hermeneutik und Dialektik* (Tübingen, 1970), vol. II, p. 48; also in Apel, *Transformation der Philosophie* (Frankfurt, 1973), vol. II.

25 *Mind, Self and Society* (Chicago, 1934), p. 327.

26 *Mündigkeit* (originally, *Mund* = mouth), here refers to one's ability as a competent, self-determining speaker – Trans.

27 J. Habermas, 'Zur Logic der Sozialwissenschaften', p. 174.

28 Gadamer, 'Rhetorik, Hermeneutik und Ideologiekritik;, p. 124.

29 Ibid., p. 129.

30 Cf. Habermas, *Protestbewegung und Hochschulreform* (Frankfurt, 1969), Introduction, p. 43, n. 6.

8

Beyond Hermeneutics: Interpretation in Late Heidegger and Recent Foucault

HUBERT L. DREYFUS

Two of the most original and influential interpreters of the contemporary world, Martin Heidegger and Michel Foucault, both deny that what they are doing should be called hermeneutics. Foucault opposes hermeneutics, which he calls exegesis or commentary, as the mistaken attempt to get at a deep truth hidden behind discourse. According to Foucault commentary seeks 'the re-apprehension through the manifest meaning of discourse of another meaning at once secondary and primary, that is, more hidden but also more fundamental'.[1] Hermeneutics thus 'dooms us to an endless task . . . [because it] rests on the postulate that speech is an act of "translation" . . . of the Word of God, ever secret, ever beyond itself.' Foucault dismisses this approach with the remark, 'For centuries we have waited in vain for the decision of the Word'.[2]

Heidegger, unlike Foucault, once had high hopes for hermeneutics. In fact his use of hermeneutic analysis in *Being and Time* modernized this approach, which he took from Dilthey (who took it from Schleiermacher), and made the hermeneutic method a respectable subject of discussion in philosophy and the human sciences. But later Heidegger characterizes the hermeneutic circle as 'superficial'[3] and he explicitly distances himself from his earlier position: '[I]n my later writings', he informs us, 'I no longer employ the term "hermeneutics" . . . I have left an earlier standpoint . . . because [it] was merely a way-station along a way.'[4] In his book on Nietzsche, Heidegger criticizes his earlier 'hermeneutic-transcendental questions' as 'not yet thought in terms of the history of Being'.[5] Instead of continuing to claim he is practising hermeneutic

Reprinted by permission of University of Massachusetts Press from *Hermeneutics: Questions and Prospects*, G. Shapiro and A. Sica (eds) (Amherst: University of Massachusetts Press, 1984), pp. 66–93, revised for this edition;

transcendental phenomenology, later Heidegger prefers to say he is simply thinking.[6] To understand what Foucault rejects and what Heidegger leaves behind, we must look in some detail at the two-stage hermeneutic analysis Heidegger introduced in *Being and Time*.

In the introduction to *Being and Time* Heidegger tells us: 'The phenomenology of *Dasein* [human being] is *hermeneutic* in the primordial signification of the world, where it designates the business of interpreting.'[7] Heidegger then sets out to show *why* phenomenology must be hermeneutic. He accepts Husserl's definition of phenomenology as a discipline that lets what is studied manifest itself as it is in itself, but he then completely reverses Husserl's notion of an 'original, intuitive' access to the phenomena. The phenomena, Heidegger points out, can be covered up; indeed, 'just because the phenomena are for the most part *not* given, there is need for phenomenology'.[8]

There are, Heidegger says, three kinds of covered-up-ness. These three forms of hiddenness delineate the kind of phenomena which are to be subjected to analysis in Division I and Division II of *Being and Time*, and foreshadow what Heidegger will later see as part of the subject matter of thinking. The first form of covered-up-ness is simply being undiscovered – 'neither known nor unknown'.[9] This is the kind of covered-up-ness we find when we investigate everyday activities. The second is 'being buried over'. 'This means that [the phenomena] has at some point been discovered but has deteriorated to the point of getting covered up again.'[10] Last, but most crucial, is the attempt to pass off the phenomenon that has covered the original phenomenon as itself the truth, in effect denying that anything has been covered up. Heidegger calls this full-fledged cover-up 'disguise', which suggests that the covering up was motivated by not wanting to see the truth, and he notes 'this covering up . . . is the most dangerous, for here the possibilities of deceiving and misleading are especially stubborn'.[11]

In *Being and Time*, Division I and II respectively are concerned with the first and last kinds of hidden phenomena. Division I takes up our everyday understanding of the world and the objects in it, and Division II investigates the meaning of human being. According to Heidegger the being of the world is so obvious that it is unnoticed in the course of our everyday activity while, the way of being of human beings is so unsettling that, just because it is constantly sensed it is constantly disguised. Moreover, the unnoticed structure of our everyday world is itself distorted by being used to help hide what human beings really are, and this distorted structure is then taken as self-evident by traditional philosophy.

The above three forms of hiddenness require two different kinds of phenomenological-hermeneutic inquiry (as well as an historical analysis, projected for Part II of *Being and Time*). One approach is employed in Division I of *Being and Time*, and another is introduced in Division II. Each of these interpretive techniques has been elaborated and applied by contemporary writers who call their work hermeneutic. In Division I Heidegger elaborates what he calls an interpretation of Dasein in its everydayness.[12] Heidegger notes that our everyday practices for coping with things, social institutions and people embody an unnoticed but pervasive interpretation of the world, the things in it, and of what counts as a normal human being. This interpretation is not something cognitive which has been explicitly handed down to us, nor did we have to figure it out in order to acquire it. We are just socialized into it. Thus it is appropriate to say, as Heidegger does, that it is neither known nor unknown.

Since the idea of an interpretation in our practices, which is unnoticed but can be made manifest, plays such an important role in Heidegger's work from *Being and Time* until his last essay, it is important to bear in mind an example. A striking illustration can be drawn from the contrasting child-rearing practices in the United States and Japan:

> [A] Japanese baby seems passive . . . He lies quietly . . . while his mother, in her care, does [a great deal of] lulling, carrying, and rocking her baby. She seems to try to soothe and quiet the child, and to communicate with him physically rather than verbally. On the other hand, the American infant is more active . . . and exploring of his environment, and his mother, in her care, does more looking at and chatting to her baby. She seems to stimulate the baby to activity and vocal response. It is as if the American mother wanted to have a vocal, active baby, and the Japanese mother wanted to have a quiet, contented baby. In terms of styles of caretaking of the mothers in the two cultures, they get what they apparently want . . . a great deal of cultural learning has taken place by three to four months of age . . . babies have learned by this time to be Japanese and American babies.[13]

This example of Japanese and American socialization suggests that our practices embody pervasive responses, discriminations, motor skills etc., which add up to an interpretation of what it is to be a person. The same is true of our interpretation of what it is to be an object. It should be clear from the Japanese example that the common understanding in our practices which Heidegger wants to reveal is not some theory, conceptual framework, or network of beliefs. Heidegger's view is thus the extreme opposite of the cognitivism one finds in Husserl, Chomsky, Piaget, Habermas and the Foucault of *The Archaeology of Knowledge*. All these modern Kantians hold that our practices are caused by a belief system, innate rules, or some other deep structure. For Heidegger, our practices are presumably simple skills picked up by imitation.[14] Heidegger puts the important difference between cognitivism and hermeneutics quite clearly when he says that what he is interested in 'is not an object of mental representation, but . . . the dominance of usage;.[15]

Because man is constituted by the *interpretation* embodied in usage or custom, Heidegger calls man's relation to the meaning of his practices, a hermeneutic relation. By emphasizing the fundamental importance of this special relation Heidegger is able to undercut the idea of a subject with mental representations of objects. Later Heidegger tells us that all notions of private experience which refer back to the 'I' were 'left behind when [he] entered into the hermeneutic relation . . .'.[16] In thus denying the philosophical importance of subjective experience and mental processing Heidegger is squarely on the side of the pragmatists and that other great original thinker of the twentieth century, Ludwig Wittgenstein. Moreover, since the understanding in our practice is not an internalized set of rules or an implicit belief system, there is nothing behind the practices which can be made explicit in order to explain them. All there is is the interpretation *in* the practices and all one can do if one wants to understand a culture is offer an interpretation of this interpretation.

The 'primordial understanding' in everyday practices and discourse, overlooked by the practitioners but recognized when pointed out to them, is the subject of much recent hermeneutic investigation. Robert Bellah in sociology[17] and Charles Taylor in political science[18] explicitly identified themselves with this type of hermeneutic concern. An offshoot of this sort of hermeneutics of the everyday is the application of the same method to other cultures, e.g., Clifford Geertz's brand of anthropology,[19] or to other epochs in our own culture, e.g., Thomas Kuhn's application of what he now explicitly calls the hermeneutic method to the understanding of nature presupposed by Aristotelian physics.[20]

Richard Rorty has defined hermeneutics as the attempt to make incommensurate discourses commensurable.[21] Anyone can define hermeneutics any way he pleases, but this definition is surely far from the one Heidegger introduced into modern philosophical discussion. Heidegger would regard attempts to interpret *alien* discourse and practices, such as we find in Geertz and Kuhn, as descendants of an earlier version of hermeneutics which presupposes his hermeneutics of everydayness. In *On the Way to Language*, he quotes Schleiermacher's remark that hermeneutics is 'the art of understanding rightly another man's language', and notes that 'broadened in the appropriate sense [hermeneutics] can mean the theory and methodology for every kind of interpretation'. He then adds that 'in *Being and Time* the term "hermeneutics" is used in a *still* broader sense' to mean 'the attempt first of all to define the nature of interpretation'.[22] Heidegger claims to be doing a sort of hermeneutics which lays the basis for all other hermeneutics by showing that human beings are *defined* by a set of meaningful social practices. Moreover, Heidegger sees that this claim is itself an interpretation. He says that 'hermeneutics, used as an adjunct word to "phenomenology", does not have its usual meaning, methodology of interpretation, but means the interpretation itself'.[23]

Thus hermeneutic phenomenology is an interpretation of human beings as essentially self-interpreting, which thereby shows why interpretation is the proper method for studying human beings. In addition, Heidegger's account, as we have seen, is supposed to be 'transcendental'. He does not discuss what it means to be a human being in specific cultures or historical periods, but attempts to lay out the general characteristics of self-interpreting being which apply at all time and all places. These structures, which have never been noticed, i.e. are covered up in the first sense of hiddenness mentioned above, turn out according to Heidegger to be isomorphic with the structure of temporality. Moreover, they reveal an unsettling groundlessness which makes everyone dimly anxious, and which the everyday practices, therefore, serve to disguise.

The interpretation which makes up Division I of *Being and Time*, thus, turns out to be only a first step on the way to uncovering the *meaning* in human practices. This gives special importance to the circular nature of hermeneutic analysis. In general, the so-called hermeneutic circle refers to the fact that in interpreting a text one must move back and forth between an overall interpretation and the details which a given reading let stand out as significant. Since the new details can in turn modify the overall interpretation, which can in turn reveal new details as significant, the circle is supposed to lead to a richer understanding of the text. As adapted by Heidegger, the phenomenological-hermeneutic circle provides the premises for a stronger methodological claim. (1) Since we must begin our analysis from within the practices we seek to interpret, our choice of phenomena to interpret is already guided by our traditional understanding of being which has made us what we are. (2) Since this traditional understanding may well pass over what is crucial, we cannot take the traditional interpretation at face value. Thus (3) we must be prepared to revise radically our first account on the basis of the phenomena which our interpretation reveals. If it turns out that the traditional interpretation of Dasein itself is a disguise, Division I will have to be totally reinterpreted by a second round of interpretation in Division II. As Heidegger puts it:

> Our analysis of Dasein . . . is . . . *provisional*. It merely brings out the being of this entity, *without interpreting its meaning*. It is rather a preparatory account by which the horizon for the most primordial way of interpreting being may be laid bare. Once we have arrived at that horizon, this preparatory analytic of Dasein will have to be repeated on a higher and authentically ontological basis.[24]

In Heidegger's hands the hermeneutic circle thus becomes a two-step downward spiral towards a deep concealed truth. As Foucault saw in his general definition of commentary, besides the everday meaning in our practice there turns out to be another meaning 'at once secondary and primary . . . more hidden but more fundamental'. In division II of *Being and Time* Heidegger turns to the hermeneutic unmasking of this concealed truth.

Division II, then, does not take the interpretation of Division I at face value, rather it sees it as being used in the motivated masking of a painful truth. Heidegger draws the moral:

> Dasein's *kind of being* thus *demands* that any ontological interpretation which sets itself the goal of exhibiting the phenomena in their primordiality, *should capture the being of the entity, in spite of this entity's own tendency to cover things up*. Existential analysis, therefore, constantly has the character of doing violence whether to the claims of the everyday interpretation, or to its complacency and its tranquilized obviousness.[25]

Whatever the truth about our being turns out to be, it is clear that in Division II Heidegger's method turns into what Paul Ricoeur has called a hermeneutic of suspicion.[26] In any such case of motivated distortion, whether one finds truth in the class struggle as revealed by Marx, or the twists and turns of the libido as uncovered by Freud, some authority which has already unmasked the concealed truth (the Marxist theorist, the therapist) must lead the self-deluded participant to see it too. In *Being and Time* this enlightened authority, already present in each person's sense of his condition, is called the voice of conscience. Moreover, in any case where the truth is repressed the individual must confirm the truth of the deep interpretation by acknowledging it, and since the person's real problem is the restrictions erected as defences against the truth, the participant's acknowledging the truth is supposed to bring about some sort of liberation. Marx promises the power released by the realization that one's class is exploited; Freud offers the control gained by recovering the repressed secrets of one's sexuality; and Heidegger claims that the realization that nothing is grounded and that there are no guidelines gives *Dasein* increased openness, flexibility and even gaiety.

It is important to be clear about what deep truth Heidegger claims to have ferreted out. It is not simply that human being is interpretation all the way down, so that our practices can never be grounded in human nature, God's will, or the structure of rationality. It is, in addition, a certain understanding of this condition as one of such radical rootlessness that everyone feels fundamentally unsettled (*unheimlich*), i.e. senses that human beings can never be at home.

Thus transcendental-hermeneutic phenomenology does not simply seek to lay out the general structure of self-interpreting being; rather it claims to force into view a substantive truth about human beings. The truth, hidden by all cultures at all times, is that man can never be at home in the world. According to Heidegger, we plunge into busily trying to make ourselves at home and secure the world precisely to cover up this truth. Indeed, this frantic everyday activity in which human beings seek to give their life some stable meaning is just what reveals everyday activity as a flight motivated by the 'pre-ontological' understanding each human being has of his or her ultimate meaninglessness.

Earlier Heidegger thus turns out to be a paradigmatic practitioner of the sort of deep hermeneutics Foucault defines and rejects. What unites these two thinkers is that, rather than continuing to use this version of the hermeneutic method in his later works, Heidegger rejects it for reasons quite similar to Foucault's. To highlight what Heidegger preserves and what he abandons when he turns away from the transcendental-hermeneutics of *Being and Time*, we can summarize his early view in six theses:

1 Human being is a self-interpreting activity. This is the hermeneutic relation.
2 This activity involves an understanding of what being means, and it is this understanding which opens a clearing in which human beings can encounter objects, institutions and other human beings. All members of a society share a pre-ontological understanding of this interpretation.
3 Everyday practices and everyday awareness takes place in this clearing which governs what everyday human activity takes for granted. These practices embody specific cultural ways of treating things as important or trivial, public or private, perceptual or imaginary, controlable or mysterious, all of which adds up to an understanding of what counts as real for us.
4 On some deep level every human being realizes that what counts as real in the everyday world is thus 'merely' an interpretation. The deep

truth is that there is no ultimate reality to which our practices do or should correspond. This is revealed to each individual in the experience of anxiety, but since this experience is unsettling, human beings try not to face it.

5 Thus human beings plunge frantically into their everyday practices and take them even more seriously in order to cover up the realization that these practices have no ultimate justification and so lack the sort of truth and utlimate seriousness that human life seems to demand.

6 By a double use of the hermeneutic circle, hermeneutic phenomenology strips away our disguises and makes manifest the pre-ontological understanding of being as *unheimlich* hidden beneath each person's everyday moods and in the public practices, thus revealing the deep truth of our condition.

Of these six theses, later Heidegger preserves only the first three. That is, he keeps the idea that members of a culture all share an understanding of being which can be brought out by a hermeneutic analysis. But later Heidegger distinguishes the *specific interpretation* of what counts as real, which everybody brought up in the practices of a particular culture at a particular time share, from the *meta-interpretation* of this public understanding. It is this meta-understanding, viz. that because Dasein is essentially self-interpreting it can never have any content of its own, which, in *Being and Time* is supposed to be revealed to each human being in an ever-present but ever-repressed sense of anxiety. Later Heidegger rejects his earlier claim that every human being is dimly aware of his or her 'nullity'. This change is reflected in his reinterpretation of the phenomenon of anxiety.

Heidegger introduced his account of anxiety as a privileged revealing experience of man's rootlessness in *Being and Time*, and elaborated it in his lecture, *What is Metaphysics?* But after his 'turning', in a new introduction to that lecture in 1949, he presents anxiety quite differently. He still holds that anxiety as a revelation of meaninglessness is no ordinary mood. It cannot be explained and removed by psychology or psychoanalysis. But it is no longer interpreted as a source of insight into the true structure of Dasein, pre-ontologically available to each human being, which hermeneutical phenomenology can uncover by violently wrenching away motivated disguises. It is now presented as the experience of the 'oblivion of being' characteristic uniquely of the modern age.[27]

On this interpretation, we moderns all feel an 'immeasurable need', and since it is painful, almost everyone flees it almost all of the time – but we do not flee because we grasp this pain's significance. In so far as there is a shared interpretation of this shared distress in our practices, it is misleading and superficial – e.g., that anxiety is the result of urbanization, repression, overwork, etc. – problems to which sociology and psychology have not yet found solutions. Heidegger no longer attempts to uncover a deep sense of what anxiety really means which this superficial understanding covers up. If there is no pre-ontological understanding of the meaning of our being, repeated turns of the hermeneutic circle will lead us nowhere. Anxiety can be seen as a special, revealing mood only if it is *given* an interpretation. Heidegger the thinker (not the hermeneutic phenomenologist with a pre-ontological understanding of the meaning of being) follows Rilke in interpreting anxiety as a specific response to the rootlessness of the contemporary technological world.[28]

Anxiety, then, is no longer interpreted as a manifestation of the essential truth, accessible to all human beings, that, since reality is relative to human practices, human beings can never find a foundation for their world, and so can never feel at home in it. On the contrary, Heidegger becomes interested in how the pre-Socratic Greeks were aware of the relation between custom and being, and yet, were at home in their world and free from modern anxiety. He even hopes to find hints in practices still left over from ancient times of how we can once again be at home in our world. Directly contradicting his early emphasis on man's essential experience of not being at home, later Heidegger strives to give us 'a vision of a new rootedness which someday might even be fit to recapture the old and now rapidly disappearing rootedness in a changed form'.[29]

Heidegger thus abandons theses 4, 5, and 6. That is, he no longer holds that human beings have a pre-ontological understanding of the deep but disguised truth that what counts as reality is relative to human practices. Some people, who he now calls wanderers, thinkers and poets, do realize that our practices determine what counts as reality and bring forth what counts as true. Moreover, in at least one period of our culture, fifth century Greece, this realization was captured in the language and practices as revealed by the fact that their word for truth was *aletheia* (unconcealedness). But this understanding is no longer for Heidegger a transcendental truth immanent in each human being and so no longer provides a criterion of success for deep hermeneutic interpretation.

Later Heidegger, however, never abandons the hermeneutics of everydayness, which is the lasting contribution of *Being and Time*; rather he historicizes it. Starting with his reinterpretation of anxiety as occasioned by our modern understanding of being, Heidegger attempts to show that each specific epoch in the development of our historical culture is a variation on a basic interpretation of reality as presence. Thus, for the early Greeks, reality was that which opened itself and took man into its presence where he was 'beheld by what is, . . . included and maintained within its openness and in that way borne along by it, to be driven about by its oppositions and marked by its discord'.[30] For Medieval Christians reality was God's presence in the world which was to be accepted, endured and interpreted like a text; while for modern man, starting with Descartes, reality was to be made present to man by being made to live up to his standards of intelligibility.

Each of these understandings of being allows different sorts of beings to show up. The Greeks encountered things in their beauty and power, and people as poets, statesmen and heroes; the Christians encountered creatures to be dominated and deciphered and people as saints and sinners; and we moderns encounter objects to be controlled and organized by subjects in order to satisfy our desires or, most recently with the increasing triumph of technology, we experience everything including ourselves as resources to be enhanced, transformed and ordered simply for the sake of ever greater efficiency and order.

Heidegger moves back and forth between our epoch and other understandings of being in our history, in order to bring out our present understanding more clearly. This recalls the circular movement between the whole and details characteristic of the hermeneutic circle, but now there is no attempt to uncover an ahistorical, hidden, deep truth. Gadamer's version of hermeneutics as a dialogue with past ways of understanding the world reflects this second stage of Heidegger's thought. But unlike Gadamer, Heidegger is not interested in these past understandings for the truth they contain – what Foucault along with Gadamer calls the Word – if that means a truth we can take up and fuse into our own horizon. One cannot enter into dialogue with practices which no longer exist in a unified, focused, way. How can there be a dialogue between the living and the dead? How could a fusion of horizons be possible when the only horizon that works now and determines truth for us is the technological horizon? Rather, for later Heidegger, the history of our understanding of being serves as a way of diagnosing how we arrived where we are, so that we can begin to mitigate the effects of our current technological understanding of reality by no longer taking it as self-evident and inevitable. When a culture's understanding of being becomes unbearable, relativizing its convictions is a first step towards an escape.

Heidegger still holds that each of the ways of understanding reality in our past, along with the correlative sorts of real things which were thus revealed, was understood pre-ontologically by each of the human beings involved and so could be made manifest by phenomenological-hermeneutic analysis of everydayness – without, of course, making any transcendental, cross-cultural a-historical claims. But, in fact, after his turn to thinking being historically, Heidegger developed new techniques of interpretation. Instead of using the hermeneutic circle – going back and forth between a general account and specific details in order to elicit the understanding of being of a particular epoch from the everyday practices of that epoch – Heidegger now finds this approach 'superficial'. It is superficial presumably because it does not take account of the fact that practices, in order to form a historical understanding of reality, must be *explicitly* shared; that is, they must be focused, organized and held up to the practitioners. This function, which later Heidegger calls 'truth setting itself to work', can be performed by what Heidegger calls a work of art. Heidegger takes as his illustration of a work of art working, the Greek temple. But he mentions several other examples of truth setting itself to work: the nearness of the god (e.g., the Hebrew Covenant), the sacrifice of a god (e.g. the Crucifixion), the act of a great political leader (e.g. Pericles), or the words of a great thinker (e.g., Parmenides). These are stabilizing and focusing events which one might call cultural paradigms. Later Heidegger holds that 'there must always be some being in the open [the clearing], something that is, in which the openness takes its stand and attains its constancy'.[31] There is no such requirement in the phenomenological hermeneutics laid out in *Being and Time*.

Once Heidegger has this insight his interpretations no longer go back and forth between details and the whole; rather he concentrates on specific entities which, during a specified epoch, incarnate for a people and for the interpreter what being means. In interpreting the practices of fifth century Greece, Heidegger describes the appearance and functioning of the Greek temple, and comments on the teachings of the pre-Socratics. In interpreting the understanding of being which allows things to appear to *us*, Heidegger interprets Nietzsche's notion of will to power and describes the hydraulic power station on the Rhine as a paradigm case of our technological drive to ever greater order and control.[32]

When we see that for later Heidegger only those practices focused in a paradigm can establish what can count as true, we can see why he was pessimistic about a saving dialogue with practices from the past. Such practices, now marginal, or as Heidegger would have said earlier, 'buried over', have no truth and reveal no reality, until they are taken up in a new shared paradigm. We must preserve such practices in the hope that they will be taken up in a new paradigm – a new god Heidegger sometimes calls it – since only such a god can save us.[33]

Thus far we have seen that later Heidegger is still interested in pointing out that human practices always embody an understanding of being, and adds to this a concern with in the specific understanding of being that our practices embody. We have also seen that his thinking leads him away from hermeneutic phenomenology because (1) the practices do not themselves necessarily contain concealed hints of their own role in establishing a clearing, and (2) even though the practices do provide the basis for an interpretation of the specific sort of clearing they produce, the hermeneutic circle does not turn out to be the best approach for making this meaning manifest.

We now turn to another important development in Heidegger's later thought – the realization that there is another kind of unnoticed meaning in our practices, for whose interpretation one needs more than the hermeneutics of everydayness, yet for understanding which the hermeneutics of suspicion may be an actual hindrance. This kind of meaning might be called the *significance* of any given understanding of being. To get at this significance an interpreter must ask how a given understanding of being developed, its cost, and, if it exacts too high a price, what can be done to change it.

Both the idea that all human practices hold a single repressed truth which it is the job of hermeneutics to uncover, and the notion that the practitioners have a pre-ontological understanding of the meaning of their current cultural practices, may distract the thinker from seeking the significance of our present understanding of reality. It should be clear that most practitioners of technology have no understanding repressed or overt of what the technological practices are doing to them. Indeed, if they were asked, most members of this culture, especially its elite scientists and administrators, would say that things are getting better and better as science and technology succeed in getting everything under control. If there is any problem, they would say, it is that we cannot control our own technology, but if we can gain control before we are blown up or polluted to death, an era of general welfare will ensue. Anxiety has no special significance in this interpretation and will be eliminated when we have better drugs and better therapy.

Heidegger offers the counter-interpretation that the cost of control is precisely the problem; that our anxiety and neediness will only increase as we achieve what he calls the 'total mobilization of all beings'. This reading of the significance of our modern understanding of being is not a phenomenological-hermeneutic unpacking of the deep meaning each practitioner represses, nor even a reading of the surface meaning of the practices the practitioners share pre-ontologically whether anyone knows it or not. It is an interpretation arising from a shared distress, which attempts to single out the paradigms which focus for all of us the technological understanding of our being in our current practices, and then to call attention to what these practices do to the quality of our lives. Later Heidegger calls the way a particular understanding of Being comes to be and pursues its course, 'its essence'. Thus to understand the essence of technology is to understand how we got this way, how technology works, and what it does to us. Those familiar with Foucault will recognize a striking parallel to what Foucault calls genealogy.

Foucault, like Heidegger, has always been interested not in the ideas subjects have in their minds, but in what unifies their practices. In his early writing Foucault sought his intelligibility in supposedly autonomous rules governing the production of discourse.[34] Later, he saw that discourse itself depends upon an intelligibility already in non-linguistic practices which it further focuses. He calls the results unified, focused intelligibility which, like the understanding of being in Heidegger 'governs' what can show up, 'power'. Using a notion of the body reminiscent of Maurice Merleau-Ponty's, he arrived at the view that these power practices are not governed by abstractable rules nor represented in a subject's mind, but are directly taken up by docile bodies.

> Power relations can materially penetrate the body in depth, without depending even on the mediation of the subject's own representations. If power takes hold of the body, this isn't through its having first to be interiorised in people's consciousness.[35]

Foucault's objection to hermeneutic in *The Birth of the Clinic* is that this sort of exegesis merely adds to the proliferation of supposedly meaningful discourse rather than elucidating meaningless discursive structures. Once he gives up his emphasis on discourse, Foucault criticizes the hermeneutics of everydayness for its misplaced emphasis on the meaning which social practices have for the practitioners. It is not that social actors fail to understand the surface significance of what they are saying and doing, but the practitioners do not know the effect of what they are doing, or worse, they have a mistaken view of these effects. Thus a hermeneutics of their pre-ontological understanding is no help in understanding what is going on.

The rejection of the participant's own interpretation of the significance of his actions, however, does *not* lead Foucault to the hermeneutics of suspicion. He continues to reject the view that participants do not have direct access to the meaning of their discourse and practices because their everyday understanding of things is a motivated cover-up. On Foucault's analysis, this position rests on the mistaken methodological assumption that there is an essential connection between everyday intelligibility and a deeper kind of intelligibility which the everyday view covers up. Foucault does not deny that some surface behaviour can be understood as a distortion of significances which the subject senses but is motivated to disguise. His basic objection to the hermeneutics of suspicion is that these secrets are mistakenly supposed to be the true and deepest meaning of the surface behaviour. Foucault seeks to demonstrate that the deeper meaning that the authority directs the participant to uncover in his practices, itself hides another, more important significance, which is not already known by the participant. Since the hidden meaning is not the final truth about what is going on, finding it is not necessarily liberating, and can, as Foucault points out, lead away from the kind of understanding which might help the participant resist pervasive practices whose only end is the ever more efficient ordering of society, and whose effects lead to cultural distress.

An understanding which makes resistance possible can only be obtained by someone who shares the participants' involvement but distances himself from it and does the hard historical work of diagnosing the history and organization of our current ways of being. The result is a pragmatically guided reading of the effect of present social practices which does not claim to correspond either to the everyday understanding of being in those practices nor to a deeper repressed understanding. Foucault follows Nietzsche in calling the interpretation of the signicance of the practices inscribed in our bodies 'genealogy'. Foucault's genealogical method, which he sometimes calls *déchiffrement*, thus turns out to be akin to Heidegger's 'thinking'.[36]

Let us now review the similarities and differences between Heidegger and Foucault which have emerged. In the course of this paper we have been led to distinguish three different ways of doing interpretation, each with its distinct subject matter, method and goals. The hermeneutics of everydayness treats social practices as a text, and by circling back and forth between details and the whole, seeks to reveal the meaning in these practices; the hermeneutics of suspicion uses the same method in an attempt to liberate the social participants by unmasking their deep meaning which the everyday practices serve to suppress; finally, thinking or deciphering focuses on specific social paradigms in order to highlight what our current practices are doing to the quality of our lives and open us to the possibility of change.

Foucault was always critical of the hermeneutics of suspicion (with the possible exception of his suggestion in *Madness and Civilization*, that society attempts to cover-up the total otherness of pure madness). Heidegger abandoned the hermeneutics of suspicion soon after the publication of *Being and Time*. Heidegger and Foucault would, indeed, both, accept one aspect of the hermeneutics of suspicion. They would agree that some people feel distress as a result of current technological and disciplinary practices, and that some people repress this distress. But both would deny that this distress is repressed because people sense its true meaning and that current practices can therefore be understood as *motivated* by the attempts to cover up this malaise. Both thinkers reject the view that human subjects, or everyday social practices, can be understood as repressing a deep truth, both because such an interpretation cannot be made plausible and because it tends to obscure rather than illuminate the nature and dangers of our practices.

Later Heidegger and Foucault are interested almost exclusively in assembling evidence that our current social practices manifest (and in no way repress) a general tendency or strategy whose effect is to turn nature and human beings into resources to be ever more efficiently organized and used. Heidegger holds that our current practices restrict a way of being receptive to beings that was defined for us by the early Greeks and continue to define our way of being human. Poets such as Holderlin, and thinkers such as Heidegger are acutely aware of this absent openness and see its loss as the cause of our present distress. Foucault is more radical. He denied that there is any truth that defines us. Consequently, he can give no account of the source of our distress. According to Foucault, some people, such as Foucault himself, suffer from the current practices of social control and others do not. That is all he can say. But he implies that in the light of some future paradigm everyone might retroactively come to share his view of our current condition as dangerous.

One question remains: What stand does each of these thinkers take on the hermeneutics of everydayness? Do they reject it along with the hermeneutics of suspicion or practise it in some new form? Here the parallel between Heidegger and Foucault breaks down. Heidegger continues throughout his work to interpret the understanding of our being in our cultural practices. He gives up the idea that this understanding is pre-ontologically given to each participant, but he looks to previous thinkers to help him trace the development of the technological understanding of being characteristic of Western society. He thus carries on an hitoricized version of the hermeneutics of everydayness developed in Division I of *Being and Time*. Heidegger would presumably endorse the hermeneutic of surface-meaning found in the works of Kuhn, Taylor, Bellah and Geertz. From his later vantage point he might point out, however, that rather than circling back and forth between details and whole, which is appropriate for a text, each writer in fact attempts to find a cultural paradigm that manifests to the society and the investigator which details of the social practices are important and what they mean. The interpretation, then, consists in taking some particular scientific achievement, political movement, exemplary persons, or cultural ritual, as a case of 'truth setting itself to work', and putting into words what this paradigm reveals.

Foucault's genealogical works are also organized around paradigms such as Bentham's panopticon model for prisons, schools, workshops etc. and the 'meticuluous rituals' of Christian and psychoanalytic confessional practices. But Foucault does not approach these social paradigms as ways of focusing the meaning of being in the practices, but rather as ways institutions concentrate and further social strategies.

Thus both Heidegger and Foucault wish to interpret the way our practices affect our lives. But for Heidegger the effect of the practices follows from their meaning so he still seeks an understanding of the meaning of being in the practices in order to understand how they work. According to Heidegger we must understand that since the pre-Socratics our culture has equated 'to be' with 'to be present', in order to see why and how we have arrived at the 'total mobilization of all beings'. Thinking presupposes the hermeneutics of our everyday understanding of being.

For Foucault, on the contrary, all that is important about our micro-practices is how they affect the people whose bodies and minds they form. He, therefore, is not interested in seeking out the understanding of being in our everyday practices. For him, such an understanding would in any case be seen as an effect of disciplinary power rather than the reverse. He thus bypasses a hermeneutic of everydayness and turns directly to a genealogy of strategies of social control.

NOTES

1 Michel Foucault, *The Order of Things* (New York: Vintage Books, 1973), p. 373.
2 Michel Foucault, *The Birth of the Clinic* (New York: Vintage Books, 1975), p. xvi.
3 Martin Heidegger, *On the Way to Language* (New York: Harper and Row, 1971), p. 51.
4 Ibid., p. 12.
5 Martin Heidegger, *Nietzsche II* (Pfullingen: Verlag Gunter Neske, 1961), p. 415.
6 Martin Heidegger, *What is Called Thinking* (New York: Harper and Row, 1954), p. 159ff.
7 Martin Heidegger, *Being and Time* (New York: Harper and Row, 1962), p. 62. All references are to the standard English translation. I have modified the translation wherever I thought necessary to preserve the sense.
8 Ibid., p. 60.
9 Ibid.
10 Ibid.
11 Ibid.
12 Ibid., p. 38.
13 W. Caudill and H. Weinstein, 'Maternal care and infant behaviour in Japan and in America', reprinted in C. S. Lavatelli and F. Stendler (eds), *Readings*

in *Child Behaviour and Development* (New York: Harcourt Brace, 1972), p. 78.

14 This non-standard reading of Heidegger is spelled out and defended in H. Dreyfus, *Being-in-the-World: A Commentary on Division I of* Being and Time (Bradford/MIT Press, forthcoming).

15 Heidegger, *On the Way to Language*, p. 33.

16 Ibid., p. 36.

17 Robert N. Bellah et al., *Habits of the Heart: Individualism and Commitment in American Life* (Berkeley, Ca: University of California Press, 1985).

18 See especially Taylor's 'Interpretation and the sciences of man', reprinted in Charles Taylor, *Philosophical Papers 2* (Cambridge: Cambridge University Press, 1985).

19 Clifford Geertz, *The Interpretation of Cultures* (New York: Harper and Row, 1973).

20 Thomas Kuhn, *The Essential Tension* (Chicago: University of Chicago Press, 1977).

21 Richard Rorty, *Philosophy and the Mirror of Nature* (Princeton, NJ: Princeton University Press, 1979).

22 Heidegger, *On the Way to Language*, p. 11.

23 Ibid., p. 11.

24 Heidegger, *Being and Time*, p. 38 (second italics mine).

25 Ibid., p. 359.

26 Ricoeur blurs his classification by including Nietzsche, who, indeed, does not take our practices at face value, among those who practise the hermeneutic of suspicion. According to Foucault's more illuminating classification, however, Nietzsche, while questioning our cultural self-interpretation, is not practising hermeneutics because he does not assume that the distorted interpretation in our cultural practices is the result of a deliberate cover-up of an undistorted one. Nietzsche's *Genealogy of Morals*, for example, questions the validity of Western morality and metaphysics but it does not trace these practices back to a refusal to face a deep truth (as in Freud) or even the refusal to face the fact that there is no deep truth (as in Heidegger). Foucault points out that for Nietzsche our current self-interpretation is not in the service of a deliberate cover-up, but rather is the result of many local power struggles.

27 Martin Heidegger, 'The way back into the ground of metaphysics', in Walter Kaufmann (ed.) *Existentialism from Dostoevsky to Sartre* (New York: Meridian Books, 1957), p. 211.

28 Martin Heidegger, 'What are poets for?', *Poetry, Language, Thought* (New York: Harper and Row, 1971).

29 Martin Heidegger, *Discourse on Thinking* (New York: Harper and Row, 1959), p. 55.

30 Martin Heidegger, 'The age of the world picture', in *The Question Concering Technology and Other Essays* (New York: Harper and Row, 1977), p. 131.

31 Heidegger, 'The origin of the work of art', in *Poetry, Language, Thought* (New York: Harper and Row, 1971), p. 61.

32 Martin Heidegger, 'The question concerning technology', in *The Question Concerning Technology and Other Essays* (New York: Harper and Row, 1977, p. 16.

33 Heidegger interview, 'Only a god can save us', *Der Spiegel*, 31 May 1976. Gadamer once told me that Heidegger was more pessimistic than he, Gadamer, was. This pessimism would apply also to Robert Bellah's and Charles Taylor's suggestion that we revive Christian communal practices. Heidegger would say that we should, indeed, try to preserve such practices, but they can only save us if they are radically transformed and integrated into a new understanding of reality.

34 For a detailed study of this method, which Foucault calls archaeology, and its difficulties see Hubert Dreyfus and Paul Rabinow, *Michel Foucault: Beyond Structuralism and Hermeneutics* (Chicago: Chicago University Press, 1982), Part I.

35 Michel Foucault, *Power/Knowledge*, ed. by Colin Gordon (New York: Pantheon, 1980), p. 186.

36 For a more detailed discussion of Foucault's revised method, its relation to archaeology and its use of paradigms, see Dreyfus and Rabinow, *Beyond Hermeneutics*, Part II.

9

Nietzsche, Genealogy, History

MICHEL FOUCAULT

1 Genealogy is gray, meticulous and patiently documentary. It operates on a field of entangled and confused parchments, on documents that have been scratched over and recopied many times.

On this basis, it is obvious that Paul Ree[1] was wrong to follow the English tendency in describing the history of morality in terms of a linear development – in reducing its entire history and genesis to an exclusive concern for utility. He assumed that words had kept their meaning, that desires still pointed in a single direction, and that ideas retained their logic; and he ignored the fact that the world of speech and desires has known invasions, struggles, plundering, disguises, ploys. From these elements, however, genealogy retrieves an indispensable restraint: it must record the singularity of events outside of any monotonous finality; it must seek them in the most unpromising places, in which we tend to feel is without history – in sentiments, love, conscience, instincts; it must be sensitive to their recurrence, not in order to trace the gradual curve of their evolution, but to isolate the different scenes where they engaged in different roles. Finally, genealogy must define even those instances where they are absent, the moment when they remained unrealized (Plato, at Syracuse, did not become Mohammed).

Genealogy, consequently, requires patience and a knowledge of details and it depends on a vast accumulation of source material. Its 'cyclopean monuments'[2] are constructed from 'discreet and apparently insignificant truths and according to a rigorous method'; they cannot be the produce of 'large and well-meaning errors'.[3] In short, genealogy demands relentless erudition. Genealogy does not oppose itself to history as the lofty and profound gaze of the philosopher might compare to the

This essay first appeared in *Hommage à Jean Hyppolite* (Paris: Presses Universitaires de France, 1971), pp. 145–72. Reprinted by permission of Cornell University Press from Michel Foucault: 'Nietzsche, Genealogy, History', in *Language, Counter-Memory, and Practice: Selected Essays and Interviews by Michel Foucault*, translated by Donald F. Bouchard and Sherry Simon, ed. Donald F. Bouchard (Ithaca, NY: Cornell University Press).

molelike perspective of the scholar; on the contrary, it rejects the metahistorical deployment of ideal significations and indefinite teleologies. It opposes itself to the search for 'origins'.

2 In Nietzsche, we find two uses of the word *Ursprung*. The first is unstressed, and it is found alternately with other terms such as *Entstehung*, *Herkunft*, *Abkunft*, *Geburt*. In *The Genealogy of Morals*, for example, *Entstehung* or *Ursprung* serve equally well to denote the origin of duty or guilty conscience,[4] and in the discussion of logic or knowledge in *The Gay Science*, their origin is indiscriminately referred to as *Ursprung*, *Entstehung*, or *Herkunft*.[5]

The other use of the word is stressed. On occasion, Nietzsche places the term in opposition to another: in the first paragraph of *Human, All Too Human* the miraculous origin (*Wunderursprung*) sought by metaphysics is set against the analyses of historical philosophy, which poses questions *über Herkunft und Anfang*. *Ursprung* is also used in an ironic and deceptive manner. In what, for instance, do we find the original basis (*Ursprung*) of morality, a foundation sought after since Plato? 'In detestable, narrowminded conclusions. *Pudenda origo*'.[6] Or in a related context, where should we seek the origin of religion (*Ursprung*), which Schopenhauer located in a particular metaphysical sentiment of the hereafter? It belongs, very simply, to an invention (*Erfindung*), a sleight-of-hand, an artifice (*Kunststück*), a secret formula, in the rituals of black magic, in the work of the *Schwarzkünstler*.[7]

One of the most significant texts with respect to the use of all these terms and to the variations in the use of *Ursprung* is the preface to the *Genealogy*. At the beginning of the text, its objective is defined as an examination of the origin of moral preconceptions and the term used is *Herkunft*. Then, Nietzsche proceeds by retracing his personal involvement with this question: he recalls the period when he 'calligraphied' philosophy, when he questioned if God must be held responsible for the origin of evil. He now finds this question amusing and properly characterizes it as a search for *Ursprung* (he will shortly use the same term to summarize Paul Ree's activity).[8] Further on, he evokes the analyses that are characteristically Nietzschean and that began with *Human, All too Human*. Here, he speaks of *Herkunhfthypothesen*. This use of the word *Herkunft* cannot be arbitrary, since it serves to designate a number of texts, beginning with *Human, All Too Human*, which deal with the origin of morality, asceticism, justice, and punishment. And yet, the word used in all these works had been *Ursprung*.[9] It would seem that at this point in the *Genealogy* Nietzsche wished to validate an opposition between *Herkunft* and *Ursprung* that did not exist ten years earlier. But immediately following the use of the two terms in a specific sense,

Nietzsche reverts, in the final paragraphs of the preface, to a usage that is neutral and equivalent.[10]

Why does Nietzsche challenge the pursuit of the origin (*Ursprung*), at least on those occasions when he is truly a genealogist? First, because it is an attempt to capture the exact essence of things, their purest possibilities, and their carefully protected identities, because this search assumes the existence of immobile forms that precede the external world of accident and succession. This search is directed to 'that which was already there', the image of a primordial truth fully adequate to its nature, and it necessitates the removal of every mask to ultimately disclose an original identity. However, if the genealogist refuses to extend his faith in metaphysics, if he listens to history, he finds that there is 'something altogether different' behind things: not a timeless and essential secret, but the secret that they have no essence or that their essence was fabricated in a piecemeal fashion from alien forms. Examining the history of reason, he learns that it was born in an altogether 'reasonable' fashion – from chance;[11] devotion to truth and the precision of scientific methods arose from the passion of scholars, their reciprocal hatred, their fanatical and unending discussions, and their spirit of competition – the personal conflicts that slowly forged the weapons of reason.[12] Further, genealogical analysis shows that the concept of liberty is an 'invention of the ruling classes'[13] and not fundamental to man's nature or at the root of his attachment to being and truth. What is found at the historical beginning of things is not the inviolable identity of their origin; it is the dissension of other things. It is disparity.[14]

History also teaches how to laugh at the solemnities of the origin. The lofty origin is no more than 'a metaphysical extension which arises from the belief that things are most precious and essential at the moment of birth.[15] We tend to think that this is the moment of their greatest perfection, when they emerged dazzling from the hands of a creator or in the shadowless light of a first morning. The origin always precedes the Fall. It comes before the body, before the world and time; it is associated with the gods, and its story is always sung as a theogony. But historical beginnings are lowly: not in the sense of modest or discreet like the steps of a dove, but derisive and ironic, capable of undoing every infatuation. 'We wished to awaken the feeling of man's sovereignty by showing his divine birth: this path is now forbidden, since a monkey stands at the entrance.'[16] Man originated with a grimace over his future development; and Zarathustra himself is plagued by a monkey who jumps along behind him, pulling on his coattails.

The final postulate of the origin is linked to the first two in being the site of truth. From the vantage point of an absolute distance, free from the restraints of positive knowledge, the origin makes possible a field of knowledge whose function is to recover it, but always in a false recognition due to the excesses of its own speech. The origin lies at a place of inevitable loss, the point where the truth of things corresponded to a truthful discourse, the site of a fleeting articulation that discourse has obscured and finally lost. It is a new cruelty of history that compels a reversal of this relationship and the abandonment of 'adolescent' quests: behind the always recent, avaricious and measured truth, it posits the ancient proliferation of errors. It is now impossible to believe that 'in the rending of the veil, truth remains truthful; we have lived long enough not to be taken in'.[17] Truth is undoubtedly the sort of error that cannot be refuted because it was hardened into an unalterable form in the long baking process of history.[18] Moreover, the very question of truth, the right it appropriates to refute error and oppose itself to appearance,[19] the manner in which it developed (initially made available to the wise, then withdrawn by men of piety to an unattainable world where it was given the double role of consolation and imperative, finally rejected as a useless notion, superfluous, and contradicted on all sides) – does this not form a history, the history of an error we call truth? Truth, and its original reign, has had a history within history from which we are barely emerging 'in the time of the shortest shadow', when light no longer seems to flow from the depths of the sky or to arise from the first moments of the day.[20]

A genealogy of values, morality, asceticism and knowledge will never confuse itself with a quest for their 'origins', will never neglect as inaccessible the vicissitudes of history. On the contrary, it will cultivate the details and accidents that accompany every beginning; it will be scrupulously attentive to their petty malice; it will await their emergence, once unmasked, as the face of the other. Wherever it is made to go, it will not be reticent – in 'excavating the depths', in allowing time for these elements to escape from a labyrinth where no truth had ever detained them. The genealogist needs history to dispel the chimeras of the origin, somewhat in the manner of the pious philosopher who needs a doctor to exorcise the shadow of his soul. He must be able to recognize the events of history, its jolts, its surprises, its unsteady victories and unpalatable defeats – the basis of all beginnings, atavisms and heredities. Similarly, he must be able to diagnose the illnesses of the body, its conditions of weakness and strength, its breakdown and resistances, to be in a position to judge philosophical discourse. History is the concrete body of a development, with its moments of intensity, its lapses, its extended periods of feverish agitation, its fainting spells; and only a metaphysician would seek its soul in the distant ideality of the origin.

3 *Entstehung* and *Herkunft* are more exact than *Ursprung* in recording the true objective of genealogy; and, while they are ordinarily translated as 'origin', we must attempt to reestablish their proper use.

Herkunft is the equivalent of stock or *descent*; it is the ancient affiliation to a group, sustained by the bonds of blood, tradition, or social class. The analysis of *Herkunft* often involves a consideration of race[21] or social type.[22] But the traits it attempts to identify are not the exclusive generic characteristics of an individual, a sentiment, or an idea, which permit us to qualify them as 'Greek' or 'English'; rather, it seeks the subtle, singular and subindividual marks that might possibly intersect in them to form a network that is difficult to unravel. Far from being a category of resemblance, this origin allows the sorting out of different traits: the Germans imagined that they had finally accounted for their complexity by saying they possessed a double soul; they were fooled by a simple computation, or rather, they were simply trying to master the racial disorder from which they had formed themselves.[24] Where the soul pretends unification or the self fabricates a coherent identity, the genealogist sets out to study the beginning – numberless beginnings whose faint traces and hints of color are readily seen by an historical eye. The analysis of descent permits the dissociation of the self, its recognition and displacement as an empty synthesis, in liberating a profusion of lost events.

An examination of descent also permits the discovery, under the unique aspect of a trait or a concept, of the myriad events through which – thanks to which, against which – they were formed. Genealogy does not pretend to go back in time to restore an unbroken continuity that operates beyond the dispersion of forgotten things; its duty is not to demonstrate that the past actively exists in the present, that it continues secretly to animate the present, having imposed a predetermined form to all its vicissitudes. Genealogy does not resemble the evolution of a species and does not map the destiny of a people. On the contrary, to follow the complex course of descent is to maintain passing events in their proper dispersion; it is to identify the accidents, the minute deviations – or conversely, the complete reversals – the errors, the false appraisals and the faulty calculations that gave birth to those things that continue to exist and have value for us; it is to discover that truth or being do not lie at the root of what we know and what we are, but the exteriority of accidents.[24] This is undoubtedly why every origin of morality from the moment it stops being pious – and *Herkunft* can never be – has value as a critique.[25]

Deriving from such a source is a dangerous legacy. In numerous instances, Nietzsche associates the term *Herkunft* and *Erbschaft*. Nevertheless, we should not be deceived into thinking that this heritage is an acquisition, a possession that grows and solidifies; rather, it is an unstable assemblage of faults, fissures and heterogeneous layers that threatens the fragile inheritor from within or from underneath: 'injustice or instability in the minds of certain men, their disorder and lack of decorum, are the final consequences of their ancestors' numberless logical inaccuracies, hasty conclusions, and superficiality.'[26] The search for descent is not the erecting of foundations: on the contrary, it disturbs what was previously considered immobile; it fragments what was thought unified; it shows the heterogeneity of what was imagined consistent with itself. What convictions and, far more decisively, what knowledge can resist it? If a genealogical analysis of a scholar were made – of one who collects facts and carefully accounts for them – his *Herkunft* would quickly divulge the official papers of the scribe and the pleadings of the lawyers – their father[27] – in their apparently disinterested attention, in the 'pure' devotion to objectivity.

Finally, descent attaches itself to the body.[28] It inscribes itself in the nervous system, in temperament, in the digestive apparatus; it appears in faulty respiration, in improper diets, in the debilitated and prostrate body of those whose ancestors committed errors. Fathers have only to mistake effects for causes, believe in the reality of an 'afterlife', or maintain the value of eternal truths, and the bodies of their children will suffer. Cowardice and hypocrisy, for their part, are the simple offshoots of error: not in a Socratic sense, not that evil is the result of a mistake, not because of a turning away from an original truth, but because the body maintains, in life as in death, through its strength or weakness, the sanction of every truth and error, as it sustains, in an inverse manner, the origin – descent. Why did men invent the contemplative life? Why give a supreme value to this form of existence? Why maintain the absolute truth of those fictions which sustain it?

> During the barbarous ages . . . if the strength of an individual declined, if he felt himself tired or sick, melancholy or satiated and, as a consequence, without desire or appetite for a short time, he became relatively a better man, that is, less dangerous. His pessimistic ideas could only take form as words or reflections. In this frame of mind, he either became a thinker and prophet or used his imagination to feed his superstitions.[29]

The body – and everything that touches it: diet, climate, and soil – is the domain of the *Herkunft*. The body manifests the stigmata of past experience and also gives rise to desires, failings and errors. These elements may join in a body where they achieve a sudden expression, but as often, their encounter is an engagement in which they efface each other, where the body becomes the pretext of their insurmountable conflict.

The body is the inscribed surface of events (traced by language and dissolved by ideas), the locus of a dissociated Self (adopting the illusion of a substantial unity), and a volume in perpetual disintegration. Genealogy, as an analysis of descent, is thus situated within the articulation of the body and history. Its task is to expose a body totally imprinted by history and the process of history's destruction of the body.

4 *Entstehung* designates *emergence*, the moment of arising. It stands as the principle and the singular law of an apparition. As it is wrong to search for descent in an uninterrupted continuity, we should avoid thinking of emergence as the final term of an historical development; the eye was not always intended for contemplation, and punishment has had other purposes than setting an example. These developments may appear as a culmination, but they are merely the current episodes in a series of subjugations: the eye initially responded to the requirements of hunting and warfare; and punishment has been subjected, throughout its history, to a variety of needs – revenge, excluding an aggressor, compensating a victim, creating fear. In placing present needs at the origin, the metaphysician would convince us of an obscure purpose that seeks its realization at the moment it arises. Genealogy, however, seeks to reestablish the various systems of subjection: not the anticipatory power of meaning, but the hazardous play of dominations.

Emergence is always produced through a particular stage of forces. The analysis of the *Entstehung* must delineate this interaction, the struggle these forces wage against each other or against adverse circumstances, and the attempt to avoid degeneration and regain strength by dividing these forces against themselves. It is in this sense that the emergence of a species (animal or human) and its solidification are secured 'in an extended battle against conditions which are essentially and constantly unfavorable'. In fact, 'the species must realize itself as a species, as something – characterized by the durability, uniformity, and simplicity of its form – which can prevail in the perpetual struggle against outsiders or the uprising of those it oppresses from within'. On the other hand, individual differences emerge at another stage of the relationship of forces, when the species has become victorious and when it is no longer threatened from outside. In this condition, we find a struggle 'of egoisms turned against each other, each bursting forth in a splintering of forces and a general striving for the sun and for the light'.[30] There are also times when force contends against itself, and not only in the intoxication of an abundance, which allows it to divide itself, but at the moment when it weakens. Force reacts against its growing lassitude and gains strength; it imposes limits, inflicts torments and mortifications; it masks these actions as a higher morality, and, in exchange, regains its strength. In this manner, the ascetic ideal was born, 'in the instinct of a decadent life which . . . struggles for its own existence'.[31] This also describes the movement in which the Reformation arose, precisely where the church was least corrupt;[32] German Catholicism, in the sixteenth century, retained enough strength to turn against itself, to mortify its own body and history, and to spiritualize itself into a pure religion of conscience.

Emergence is thus the entry of forces; it is their eruption, the leap from the wings to center stage, each in its youthful strength. What Nietzsche calls the *Entstehungsherd*[33] of the concept of goodness is not specifically the energy of the strong or the reaction of the weak, but precisely this scene where they are displayed superimposed or face-to-face. It is nothing but the space that divides them, the void through which they exchange their threatening gestures and speeches. As descent qualifies the strength or weakness of an instinct and its inscription on a body, emergence designates a place of confrontation but not as a closed field offering the spectacle of a struggle among equals. Rather, as Nietzsche demonstrates in his anlaysis of good and evil, it is a 'non-place', a pure distance, which indicates that the adversaries do not belong to a common space. Consequently, no one is responsible for an emergence; no one can glory in it, since it always occurs in the interstice.

In a sense, only a single drama is ever staged in this 'non-place', the endlessly repeated play of dominations. The domination of certain men over others leads to the differentiation of values;[34] class domination generates the idea of liberty,[35] and the forceful appropriation of things necessary to survival and the imposition of a duration not intrinsic to them account for the origin of logic.[36] This relationship of domination is no more a 'relationship' than the place where it occurs is a place; and, precisely for this reason, it is fixed, throughout its history, in rituals, in meticulous procedures that impose rights and obligations. It establishes marks of its power and engraves memories on things and even within bodies. It makes itself accountable for debts and gives rise to the universe of rules, which is by no means designed to temper violence, but rather to satisfy it. Following traditional beliefs, it would be false to think that total war exhausts itself in its own contradictions and ends by renouncing violence and submitting to civil laws. On the contrary the law is a calculated and relentless pleasure, delight in the promised blood, which permits the perpetual instigation of new dominations and the staging of meticulously repeated scenes of violence. The desire for peace, the serenity of compromise, and the tacit acceptance of the law, far from representing a major moral conversion or a utilitarian calculation that gave rise to the law, are but its result and, in point of fact, its perversion: 'guilt, conscience, and duty had their threshold of emergence in the right to secure obligations; and their inception, like that of any major event on earth, was saturated in blood.[37] Humanity does not gradually progress from combat to combat until it arrives at universal reciprocity, where the rule of law finally replaces warfare; humanity installs each of its violences in a system of rules and thus proceeds from domination to domination.

The nature of these rules allows violence to be inflicted on violence and the resurgence of new forces that are sufficiently strong to dominate those in power. Rules are empty in themselves, violent and unfinalized; they are impersonal and can be bent to any purpose. The successes of history belong to those who are capable of seizing these rules, to replace those who had used them, to disguise themselves so as to pervert them, invert their meaning, and redirect them against those who had initially imposed them; controlling this complex mechanism, they will make it function so as to overcome the rulers through their own rules.

The isolation of different points of emergence does not conform to the successive configurations of an identical meaning; rather, they result from substitutions, displacements, disguised conquests and systematic reversals. If interpretation were the slow exposure of the meaning hidden in an origin, then only metaphysics could interpret the development of humanity. But if interpretation is the violent or surreptitious appropriation of a system of rules, which in itself has no essential meaning, in order to impose a direction, to bend it to a new will, to force its participation in a different game, and to subject it to secondary rules, then the development of humanity is a series of interpretations. The role of genealogy is to record its history: the history of morals, ideals, and metaphysical concepts, the history of the concept of liberty or of the ascetic life; as they stand for the emergence of different interpretations, they must be made to appear as events on the stage of historical process.

5 How can we define the relationship between genealogy, seen as the examination of *Herkunft* and *Entstehung*, and history in the traditional sense? We could, of course, examine Nietzsche's celebrated apostrophes against history, but we will put these aside for the moment and consider those instances when he conceives of genealogy as 'wirkliche Historie', or its more frequent characterization as historical 'spirit' or 'sense'.[38] In fact, Nietzsche's criticism, beginning with the second of the *Untimely Meditations*, always questioned the form of history that reintroduces (and always assumes) a suprahistorical perspective: a history whose function is to compose the finally reduced diversity of time into a totality fully closed upon itself; a history that always encourages subjective recognitions and attributes a form of

reconciliation to all the displacements of the past; a history whose perspective on all that precedes it implies the end of time, a completed development. The historian's history finds its support outside of time and pretends to base its judgments on an apocalyptic objectivity. This is only possible, however, because of its belief in eternal truth, the immortality of the soul, and the nature of consciousness as always identical to itself. Once the historical sense is mastered by a supra-historical perspective, metaphysics can bend it to its own purpose and, by aligning it to the demands of objective science, it can impose its own 'Egyptianism'. On the other hand, the historical sense can evade metaphysics and become a privileged instrument of genealogy if it refuses the certainty of absolutes. Given this, it corresponds to the acuity of a glance that distinguishes, separates and disperses, that is capable of liberating divergence and marginal elements – the kind of dissociating view that is capable of decomposing itself, capable of shattering the unity of man's being through which it was thought that he could extend his sovereignty to the events of his past.

Historical meaning becomes a dimension of 'wirkliche Historie' to the extent that it places within a process of development everything considered immortal in man. We believe that feelings are immutable, but every sentiment, particularly the noblest and most disinterested, has a history. We believe in the full constancy of instinctual life and imagine that it continues to exert its force indiscriminately in the present as it did in the past. But a knowledge of history easily disintegrates this unity, depicts its wavering course, locates it moments of strength and weakness, and defines its oscillating reign. It easily seizes the slow elaboration of instincts and those movements where, in turning upon themselves, they relentlessly set about their self-destruction.[39] We believe, in any event, that the body obeys the exclusive laws of physiology and that it escapes the influence of history, but this too is false. The body is molded by a great many distinct regimes; it is broken down by the rhythms of work, rest and holidays; it is poisoned by food or values, through eating habits or moral laws; it constructs resistances.[40] 'Effective' history differs from traditional history in being without constants. Nothing in man – not even his body – is sufficiently stable to serve as the basis for self-recognition or for understanding other men. The traditional devices for constructing a comprehensive view of history and for retracing the past as a patient and continuous development must be systematically dismantled. Necessarily, we must dismiss those tendencies that encourage the consoling play of recognitions. Knowledge, even under the banner of history, does not depend on 'rediscovery', and it emphatically excludes the 'rediscovery of ourselves'. History becomes 'effective' to the degree that it introduces discontinuity into our very being – as it divides our emotions, dramatizes our instincts, multiplies our body and sets it against itself. 'Effective' history deprives the self of the reassuring stability of life and nature, and it will not permit itself to be transported by a voiceless obstinacy towards a millenial ending. It will uproot its traditional foundations and relentlessly disrupt its pretended continuity. This is because knowledge is not made for understanding; it is made for cutting.[41]

From these observations, we can grasp the particular traits of historical meaning as Nietzsche understood it – the sense which opposes 'wirkliche Historie' to traditional history. The former transposes the relationship ordinarily established between the eruption of an event and necessary continuity. An entire historical tradition (theological or rationalistic) aims at dissolving the singular event into an ideal continuity – as a teleological movement or a natural process. 'Effective' history, however, deals with events in terms of their most unique characteristics, their most acute manifestations. An event, consequently, is not a decision, a treaty, a reign, or a battle, but the reversal of a relationship of forces, the usurpation of power, the appropriation of a vocabulary turned against those who had once used it, a feeble domination that poisons itself as it grows lax, the entry of a masked 'other'. The forces operating in history are not controlled by destiny or regulative mechanisms, but respond to haphazard conflicts.[42] They do not manifest the successive forms of a primordial intention and their attraction is not that of a conclusion, for they always appear through the singular randomness of events. The inverse of the Christian world, spun entirely by a divine spider, and different from the world of the Greeks, divided between the realm of will and the great cosmic folly, the world of effective history knows only one kingdom, without providence or final cause, where there is only 'the iron hand of necessity shaking the dice-box of chance'.[43] Chance is not simply the drawing of lots, but raising the stakes in every attempt to master chance through the will to power, and giving rise to the risk of an even greater chance.[44] The world we know is not this ultimately simple configuration where events are reduced to accentuate their essential traits, their final meaning, or their initial and final value. On the contrary, it is a profusion of entangled events. If it appears as a 'marvelous motley, profound and totally meaningful', this is because it began and continues its secret existence through a 'host of errors and phantams'.[45] We want historians to confirm our belief that the present rests upon profound intentions and immutable necessities. But the true historical sense confirms our existence among countless lost events, without a landmark or a point of reference.

Effective history can also invert the relationship that traditional history, in its dependence on metaphysics, establishes between proximity and distance. The latter is given to a contemplation of distances and heights: the noblest periods, the highest forms, the most abstract ideas, the purest individualities. It accomplishes this by getting as near as possible, placing itself at the foot of its mountain peaks, at the risk of adopting the famous perspective of frogs. Effective history, on the other hand, shortens its vision to those things nearest to it – the body, the nervous system, nutrition, digestion, and energies; it unearths the periods of decadence and if it chances upon lofty epochs, it is with the suspicion – not vindictive but joyous – of finding a barbarous and shameful confusion. It has no fear of looking down, so long as it is understood that it looks from above and descends to seize the various perspectives, to disclose dispersions and differences, to leave things undisturbed in their own dimension and intensity. It reverses the surreptitious practice of historians, their pretension to examine things furthest from themselves, the grovelling manner in which they approach this promising distance (like the metaphysicians who proclaim the existence of an afterlife, situated at a distance from this world, as a promise of their reward). Effective history studies what is closest, but in an abrupt dispossession, so as to seize it at a distance (an approach similar to that of a doctor who looks closely, who plunges to make a diagnosis and to state its difference). Historical sense has more in common with medicine than philosophy; and it should not suprise us that Nietzsche occasionally employs the phrase 'historically and physiologically',[46] since among the philosopher's idiosyncracies is a complete denial of the body. This includes, as well, 'the absence of historical sense, a hatred for the idea of development, Egyptianism', the obstinate 'placing of conclusions at the beginning', of 'making last things first'.[47] History has a more important task than to be a handmaiden to philosophy, to recount the necessary birth of truth and values; it should become a differential knowledge of energies and failings, heights and degenerations, poisons and antidotes. Its task is to become a curative science.[48]

The final trait of effective history is its affirmation of knowledge as perspective. Historians take unusual pains to erase the elements in their work which reveal their grounding in a particular time and place, their preferences in a controversy – the unavoidable obstacles of their passion. Nietzsche's version of historical sense is explicit in its perspective and acknowledges its system of injustice. Its perception is slanted, being a deliberate appraisal, affirmation, or negation; it reaches the lingering and poisonous traces in order to prescribe the best antidote. It is not given to a discreet effacement before the objects it observes and does not submit itself to their processes; nor does it seek laws, since it gives equal weight to its own sight and to its objects. Through the historical sense, knowledge is allowed to create its own genealogy in the act of cognition;

and 'wirkliche Historie' composes a genealogy of history as the vertical projection of its position.

6 In this context, Nietzsche links historical sense to the historian's history. They share a beginning that is similarly impure and confused, share the same sign in which the symptoms of sickness can be recognized as well as the seed of an exquisite flower.[49] They arose simultaneously to follow their separate ways, but our task is to trace their common genealogy.

The descent (*Herkunft*) of the historian is unequivocal: he is of humble birth. A characteristic of history is to be without choice: it encourages thorough understanding and excludes qualitative judgments – a sensitivity to all things without distinction, a comprehensive view excluding differences. Nothing must escape it and, more importantly, nothing must be excluded. Historians argue that this proves their tact and discretion. After all, what right have they to impose their tastes and preferences when they seek to determine what actually occurred in the past? Their mistake is to exhibit a total lack of taste, the kind of crudeness that becomes smug in the presence of the loftiest elements and finds satisfaction in reducing them to size. The historian is insensitive to the most disgusting things; or rather, he especially enjoys those things that should be repugnant to him. His apparent serenity follows from his concerted avoidance of the exceptional and his reduction of all things to the lowest common denominator. Nothing is allowed to stand above him; and underlying his desire for total knowledge is his search for the secrets that belittle everything: 'base curiosity'. What is the source of history? It comes from the plebs. To whom is it addressed? To the plebs. And its discourse strongly resembles the demagogue's refrain: 'No one is greater than you and anyone who presumes to get the better of you – you who are good – is evil.' The historian, who functions as his double, can be heard to echo: 'No past is greater than your prsent, and, through my meticulous erudition, I will rid you of your infatuations and transform the grandeur of history into pettiness, evil, and misfortune.' The historian's ancestry goes back to Socrates.

This demagogy, of course, must be masked. It must hide its singular malice under the cloak of universals. As the demagogue is obliged to invoke truth, laws of essences and eternal necessity, the historian must invoke objectivity, the accuracy of facts, and the permanence of the past. The demagogue denies the body to secure the sovereignty of a timeless idea and the historian effaces his proper individuality so that others may enter the stage and reclaim their own speech. He is divided against himself: forced to silence his preferences and overcome his distaste, to blur his own perspective and replace it with the fiction of a universal geometry, to mimic death in order to enter the kingdom of the dead, to adopt a faceless anonymity. In this world where he has conquered his individual will, he becomes a guide to the inevitable law of a superior will. Having curbed the demands of his individual will in his knowledge, he will disclose the form of an eternal will in his object of study. The objectivity of historians inverts the relationships of will and knowledge and it is, in the same stroke, a necessary belief in Providence, in final causes and teleology – the beliefs that places the historian in the family of ascetics. 'I can't stand these lustful eunuchs of history, all the seductions of an ascetic ideal; I can't stand these blanched tombs producing life or those tired and indifferent beings who dress up in the part of wisdom and adopt an objective point of view.'[50]

The *Entstehung* of history is found in nineteenth-century Europe: the land of interminglings and bastardy, the period of the 'man-of-mixture'. We have become barbarians with respect to those rare moments of high civilization: cities in ruin and enigmatic monuments are spread out before us; we stop before gaping walls; we ask what gods inhabited these empty temples. Great epochs lacked this curiosity, lacked our excessive deference; they ignored their predecessors: the classical period ignored Shakespeare. The decadence of Europe presents an immense spectacle (while stronger periods refrained from such exhibitions), and the nature of this scene is to represent a theater; lacking monuments of our own making, which properly belong to us, we live among crowded scenes. But there is more. Europeans no longer know themselves; they ignore their mixed ancestries and seek a proper role. They lack individuality. We can begin to understand the spontaneous historical bent of the nineteenth century: the anemia of its forces and those mixtures that effaced all its individual traits produced the same results as the mortifications of asceticism; its inability to create, its absence of artistic works, and its need to rely on past achievements forced it to adopt the base curiosity of plebs.

If this fully represents the genealogy of history, how could it become, in its own right, a genealogical analysis? Why did it not continue as a form of demagogic or religious knowledge? How could it change roles in the same stage? Only by being seized, dominated, and turned against its birth. And it is this movement which properly describes the specific nature of the *Entstehung*: it is not the unavoidable conclusion of a long preparation, but a scene where forces are risked in the chance of confrontations, where they emerge triumphant, where they can also be confiscated. The locus of emergence for metaphysics was surely Athenian demagogy, the vulgar spite of Socrates and his belief in immortality, and Plato could have seized this Socratic philosophy to turn it against itself. Undoubtedly, he was often tempted to do so, but his defeat lies in its consecration. The problem was similar in the nineteenth century: to avoid doing for the popular asceticism of historians what Plato did for Socrates. This historical trait should not be founded upon a philosphy of history, but dismantled beginning with the things it produced; it is necessary to master history so as to turn it to genealogical uses, that is, strictly anti-Platonic purposes. Only then will the historical sense free itself from the demands of a suprahistorical history.

7 The historical sense gives rise to three uses that oppose and correspond to the three Platonic modalities of history. The first is parodic, directed against reality, and opposes the theme of history as reminiscence or recognition; the second is dissociative, directed against identity, and opposes history given as continuity or representative of a tradition; the third is sacrificial, directed against truth, and opposes history as knowledge. They imply a use of history that severs its connection to memory, its metaphysical and anthropological model, and constructs a counter-memory – a transformation of history into a totally different form of time.

First, the parodic and farcical use. The historian offers this confused and anonymous European, who no longer knows himself or what name he should adopt, the possibility of alternate identities, more individualized and substantial than this own. But the man with historical sense will see that this substitution is simply a disguise. Historians supplied the Revolution with Roman prototypes, romanticism with knight's armor, and the Wagnerian era was given the sword of a German hero – ephemeral props that point to our own unreality. No one kept them from venerating these religions, from going to Bayreuth to commemorate a new afterlife; they were free, as well, to be transformed into street-vendors of empty identities. The new historian, the genealogist, will know what to make of this masquerade. He will not be too serious to enjoy it; on the contrary, he will push the masquerade to its limit and prepare the great carnival of time where masks are constantly re-appearing. No longer the identification of our faint individuality with the solid identities of the past, but our 'unrealization' through the excessive choice of identities – Frederick of Hohenstaufen, Caesar, Jesus, Dionysus, and possibly Zarathustra. Taking up these masks, revitalizing the buffoonery of history, we adopt an identity whose unreality surpasses that of God who started the charade. 'Perhaps, we can discover a realm where originality is again possible as parodists of history and buffoons of God.'[51] In this, we recognize the parodic double of what the second of the *Untimely Meditations* called 'monumental history': a history given to reestablishing the high points of historical development and their maintenance in a perpetual presence, given to the recovery of works, actions and creations through the monogram of their personal essence. But in 1874, Nietzsche accused this history, one totally devoted to veneration, of barring access to the actual intensities and creations of life. The parody of his last texts serves to emphasize that 'monumental history' is itself a parody. Genealogy is history in the form of a concerted carnival.

The second use of history is the systematic dissociation of identity. This is necessary because this rather weak identity, which we attempt to support and to unify under a mask, is in itself only a parody; it is plural; countless spirits dispute its possession; numerous systems intersect and compete. The study of history makes one 'happy, unlike the metaphysicians, to possess in oneself not an immortal soul but many mortal ones'.[52] And in each of these souls, history will not discover a forgotten identity, eager to be reborn, but a complex system of distinct and multiple elements unable to be mastered by the powers of synthesis: 'it is a sign of superior culture to maintain, in a fully conscious way, certain phases of its evolution which lesser men pass through without thought. The initial result is that we can understand those who resemble us as completely determined systems and as representative of diverse cultures, that is to say, as necessary and capable of modification. And in return, we are able to separate the phases of our own evolution and consider them individually'.[53] The purpose of history, guided by genealogy, is not to discover the roots of our identity but to commit itself to its dissipation. It does not seek to define our unique threshold of emergence, the homeland to which metaphysicians promise a return; it seeks to make visible all of those discontinuities that cross us. 'Antiquarian history', according to the *Untimely Meditations*, pursues opposite goals. It seeks the continuities of soil, language, and urban life in which our present is rooted and, 'by cultivating in a delicate manner that which existed for all time, it tries to conserve for posterity the conditions under which we were born'.[54] This type of history was objected to in the *Meditations* because it tended to block creativity in support of the laws of fidelity. Somewhat later – and already in *Human, All Too Human* – Nietzsche reconsiders the task of the antiquarian, but with an altogether different emphasis. If genealogy in its own right gives rise to questions concerning our native land, native language, or the laws that govern us, its intention is to reveal the heterogenous systems which, masked by the self, inhibit the formation of any form of identity.

The third use of history is the sacrifice of the subject of knowledge. In appearance, or rather, according to the mask it bears, historical consciousness is neutral, devoid of passions and committed solely to truth. But if it examines itself and if, more generally, it interrogates the various forms of scientific consciousness in its history, it finds that all these forms and transformations are aspects of the will to knowledge: instinct, passion, the inquisitor's devotion, cruel subtlety and malice. It discovers the violence of a position that sides against those who are happy in their ignorance, against the effective illusions by which humanity protects itself, a position that encourages the dangers of research and delights in disturbing discoveries.[55] The historical analysis of this rancorous will to knowledge[56] reveals that all knowledge rests upon injustice (that there is no right, not even in the act of knowing, to truth or foundation for truth) and that the instinct for knowledge is malicious (something murderous, opposed to the happiness of mankind). Even in the greatly expanded form it assumes today, the will to knowledge does not achieve a universal truth; man is not given an exact and serene mastery of nature. On the contrary, it ceaselessly multiplies the risks, creates dangers in every area; it breaks down illusory defences; it dissolves the unity of the subject; it releases those elements of itself that are devoted to its subversion and destruction. Knowledge does not slowly detach itself from its empirical roots, the initial needs from which it arose, to become pure speculation subject only to the demands of reason; its development is not tied to the constitution and affirmation of a free subject; rather, it creates a progressive enslavement of its instinctive violence. Where religions once demanded the sacrifice of bodies, knowledge now calls for experimentation on ourselves,[57] calls us to the sacrifice of the subject of knowledge.

> The desire for knowledge has been transformed among us into a passion which fears no sacrifice, which fears nothing but its own extinction. It may be that mankind will eventually perish from this passion for knowledge. If not through passion, then through weakness. We must be prepared to state our choice: do we wish humanity to end in fire and light or to end on the sands?[58]

We should now replace the two great problems of nineteenth-century philosophy, passed on by Fichte and Hegel (the reciprocal basis of truth and liberty and the possibility of absolute knowledge), with the theme that 'to perish through absolute knowledge may well form a part of the basis of being'.[59] This does not mean, in terms of a critical procedure, that the will to truth is limited by the intrinsic finitude of cognition, but that it loses all sense of limitations and all claim to truth in its unavoidable sacrifice of the subject of knowledge.

> It may be that there remains one prodigous idea which might be made to prevail over every other aspiration, which might overcome the most victorious: the idea of humanity sacrificing itself. It seems

> indisputable that if this new constellation appeared on the horizon, only the desire for truth, with its enormous prerogatives, could direct and sustain such a sacrifice. For to knowledge, no sacrifice is too great. Of course, this problem has never been posed.[60]

The *Untimely Mediations* discussed the critical use of history: its just treatment of the past, its decisive cutting of the roots, its rejection of traditional attitudes of reverence, its liberation of man by presenting him with other origins than those in which he prefers to see himself. Nietzsche, however, reproached critical history for detaching us from every real source and for sacrificing the very movement of life to the exclusive concern for truth. Somewhat later, as we have seen, Nietzsche reconsiders this line of thought he had at first refused, but directs it to altogether different ends. It is no longer a question of judging the past in the name of a truth that only we can possess in the present; but risking the destruction of the subject who seeks knowledge in the endless deployment of the will to knowledge.

In a sense, genealogy returns to the three modalities of history that Nietzsche recognized in 1874. It returns to them in spite of the objections that Nietzsche raised in the name of the affirmative and creative powers of life. But they are metamorphosized; the veneration of monuments becomes parody; the respect for ancient continuities becomes systematic dissociation; the critique of the injustices of the past by a truth held by men in the present becomes the destruction of the man who maintains knowledge by the injustice proper to the will to knowledge.

NOTES

1 See Nietzsche's Preface to *The Genealogy of Morals* in *Basic Writings of Nietzsche*, ed. and tr. Walter Kaufman, New York: Modern Library, 1968, pp. 4, 7 – Trans.

2 *The Gay Science*, tr. Walter Kaufman, New York: Random House, 1974, p. 7.

3 *Human, All Too Human*, p. 3.

4 *The Genealogy*, II, pp. 6, 8.

5 *The Gay Science*, pp. 110, 111, 300.

6 *The Dawn*, New York: Gordon Press, 1974, p. 102; ('Shameful origin' – Trans.).

7 *The Gay Science*, pp. 151, 353; and also *The Dawn*, p. 62; *The Genealogy*, I, p. 14; *Twilight of the Idols*, 'The Great Errors', in *The Portable Nietzsche*, ed. and tr. Walter Kaufman, New York: Viking Press, 1954, p. 7. (*Schwarzkünstler* is a black magician – Trans.)

8 Paul Ree's text was entitled *Ursprung der Moralischen Empfindungen*.

9 In *Human, All Too Human*, New York: Gordon Press, 1974, aphorism 92 was entitled *Ursprung der Gerechtigkeit*.
10 In the main body of *The Genealogy*, '*Ursprung*' and '*Herkunft*' are used interchangeably in numerous instances (I, p. 2; II, pp. 8, 11, 12, 16, 17).
11 *The Dawn*, p. 123.
12 *Human, All Too Human*, p. 34.
13 *The Wanderer and his Shadow*, in *The Complete Works of Nietzsche*, New York: Gordon Press (n.d.), p. 9.
14 A wide range of key terms, found in *The Archaeology of Knowledge*, are related to this theme of 'disparity': the concepts of series, discontinuity, divisions, and difference. If the *same* is found in the realm and movement of dialectics, the *disparate* presents itself as an 'event' in the world of chance. For a more detailed discussion, see 'Theatrum Philosophicum', *Language, Counter-Memory, and Practice*, trans. D. F. Bouchard (Ithaca, N.J.), 1977, pp. 180, 193–6 – Trans.
15 *The Wanderer and his Shadow*, p. 3.
16 *The Dawn*, p. 49.
17 *Nietzsche contra Wagner*, p. 99.
18 *The Gay Science*, pp. 265 and 110.
19 See 'Theatrum Philosophicum', pp. 167–8, for a discussion of the development of truth; and also 'History of Systems of Thought: Summary of a Course at the Collège de France, 1970–1971', pp. 202–4 – Trans.
20 *Twilight of the Idols*, 'How the world of truth becomes a fable'.
21 For example, *The Gay Science*, p. 135; *Beyond Good and Evil*, pp. 200, 242, 244; *The Genealogy*, I, p. 5.
22 *The Gay Science*, pp. 348–9; *Beyond Good and Evil*, aphorism 260.
23 *Beyond Good and Evil*, 244.
24 *The Genealogy*, III, p. 17. The *abkunft* of feelings of depression.
25 *Twilight*, 'Reasons for philosophy'.
26 *The Dawn*, p. 247.
27 *The Gay Science*, pp. 348–9.
28 Ibid., p. 200.
29 *The Dawn*, p. 42.
30 *Beyond Good and Evil*, 262.
31 *The Genealogy*, III, p. 13.
32 *The Gay Science*, p. 148. It is also to an anemia of the will that one must attribute the *Entstehung* of Buddhism and Christianity, p. 347.
33 *The Genealogy*, I, p. 2.
34 *Beyond Good and Evil*, 260; cf. also *The Genealogy*, II, p. 12.
35 *The Wanderer*, p. 9.
36 *The Gay Science*, p. 111.
37 *The Genealogy*, II, p. 6.
38 *The Genealogy*, Preface, p. 7; and I, p. 2. *Beyond Good and Evil*, 224.
39 *The Gay Science*, p. 7.
40 Ibid.
41 This statement is echoed in Foucault's discussion of 'differentiations' in *The Archaeology of Knowledge*, pp. 130–1, 206 – Trans.

42 *The Genealogy*, II, p. 12.
43 *The Dawn*, p. 130.
44 *The Genealogy*, II, p. 12.
45 *Human, All Too Human*, p. 16.
46 *Twilight*, p. 44.
47 *Twilight*, 'Reason within philosophy', pp. 1 and 4.
48 *The Wanderer*, p. 188. (This conception underlies the task of *Madness and Civilization* and *The Birth of the Clinic* even though it it is not found as a conscious formulation until *The Archaeology of Knowledge* – Trans.)
49 *The Gay Science*, p. 337.
50 *The Genealogy*, III, p. 26.
51 *Beyond Good and Evil*, 223.
52 *The Wanderer*, (Opinions and Mixed Statements), p. 17.
53 *Human, All Too Human*, p. 274.
54 *Untimely Meditations*, II, p. 3.
55 Cf. *The Dawn*, pp. 429 and 432; *The Gay Science*, p. 333; *Beyond Good and Evil*, 229–30.
56 'Vouloir-savoir': the phrase in French means both the will to knowledge and knowledge as revenge – Trans.
57 *The Dawn*, p. 501.
58 Ibid., p. 429.
59 *Beyond Good and Evil*, 39.
60 *The Dawn*, p. 45.

10

Method, Social Science and Social Hope

RICHARD RORTY

SCIENCE WITHOUT METHOD

Galileo and his followers discovered, and subsequent centuries have amply confirmed, that you get much better predictions by thinking of things as masses of particles blindly bumping each other than by thinking of them as Aristotle thought of them – animistically, teleologically and anthropomorphically. They also discovered that you get a better handling on the universe by thinking of it as infinite and cold and comfortless than by thinking of it as finite, homey, planned and relevant to human concerns. Finally, they discovered that if you view planets or missiles or corpuscles as point-masses, you can get nice simple predictive laws by looking for nice simple mathematical ratios. These discoveries are the basis of modern technological civilization. We can hardly be too grateful for them. But they do not, *pace* Descartes and Kant, point any epistemological moral. They do not tell us anything about the nature of science or rationality. In particular, they did not result from the use of, nor do they exemplify, something called 'the scientific method'.

The tradition we call 'modern philosphy' asked itself 'How is it that science has had so much success? What is the secret of this success?'. The various bad answers to these bad questions have been variations on a single charming but uncashable metaphor: viz., the New Science discovered the language which nature itself uses. When Galileo said that the Book of Nature was written in the language of mathematics, he meant that his new reductionistic, mathematical vocabulary did not just *happen* to work, but that it worked *because* that was the way things

Reprinted by permission of *Canadian Journal of Philosophy* from Richard Rorty, 'Method, Social Science and Social Hope', *Canadian Journal of Philosophy*, XI, no. 4 (December 1981), pp. 569–88. This article reappeared in Richard Rorty, *Consequences of Pragmatism* (Minneapolis: University of Minnesota Press, 1982), pp. 191–210.

really were. He meant that the vocabulary worked because it fitted the universe as a key fits a lock. Ever since philosophers have been trying and failing, to give sense to these notions of 'working *because*', and 'things as they *really are*'.

Descartes explicated these notions in terms of the natural clarity and distinctness of Galilean ideas – ideas which, for some reason, had been foolishly overlooked by Aristotle. Locke, struck by the indistinctness of this notion of 'clarity', thought he might do better with a program of reducing complex ideas to simple. To make this program relevant to current science, he used an *ad hoc* distinction between ideas which resemble their objects and those which do not. This distinction was so dubious as to lead us, via Berkeley and Hume, to Kant's rather desperate suggestion that the key only worked because we had, behind our own backs, constructed the lock it was to fit. In retrospect, we have come to see Kant's suggestion as giving the game away. For his transcendental idealism opened the back door to all the teleological, animistic, Aristotelian notions which the intellectuals had repressed for fear of being old-fashioned. The speculative idealists who succeeded Kant dropped the notion of finding nature's secrets. They substituted the notion of making worlds by creating vocabularies, a notion echoed in our century by maverick philosophers of science like Cassirer and Goodman.

In an effort to avoid these so-called 'excesses of German idealism', a host of philosophers – roughly classifiable as 'positivist' – have spent the last hundred years trying to use notions like 'objectivity', 'rigor', and 'method' to isolate science from nonscience. They have done this because they thought that the idea that we can explain scientific success in terms of discovering Nature's Own Language must, *somehow*, be right – even if the metaphor could *not* be cashed, even if neither realism nor idealism could explain just what the imagined 'correspondence' between nature's language and current scientific jargon could consist in. Very few thinkers have suggested that maybe science does not *have* a secret of success – that there is *no* metaphysical or epistemological or transcendental explanation of why Galileo's vocabulary has worked so well so far, any more than there is explanation of why the vocabulary of liberal democracy has worked so well so far. Very few have been willing to abjure the notions that 'the mind' or 'reason' has a nature of its own, that discovery of this nature will give us a 'method', and that following that method will enable us to penetrate beneath the appearances and see nature 'in its own terms'.[1]

The importance of Kuhn seems to me to be that, like Dewey, he is one of these few. Kuhn and Dewey suggest we give up the notion of science traveling towards an end called 'correspondence with reality' and instead say *merely* that a given vocabulary works better than another for a given purpose. If we accept their suggestion, we shall not be inclined to ask 'What method do scientists use?' Or, more precisely, we shall say that within what Kuhn calls 'normal science' – puzzle-solving – they use the same banal and obvious methods all of us use in every human activity. They check off examples against criteria; they fudge the counter-examples enough to avoid the need for new models; they try out various guesses, formulated within the current jargon, in the hope of coming up with something which will cover the unfudgeable cases. We shall not think there is or could be an epistemologically pregnant answer to the question 'What did Galileo do right that Aristotle did wrong?', any more than we should expect such an answer to the questions 'What did Plato do right that Xenophon did wrong?' or 'What did Mirabeau do right that Louis XVI did wrong?'. We shall just say that Galileo had a good idea, and Aristotle a less good idea; Galileo was using some terminology which helped and Aristotle wasn't. Galileo's terminology was the *only* 'secret' he had – he didn't pick that terminology because it was 'clear' or 'natural', or 'simple', or in line with the categories of the pure understanding. He just lucked out.

The moral which seventeenth-century philosophers *should* have drawn from Galileo's success was a Whewellian and Kuhnian one: viz., that scientific breakthroughs are not so much a matter of deciding which of various alternative hypotheses are true, but of finding the right jargon in which to frame hypotheses in the first place. But, instead, as I have said, they drew the moral that the new vocabulary was the one nature had always *wanted* to be described in. I think they drew this moral for two reasons. First, they thought that the fact that Galileo's vocabulary was devoid of metaphysical comfort, moral significance and human interest was a reason why it worked. They vaguely thought that it was *because* the Galilean scientist was able to face up to the frightening abysses of infinite space that he was being so successful. They identified his distance from common sense and from religious feeling – his distance from decisions about how men should live – as part of the secret of his success. So, they said, the more metaphysically comfortless and morally insignificant our vocabulary, the likelier we are to be 'in touch with reality' or to be 'scientific', or to describe reality as it wants to be described and thereby get it under control. Second, they thought the only way to eliminate 'subjective' notions – those expressible in *our* vocabulary but not in nature's – was to eschew terms which could not be definitionally linked to those in Galileo's and Newton's vocabularies, terms denoting 'primary qualities'.

These intertwined mistakes – the notion that a term is more likely to 'refer to the real' if it is morally insignificant and if it occurs in true, predictively useful generalizations – give substance to the idea of 'scientific method' as (in Bernard Williams's phrase)[2] the search for 'an absolute conception of reality'. This is reality conceived as somehow represented by representations which are not merely ours but its own, as it looks to itself, as it would describe itself if it could. Williams, and others who take Cartesianism seriously, not only think this notion is unconfused but regard it as one of our intuitions about the nature of knowledge. On my account, by contrast, it is merely one of our intuitions about what counts as being philosophical. It is the Cartesian form of the archetypal philosophical fantasy – first spun by Plato – of cutting through all description, all representation, to a state of consciousness which, *per impossibile*, combines the best features of inarticulate confrontation with the best features of linguistic formulation. This fantasy of discovering, and somehow *knowing* that one has discovered, Nature's Own Vocabulary *seemed* to become more concrete when Galileo and Newton formulated a comprehensive set of predictively useful universal generalizations, written in suitably 'cold', 'inhuman', mathematical terms. From their time to the present, the notions of 'rationality', 'method', and 'science' have been bound up with the search for such generalizations.

Without this model to go on, the notion of 'a scientific method', in its modern sense, could not have been taken seriously. The term 'method' would have retained the sense it had in the period prior to the New Science, for people like Ramus and Bacon. In that sense, to have a method was simply to have a good comprehensive list of topics or headings – to have, so to speak, an efficient filing system. In its post-Cartesian philosophical sense, however, it does not mean simply ordering one's thoughts, but *filtering* them in order to eliminate 'subjective' or 'noncognitive' or 'confused' elements, leaving only the thoughts which are Nature's Own. This distinction between the parts of one's mind which do and don't correspond to reality is, in the epistemological tradition, confused with the distinction between rational and irrational ways of doing science. If 'scientific method' means merely being rational in some given area of inquiry, then it has a perfectly reasonable 'Kuhnian' sense – it means obeying the normal conventions of your discipline, not fudging the data *too* much, not letting your hopes and fears influence your conclusions unless those hopes and fears are shared by all those who are in the same line of work, being open to refutation by experience, not blocking the road of inquiry. In this sense, 'method' and 'rationality', are names for a suitable balance between respect for the opinions of one's fellows and respect for the stubbornness of sensation. But epistemologically centered philosophy has wanted notions of 'method' and 'rationality' which signify more than good epistemic manners, notions which describe the way in which the mind is naturally fitted to learn Nature's Own Language.

If one believes, as I do, that the traditional ideas of 'an absolute ("objective") conception of reality' and of 'scientific method' are neither clear nor useful, then one will see the interlocked questions 'What should be the method of the social sciences?' and 'What are the criteria of an objective moral theory?' as badly posed. In the remainder of this paper, I want to say in detail why I think these are bad questions, and to recommend a Deweyan approach to both social science and morality, one which emphasizes the utility of narratives and vocabularies rather than the objectivity of laws and theories.

'VALUE-FREE' SOCIAL SCIENCE AND 'HERMENEUTIC' SOCIAL SCIENCE

There has recently been a reaction against the idea that students of man and society will be 'scientific' only if they remain faithful to the Galilean model – if they find 'value-neutral', purely descriptive terms in which to state their predictive generalizations, leaving evaluation to 'policy-makers'. This had led to a revival of Dilthey's notion that to understand human beings 'scientifically' we must apply non-Galilean, 'hermeneutic' methods. From the point of view I wish to suggest, the whole idea of 'being scientific' or of choosing between 'methods' is confused. Consequently, the question about whether social scientists should seek value-neutrality along Galilean lines, or rather should try for something more cozy, Aristotelian, and 'softer' – a distinctive 'method of the human sciences' – seems to me misguided.

One reason this quarrel has developed is that it has become obvious that *whatever* terms are used to describe human beings *become* 'evaluative' terms. The suggestion that we segregate the 'evaluative' terms in a language and use their absence as one criterion for the 'scientific' character of a discipline or a theory cannot be carried out. For there is no way to prevent anybody using *any* term 'evaluatively'. If you ask somebody whether he is using 'repression' or 'primitive' or 'working class' normatively or descriptively, he might be able to answer in the case of a given statement, made on a given occasion. But if you ask him whether he uses the term only when he is describing, only when he is engaging in moral reflection, or both, the answer is almost always going to be 'both'. Further – and this is the crucial point – unless the answer *is* 'both', it is just not the sort of term which will do us much good in social science. Predictions will do 'policy-making' no good if they are not phrased in the terms in which policy can be formulated.

Suppose we picture the 'value-free' social scientist walking up to the divide between 'fact' and 'value' and handing his predictions to the policy-makers who live on the other side. They will not be of much use unless they contain some of the terms which the policy-makers use among themselves. What the policy-makers would like, presumably, are rich juicy predictions like 'If basic industry is socialized, the standard of living will [or won't] decline', 'If literacy is more widespread, more [or fewer] honest people will be elected to office', and so on. They would like hypothetical sentences whose consequences are phrased in terms which might occur in morally urgent recommendations. When they get predictions phrased in the sterile jargon of 'quantified' social sciences ('maximizes satisfaction', 'increases conflict', etc.), they either tune out, or, more dangerously, begin to use the jargon in moral deliberation. The desire for a new, 'interpretative' social science seems to me best understood as a reaction against the temptation to formulate social policies in terms so thin as barely to count as 'moral' at all – terms which never stray far from definitional links with 'pleasure', 'pain', and 'power'.

The issue between those who hanker after 'objective', 'value-free', 'truly scientific' social science and those who think this should be replaced with something more hermeneutical is misdescribed as a quarrel about 'method'. A quarrel about method requires a common goal, and disagreement about the means for reaching it. But the two sides to this quarrel are not disagreeing about how to get more accurate predictions of what will happen if certain policies are adopted. Neither side is very good at making such predictions, and if anybody ever did find a way of making them both sides would be equally eager to incorporate this strategy in their view. The nature of the quarrel is better, but still misleadingly, seen as one between the competing goals, of 'explanation' and 'understanding'. As this contrast has developed in recent literature, it is a contrast between the sort of jargon which permits Galilean-style generalizations, and Hempelian specification of confirming and disconfirming instances of such generalizations, and the sort which sacrifices this virtue for the sake of describing in roughly the same vocabulary as one evaluates (a 'teleological' vocabulary, crudely speaking).

This contrast is real enough. But it is not an issue to be resolved, only a difference to be lived with. The idea that explanation and understanding are opposed ways of doing social science is as misguided as the notion that microscopic and macroscopic descriptions of organisms are opposed ways of doing biology. There are lots of things you want to do with bacteria and cows for which it is very useful to have biochemical descriptions of them; there are lots of things you want to do with them for which such descriptions would be merely a nuisance. Similarly, there are lots of things you want to do with human beings for which descriptions of them in nonevaluative, 'inhuman' terms are very useful; there are others (e.g., thinking of them as your fellow-citizens) in which such descriptions are not. 'Explanation' is merely the sort of understanding one looks for when one wants to predict and control. It does not contrast with something else called 'understanding' as the abstract contrasts with the concrete, or the artificial with the natural, or the 'repressive' with the 'liberating'. To say that something is better 'understood' in one vocabulary than another is always an ellipsis for the claim that a description in the preferred vocabulary is more useful for a certain purpose. If the purpose is prediction, then one will want one sort of vocabulary. If it is evaluation, one may or may not want a different sort of vocabulary. (In the case of evaluating artillery fire, for example, the predictive vocabulary of ballistics will do nicely. In the case of evaluating human character, the vocabulary of stimulus and response is beside the point.)

To sum up this point: there are two distinct requirements for the vocabulary of the social sciences:

1 it should contain descriptions of situations which facilitate their prediction and control;
2 it should contain descriptions which help one decide what to do.

Value-free social science assumed that a thin 'behavioristic' vocabulary met the first requirement. This assumption has not panned out very well; the last fifty years of research in social sciences have not notably increased our predictive abilities. But even if it *had* succeeded in offering predictions, this would not *necessarily* have helped fulfill the second requirement. It would not necessarily have been useful in deciding what to do. The debate between friends of value-freedom and friends of hermeneutics has often taken for granted that neither requirement can be satisfied unless the other is also. Friends of hermeneutics have protested that Behaviorese was inappropriate for 'understanding' people – meaning that it could not catch what they were 'really' doing. But this is a misleading way of saying it is not a good vocabulary for moral reflection. We just don't want to be the sort of policy-makers who use those terms for deciding what to do to our fellow-humans. Conversely, friends of value-freedom, insisting that as soon as social science finds its Galileo (who is somehow known in advance to be a behaviorist) the first requirement will be satisified, have argued that it is our duty to start making policy decisions in suitably thin terms – so that our 'ethics' may be 'objective' and 'scientifically based'. For only in that way will we be able to make maximal use of all those splendid predictions which will shortly be coming our way. Both sides made the same mistake in thinking that there is some intrinsic connection between the two requirements. It is a mistake to think that when we know how to deal justly and honorably with a person or a society we *thereby* know how to predict and control him or her or it, and a mistake to think that ability to predict and control is *necessarily* an aid to such dealing.

To be told that only a certain vocabulary is *suited* to human beings or human societies, that only *that* vocabulary permits us to 'understand' them, is the seventeenth-century myth of Nature's Own Vocabulary all over again. If, with Dewey, one sees vocabularies as instruments for coping with things rather than representations of their intrinsic natures, then one will not think that there is an intrinsic connection, nor an intrinsic *lack* of connection, between 'explanation' and 'understanding' – between being able to predict and control people of a certain sort and being able to sympathize and associate with them, to view them as fellow-citizens. One will not think that there are two 'methods' – as for explaining somebody's behavior and another for understanding his nature.

EPISTEMIC AND MORAL PRIVILEGE

The current movement to make the social sciences 'hermeneutical' rather than Galilean makes a reasonable, Deweyan point if it is taken as saying: narratives as well as laws, redescriptions as well as predictions, serve a useful purpose in helping us deal with the problems of society. In this sense, the movement is a useful protest against the fetishism of old-fashioned, 'behaviorist' social scientists who worry about whether they are being 'scientific'. But this protest goes too far when it waxes philosophical and begins to draw a principled distinction between man and nature, announcing that the ontologial difference dictates a methodological difference. Thus, for example, when it is said that 'interpretation begins from the postulate that the web of meaning constitutes human existence',[3] this suggests that fossils (for example) might get constituted *without* a web of meanings. But once the relevant sense of 'constitution' is distinguished from the physical sense (in which houses are 'constituted out of' bricks), the claim that 'X constitutes Y' reduces to the claim that you can't know anything about Y without knowing a lot about X. To say that human beings would not be human, would be merely animal, unless they talked a lot is true enough. If you can't figure out the relation between a person, the noises he makes and other persons, then you won't know much about him. But one could equally well say that fossils wouldn't be fossils, would be merely rocks, if we couldn't grasp their relations to lots of other fossils. Fossils are constituted *as* fossils by a web of relationships to other fossils and to the speech of the paleontologists who describe such relationships. If you can't grasp some of these relationships, the fossil will remain, to you, a mere rock. *Anything* is, for purposes of being inquired into, 'constituted' by a web of meanings.

To put this another way: if we think of the fossil record as a text, then we can say that paleontology, in its early stages, followed 'interpretive' methods. That is, it cast around for some way of making sense of what had happened by looking for a vocabulary in which a puzzling object could be related to other, more familiar objects, so as to become intelligible. Before the discipline became 'normalized', nobody had any clear idea of what sort of thing might be relevant to predicting where similar fossils might be found. To say that 'Paleontology is now a science' means something like 'Nobody now has any doubts about what sorts of questions you are supposed to ask, and what sort of hypotheses you can advance, when confronted with a puzzling fossil'. On my view, being 'interpretive' or 'hermeneutical' is not having a special method but simply casting about for a vocabulary which might help. When Galileo came up with his mathematicized vocabulary, he was successfully concluding an inquiry which was, in the only sense I can give the term, hermeneutical. The same goes for Darwin. I do not see any interesting differences between what they were doing and what biblical exegetes, literary critics, or historians of culture do. So I think that it would do no harm to adopt the term 'hermeneutics' for the sort of by-guess-and-by-God hunt for new terminology which characterizes the initial stages of any new line of inquiry.

But although this would do no harm, it also would do no particular good. It is no more useful to think of people or fossils on the model of texts than to think of texts on the model of people or of fossils. It only appears more useful if we think that there is something *special* about texts – e.g., that they are 'intentional' or 'intelligible only holistically'. But I do not think – *pace*, e.g. Searle's notion of 'intrinsic intentionality' – that 'possessing intentionality' means more than 'suitable to be described anthropomorphically, as if it were a language-user'.[4] The relation, on my view, between actions and movements, noises and assertions, is that each is the other described in an alternative jargon. Nor do I see that explanation of fossils is less holistic than explanation of texts – in both cases one needs to bring the object into relation with many other different sorts of objects in order to tell a coherent narrative which will incorporate the initial object.

Given this attitude, it behoves me to offer an explanation of why some people *do* think that texts are very different from fossils. I have suggested elsewhere, in arguing against Charles Taylor,[5] that such people make the mistaken assumption that somebody's *own* vocabulary is always the best vocabulary for understanding what he is doing, that his own explanation of what's going on is the one we want. This mistake seems to me a special case of the confused notion that science tries to learn the vocabulary which the universe uses to explain itself to itself. In both cases, we are thinking of our explanandum as if it were our epistemic equal or superior. But this is not always correct in the case of our fellow-humans, and it is merely a relic of pre-Galilean anthropomorphism in the case of nature. There are, after all, cases in which the other people's, or culture's, explanation of what it's up to is so primitive, or so nutty, that we brush it aside. The only general hermeneutical rule is that it's always wise to ask what the subject *thinks* it's up to before formulating our own hypotheses. But this is an effort at saving time, not a search for the 'true meaning' of the behavior. If the explanandum can come up with a good vocabulary for explaining its own behavior, this saves us the trouble of casting about for one ourselves. From this point of view, the only difference between an inscription and a fossil is that we can imagine coming across another inscription which is a gloss on the first. By contrast, we shall describe the relation between the first fossil and the one next door, even though perhaps equally illuminating, in a nonintentional vocabulary.

In addition to the mistake of thinking that a subject's own vocabulary is always relevant to explaining him, philosophers who make a sharp distinction between man and nature are, like the postivists, bewitched by the notion that the irreducibility of one vocabulary to another implies something ontological. Yet the discovery that we can or cannot reduce a language containing terms like 'is about', 'is true of', 'refers to', etc., or one which contains 'believes' or 'intends', to a language which is extensional and 'empiricist' would show us nothing at all about how to predict, or deal with, language-users or intenders. Defenders of Dilthey make a simple inversion of the mistake made, e.g., by Quine, who thinks there can be no 'fact of the matter' about intentional states of affairs because different such states can be attributed without making a difference to the elementary particles. Quine thinks that, if a sentence can't be paraphrased in the sort of vocabulary which Locke and Boyle would have liked, it doesn't stand for anything real. Diltheyans who exaggerate the diferences between the *Geistes-* and the *Naturwissenschaften* think that the fact that it can't be paraphrased is a hint about a distinctive metaphysical or epistemic status, or the need for a distinctive methodological strategy. But surely all that such irreducibility shows is that one particular vocabulary (Locke's and Boyle's) is not going to be helpful for doing certain things with certain explananda (e.g., people and cultures). This shows as little, to use, Hilary Putnam's analogy, as the fact that if you want to know why a square peg doesn't fit into a round hole you had better *not* describe the peg in terms of the positions of its constituent elementary particles.

The reason definitional irreducibility acquires this illusionary importance, it seems to me, is that it *is* important to make a *moral* distinction between the brutes and ourselves. So, looking about for relevantly distinct behavior, we have traditionally picked our ability to *know*. In previous centuries, we made the mistake of hypostatizing cognitive behavior as the possession of 'mind' or 'consciousness' or 'ideas' and then insisting on the irreducibility of mental representations to their physiological correlates. When this became *vieux jeu*, we switched from mental representations to linguistic representations. We switched from Mind to Language as the name of a quasi-substance or quasi-power which made us morally different. So recent defenders of human dignity have been busy proving the irreducibility of the semantic instead of the irreducibility of the psychical. But all the Ryle-Wittgenstein sorts of arguments against the ghost in the machine work equally well against the ghost between the lines – the notion that having been penned by a human hand imparts a special something, textuality, to inscriptions, something which fossils can never have.

As long as we think of knowledge as representing reality rather than coping with it, mind or language will continue to seem numinous. 'Materialism' or 'behaviorism' and the Galilean style, may continue to seem morally dubious. We shall be struck with this notion of 'representing' or 'corresponding to' reality as long as we think that there is some analogy between calling things by their 'right' – i.e., their conventional – names and finding the 'right' – i.e., Nature's Own – way of describing them. But if we could abandon this metaphor, and the vocabulary of representation which goes with it – as Kuhn and Dewey suggest we might – then we would not find language or mind mysterious, nor 'materialism' or 'behaviorism' particularly dangerous. If the line I am taking is correct, we need to think of our distinctive moral status as just *that*, rather than as 'grounded' on our possession of mind, language, culture, feeling, intentionality, textuality, or anything else. All these numinous notions are just expressions of our awareness that we are members of a moral community, phrased in one or another pseudo-explanatory jargon. This awareness is something which cannot be further 'grounded' – it is simply taking a certain point of view on our fellow-humans. The question of whether it is an 'objective' point of view is not to any point.

This can be made a bit more concrete as follows. I said that, *pace* Taylor, it was a mistake to think of somebody's own account of his behavior or culture as epistemically privileged. He might have a good account of what he's doing or he might not. But it is *not* a mistake to think of it as morally privileged. We have a duty to listen to his account, not because he has privileged access to his own motives but because he is a human being like ourselves. Taylor's claim that we need to look for *internal* explanations of people or cultures or texts takes civility as a methodological strategy. But civility is not a method, it is simply a virtue. The reason why we invite the moronic psychopath to address the court before being sentenced is not that we hope for better explanations than expert psychiatric testimony has offered. We do so because he is, after all, one of us. By asking for his own account in his own words, we hope to decrease our chances of acting badly. What we hope for from social scientists is that they will act as interpreters for those with whom we are not sure how to talk. This is the same thing we hope for from our poets and dramatists and novelists.

Just as I argued in the previous section of this paper that it is a mistake to think that there is a principled distinction between explanation and understanding, or between two methods, one appropriate for nature and the other for man, I have been arguing in this section that the notion that we know *a priori* that nature and man are distinct sorts of objects is a mistake. It is a confusion between ontology and morals. There are lots of useful vocabularies which ignore the nonhuman/human or thing/person distinctions. There is at least one vocabulary – the moral – and possibly many more, for which these distinctions are basic. Human beings are no more 'really' described in the latter sort of vocabulary than in the former. Objects are not 'more objectively' described in any vocabulary than in any other. Vocabularies are useful or useless, good or bad, helpful or misleading, sensitive or coarse, and so on; but they are not 'more objective' or 'less objective' nor more or less 'scientific'.

UNGROUNDED HOPE: DEWEY VS FOUCAULT

The burden of my argument so far has been that if we get rid of traditional notions of 'objectivity' and 'scientific method' we shall be able to see the social sciences as continuous with literature – as interpreting other people to us, and thus enlarging and deepening our sense of community. We shall see the anthropologists and historians as having made it possible for us – educated, leisured policy-makers of the West – to see any exotic specimen of humanity as also 'one of us'. We shall see the sociologists as having done the same for the poor (and various other sorts of nearby outsiders), and the psychologists as having done the same for the eccentric and the insane. This is not all that the social sciences have done, but it is perhaps the most important thing. If we emphasize this side of their achievement, then we shall not object to their sharing a narrative and anecdotal style with the novelist and the journalist. We shall not worry about how this style is related to the

'Galilean' style which 'quantified behavioural science' has tried to emulate. We shall not think either style particularly appropriate or inappropriate to the study of man. For we shall not think that 'the study of man' or 'the human sciences' have a nature, any more than we think that man does. When the notion of knowledge as representation goes, then the notion of inquiry as split into discrete sectors with discrete subject matter goes. The lines between novels, newspaper articles and sociological research get blurred. The lines between subject matters are drawn by refrence to current practical concerns, rather than putative ontological status.

Once this pragmatist line is adopted, however, there are still two ways to go. One can emphasize, as Dewey did, the moral importance of the social sciences – their role in widening and deepening our sense of community and of the possibilities open to this community. Or one can emphasize, as Michel Foucault does, the way in which the social sciences have served as instruments of 'the disciplinary society', the connection between knowledge and power rather than that between knowledge and human solidarity. Much present-day concern about the status and the role of the social sciences comes out of the realization that in addition to broadening the sympathies of the educated classes, the social sciences have also helped them manipulate all the other classes (not to mention, so to speak, helping them manipulate themselves). Foucault's is the best account of this dark side of the social sciences. Admirers of Habermas and of Foucault join in thinking of the 'interpretative turn' in the social sciences as a turn against their use as 'instruments of domination', as tools for what Dewey called 'social engineering'. This has resulted in a confusing quasi-politicization of what was already a factitious 'methodological' issue. In this final section, I want to argue that one should not attribute undue importance to the 'Galilean-vs.-hermeneutic' or 'explanation-vs.-understanding' contrasts by seeing them as parallel with the contrast between 'domination' and 'emancipation'. We should see Dewey and Foucault as differing not over a theoretical issue, but over what we may hope.

Dewey and Foucault make exactly the same criticism of the tradition. They agree, right down the line, about the need to abandon traditional notions of rationality, objectivity, method, and truth. They are both, so to speak, 'beyond method'. They agree that rationality is what history and society make it – that there is no overarching ahistorical structure (the Nature of Man, the laws of human behavior, the Moral Law, the Nature of Society) to be discovered. They share the Whewellian and Kuhnian notion of Galilean Science – as exemplifying the power of new vocabularies rather than offering the secret of scientific success. But Dewey emphasizes that this move 'beyond method' gives mankind an opportunity to grow up, to be free to make itself, rather than seeking direction from some imagined outside source (one of the ahistorical structures mentioned above). His experimetnalism asks us to see knowledge-claims as proposals about what actions to try out next:

> The elaborate systems of science are born not of reason but of impulses at first slight and flickering; impulses to handle, to move about, to hunt, to uncover, to mix things separated and divide things combined, to talk and to listen. Method is their effectual organization into continuous dispositions of inquiry, development, and testing. . . . Reason, the rational attitude, is the resulting disposition.[6]

Foucault also moves beyond the traditional ideals of method and rationality as antecedent constraints upon inquiry, but he views this move as the Nietzschean realization that all knowledge-claims are moves in a power-game: 'We are subject to the production of truth through power, and we cannot exercise power except through the production of truth.'[7]

Here we have two philosophers saying the same thing but putting a different spin on it. The same phenomenon is found in their respective predecessors. James and Nietzsche (as Arthur Danto has pointed out[8]) developed the same criticisms of traditional notions of truth, and the same 'pragmatic' (or 'perspectivalist') alternative. James jovially says that 'ideas become true just in so far as they help us to get into satisfactory relation with other parts of our experience',[9] and Dewey follows this up when he says that 'rationality is the attainment of a working harmony among diverse desires'.[10] Nietzsche says that 'the criterion of truth resides in the enhancement of the feeling of power'[11] and that

> [the] mistake of philosophy is that, instead of seeing logic and the categories of reasons as means for fixing up the world for utilitarian ends . . . one thinks that they give one a criterion of truth about *reality*.[12]

Foucault follows this up by saying that 'we should not imagine that the world presents us with a legible face . . . [we] must conceive discourse as a violence that we do to things'.[13] The arguments which James and Dewey on the one hand, and Nietzsche and Foucault on the other, present for these identical views are as similar as the tone of each is different. Neither pair has any arguments except that usual 'idealist' ones, familar since Kant, against the notion of knowledge as correspondence to nonrepresentations (rather than coherence among representations). These are the arguments in whose direction I gestured in the first section of this paper, when I said that all attempts to cash Galileo's metaphor of Nature's Own Language had failed. Since the cash-value of a philosophical conclusion is the pattern of argument around it, I do not think that we are going to find any *theoretical* differences which divide these two pairs of philosophers from each other.

Is the difference then *merely* one of tone – an ingenuous Anglo-Saxon pose as opposed to a self-dramatizing Continental one? The difference could be better put in terms of something like 'moral outlook'. One is reminded of the famous passage in Wittgenstein:

> If good or bad willing changes the world, it can only change the limits of the world, not the facts; not the things that can be expressed in language. In brief, the world must thereby become quite another. It must so to speak wax or wane as a whole. The world of the happy is quite another than that of the unhappy.[14]

But again, 'good and bad willing', 'happy and unhappy' are not right for the oppositon we are trying to describe. 'Hopeful' and 'hopeless' are a bit better. Ian Hacking winds up a discussion of Foucault by saying:

> 'What is man?' asked Kant. 'Nothing,' says Foucault. 'For what then may we hope?' asks Kant. Does Foucault give the same *nothing* in reply? To think so is to misunderstand Foucault's reply to the question about Man. Foucault said that the concept Man is a fraud, not that you and I are as nothing. Likewise the concept Hope is all wrong. The hopes attributed to Marx and Rousseau are perhaps part of that very concept Man, and they are a sorry basis for optimism. Optimism, pessimism, nihilism and the like are all concepts that make sense only within the idea of a transcendental or enduring subject. Foucault is not in the least incoherent about all this. If we're not satisfied, it should not be because he is pessimistic. It is because he has given no surrogate for whatever it is that springs eternal in the human breast.[15]

What Foucault doesn't give us is what Dewey wanted to give us – a kind of hope which doesn't *need* reinforcement from 'the idea of a transcendental or enduring subject'. Dewey offered ways of using words like 'truth', 'rationality', 'progress', 'freedom', 'democracy', 'culture'. 'art', and the like which presupposed neither the ability to use the familiar vocabulary of what Foucault calls 'the classic age', nor that of the nineteenth-century French intellectuals (the vocabulary of 'man and his doubles').

Foucault sees no middle ground, in thinking about the social sciences, between the 'classic' Galilean conception of 'behavioral sciences' and the French notion of '*sciences de l'homme*'. It was just such a middle ground that Dewey proposed, and which inspired the social sciences in America before the failure of nerve which turned them 'behavioral'. More generally, the recent reaction in faviour of hermeneutical social sciences which I discussed earlier has taken for granted that if we don't want something like Parsons, we have to take something like Foucault; i.e., that overcoming the deficiences of Weberian *Zweckrationalität* requires going all the way, repudiating the 'will to truth'. What Dewey suggested was that we keep the will to truth and the optimism that goes with it, but free them from the behaviorist notion that Behaviorese is Nature's Own Language *and* from the notion of man as 'transcendental or enduring subject'. For, in Dewey's hands, the will to truth is not the urge to dominate but the urge to create, to 'attain working harmony among diverse desires'.

This may sound too pat, too good to be true. I suggest that the reason we find it so is that we are convinced that liberalism requires the notion of a common human nature, or a common set of moral principles which binds us all, or some other descendent of the Christian notion of the Brotherhood of Man. So we have come to see liberal social hope – such as Dewey's – as inherently self-deceptive and philosophically naive. We think that, once we have freed ourselves from the various illusions which Nietzsche diagnosed, we *must* find ourselves all alone, without the sense of community which liberalism requires. Perhaps, as Hacking says, Nietzsche and Foucault are not saying that you and I are as nothing, but they do seem to hint that you and I together, as *we*, aren't much – that human solidarity goes when God and his doubles go. Man as Hegel thought of him, as the Incarnation of the Idea, doubtless does have to go. The proletariat as the Redeemed Form of Man has to go, too. But there seems no particular reason why, after dumping Marx, we have to keep on repeating all the nasty things about bourgeois liberalism which he taught us to say. There is no inferential connection between the disappearance of the transcendental subject – of 'man' as something having a nature which society can repress or understand – and the disappearance of human solidarity. Bourgeois liberalism seems to me the best example of this solidarity we have yet achieved, and Deweyan pragmatism the best articulation of it.[16]

The burden of my argument here is that we should see Dewey as having already gone the route Foucault is traveling, and as having arrived at the point Foucault is still trying to reach – the point at which we can make philosophical and historical ('genealogial') reflection useful to those, in Foucault's phrase. 'whose fight is located in the fine meshes of the webs of power'. Dewey spent his life trying to lend a hand in these little fights, and in the course of doing so he worked out the vocabulary and rhetoric of American 'pluralism'. This rhetoric made the first generation of American social scientists think of themselves as apostles of a new form of social life. Foucault does not, as far as I can see, do more than update Dewey by warning that the social scientists have often been, and are always likely to be, co-opted by the bad guys. Reading Foucault reinforces the disillusion which American intellectuals have suffered during the last few decades of watching the 'behavioralized' social sciences team up with the state.

The reason why it may appear that Foucault has something new and distinctive to add to Dewey is that he is riding the crest of a powerful but vaguely-defined movement which I have elsewhere described as 'textualism' – the movement which suggests, as Foucault puts it at the end of *The Order of Things*, that 'Man is in the process of perishing as the being of language continues to shine ever brighter upon our horizon'.[18] Another reason is that Foucault is attempting to transform political discourse by seeing 'power' as not intrinsically repressive – because, roughly, there is no naturally good self to repress. But Dewey, it seems to me, had already grasped both points. Foucault's vision of discourse as a network of power-relations isn't very different from Dewey's vision of it as instrumental, as one element in the arsenal of tools people use for gratifying, synthesizing, and harmonizing their desires. Dewey had learned from Hegel what Foucault learns from Nietzsche – that there is nothing much to 'man' except one more animal, until culture, the meshes of power, begin to shape him into something else. For Dewey too there is nothing Rousseauian to be 'repressed'; 'repression' and 'liberation' are just names for the sides of the structures of power we like and the sides we don't like. Once 'power' is freed from its connotation of 'repression', then Foucault's 'structures of power' will not seem much different from Dewey's 'structures of culture'. 'Power' and 'culture' are equipollent indications of the social forces which make us more than animals – and which, when the bad guys take over, can turn us into something worse and more miserable than animals.

These remarks are not meant to downgrade Foucault – who seems to me one of the most interesting philosophers alive –but just to insist that we go slow about assuming that the discovery of things like 'discourse', 'textuality', 'speech-acts', and the like have radically changed the philosphical scene. The current vogue of 'hermeneutics' is going to end soon, and badly, if we advertise these new notions as more than they are – namely, one more jargon which tries to get out from under some of the mistakes of the past. Dewey had his own jargon – popular at the time, but now a bit musty – for the same purpose. But the difference in jargon should not obscure the common aim. This is the attempt to free mankind from Nietzsche's 'longest lie', the notion that outside the haphazard and perilous experiments we perform there lies something (God, Science, Knowledge, Rationality, or Truth) which will, if only we perform the correct rituals, step in to save us. Although Foucault and Dewey are trying to do the same thing, Dewey seems to me to have done it better, simply because his vocabulary allows room for unjustifiable hope, and an ungroundable but vital sense of human solidarity.

NOTES

1 I expand on these points in 'A Reply to Dreyfus and Taylor', *Review of Metaphysics*, XXIV (1980), 39–46, and in the ensuing discussion, pp. 47–55.

2 Cf. Bernard Williams, *Descartes: The Project of Pure Enquiry* (London and New York: Penguin Books, 1978), pp. 64ff.

3 Paul Rabinow and William M. Sullivan, 'The Interpreting Turn: Emergence of an Approach' in *Interpretive Social Science*, ed. Rabinow and Sullivan (Berkeley, Ca: University of California Press, 1979), p. 5.

4 See the discussion of Searle's 'Minds, Brains and Programs' in *The Behavioral and Brain Sciences*, 3 (1980), 417–57, esp. my 'Searle and the Secret Powers of the Brain' at pp. 445–6 and Searle's 'Intrinsic Intentionality' at pp. 450–6.

5 See the material cited in n. 1 above

6 John Dewey, *Human Nature and Conduct* (New York: Modern Library, 1930), p. 196.

7 Michel Foucault, *Power/Knowledge* (Brighton: Harvester Books, 1980), p. 93.

8 Arthur Danto, *Nietzsche as Philosopher* (New York: Macmillan, 1965), ch. 3.

9 William James, *Pragmatism* (New York: Longmans Green, 1947), p. 58.

10 Dewey, *Human Nature*, p. 196.

11 Friedrich Nietzsche, *The Will to Power*, trans. Kaufmann (New York: Random House, 1967), p. 290.

12 Friederich Nietzsche, *Werke*, ed. Schlechta, III, p. 318.

13 Michel Foucault, *The Archaeology of Knowledge* (New York: Harper and Row, 1972), p. 229.

14 Ludwig Wittgenstein, *Tractatus Logico-Philosophicus*, 6.42.

15 Ian Hacking, review of Foucault's *Power/Knowledge* in *New York Review of Books*, April 1981.

16 Dewey seems to me the twentieth-century counterpart of John Stuart Mill, whose attempt to synthesize Coleridge with Bentham is paralleled by Dewey's attempt to synthesize Hegel with Mill himself. In a brilliant

critique of liberalism, John Dunn describes Mill as attempting to combine the 'two possible radical intellectual strategies open to those who aspire to rescue liberalism as a coherent political option':

> One is to shrink liberalism to a more or less pragmatic and sociological doctrine about the relations between types of political and social order and the enjoyment of political liberties. The version of liberalism which embraces this option is usually today termed 'pluralism', a conception . . . which is still in effect the official intellectual ideology of American society. The second possible radical strategy is simply to repudiate the claims of sociology, to take an epistemological position of such stark scepticism that the somewhat over-rated causal status of sociology can safely be viewed with limited scorn (*Western Political Values in the Face of the Future* [Cambridge: Cambridge University Press, 1979], pp. 47–8).

Dunn thinks Mill's attempt to 'integrate intellectual traditions so deeply and explicitly inimical to one another' failed, and that modern pluralism fails also:

> Modern pluralism is thus at least sufficiently sociologically self-aware not to blanch from the insight that a liberal polity is the political form of bourgeois capitalist society. But the price which it has paid, so far pretty willingly, for this self-awareness, is the surrender of any plausible overall intellectual frame, uniting epistemology, psychology and political theory, which explains and celebrates the force of such political commitments (*ibid*., p. 49).

My view is that such an overall intellectual frame was exactly what Dewey gave us, and that he did so precisely by carrying out Mill's combination of strategies. (For some links between Rawls [who is Dunn's favorite example of modern pluralism] and Dewey, see Rawls's Dewey Lectures, 'Kantian Constructivism in Moral Theory', *Journal of Philosophy* LXXVII (1980), 515–72. Note esp. p. 542, on a conception of justice which swings free of religious, philosophical or moral doctrines, and *Weltanschauungen* generally. See also p. 519 for Rawls's repudiation of an 'epistemologial problem', and his doctrine of 'moral facts' as 'constructed'.) Dunn seems to me right in saying that liberalism has little useful to say about contemporary global politics, but wrong in pinning the blame for this on its lack of a philosophical synthesis of the old, Kantian, unpragmatic sort. On my view, we should be more willing than we are to celebrate bourgeois capitalist society as the best polity actualized so far, while regretting that it is irrelevant to most of the problems of most of the population of the planet.

17 Foucault, *The Order of Things* (New York: Random House, 1973), p. 386.

Index

Index by Justyn Balinski